Finding Home

Finding Home

✳

WRITING ON
NATURE AND CULTURE
FROM ORION MAGAZINE

EDITED AND WITH AN INTRODUCTION BY

PETER SAUER

BEACON PRESS
BOSTON

BEACON PRESS
25 Beacon Street
Boston, Massachusetts 02108-2892

Beacon Press books
are published under the auspices of
the Unitarian Universalist Association of Congregations.

"The American Geographies," © 1989 by Barry Lopez, reprinted by
permission of Sterling Lord Literistic; "A Child's Sense of Wildness" by Gary
Nabhan appeared in another form in *Northern Lights*; "Tokens of Mystery,"
© 1987 by Scott Russell Sanders; "Days at Bear River," from
Refuge: An Unnatural History of Time and Place by Terry Tempest Williams,
© 1991 by Terry Tempest Williams, reprinted by permission
of Pantheon Books, a division of Random House, Inc.; all other
material reprinted by permission of the author.

Library of Congress Cataloging-in-Publication Data

Finding home : writing on nature and culture from Orion magazine /
    edited and with an introduction by Peter Sauer.
      p.   cm. — (The Concord library)
    Includes bibliographical references.
    ISBN 0-8070-8518-9.—ISBN 0-8070-8519-7 (pbk.)
      1. Man—Influence on nature.   2. Human ecology—Philosophy.
3. Natural history.   4. Nature.   I. Sauer, Peter H.   II. Orion (New York, N.Y.)   III. Series.
GF75.F56   1992
508—dc20   91-40603
                                                                        CIP

PRINTED IN THE UNITED STATES OF AMERICA

99 98   8 7 6 5 4 3

Text design by Janis Owens

Contents

✳

PART THREE

Other Walls, Other Wildness

✳

PART FOUR

A Child's Sense of Wildness

✳

Contents

Introduction

✳

I

"Nature"—the way we understand the natural world—is changing, and this transformation carries with it all the makings of a cultural revolution.

A society's conceptual relationship to nature is at the core of its culture: it is a relationship that underlies what we believe and how we live. Profound changes in nature—drought, deforestation, or the outbreak of disease, as experienced by the Incans, Mesopotamians, Algonquians, and countless others—appear from an archaeological distance to have happened suddenly. The records of these times contain little information about what the people thought as they adjusted their lives to nature's new behavior, nor of the bewilderment they must have experienced as these cataclysms unfolded in their lifetimes.

We live now, too, during a time and in a society in which there is a growing consensus that nature is changing; that global warming is real, that the natural world has been fundamentally altered by humankind. Although we argue whether nature is restorable or beyond recovery, the certainty of change is a constant aspect of our lives. It influences planning for the rising sea waters in our harbor cities. It stimulates international agreements on the control of air pollutants. It manifests itself in how we treat our garbage, in what we decide are our local politics. These are the adjustments we must make in response to the changes we perceive in nature.

The source of our bewilderment, however, is an underlying uncertainty about our changing relationship to nature. The adjustments we make in how we live are minor compared to those we face in what we believe—compared to the challenge of forging a new relationship to nature. Scarcely a decade ago, Americans believed nature flowed toward a balanced state with the inevitability of a great river. We might disturb the flow, but in the end nature would "heal itself" and run to wilderness. We treasured wilderness and invented national parks as its sanctuaries. Nature had become for us an almost godlike companion. We sought coexistence, and a respectful distance, "stepping lightly" in the companion's vicinity.

Now it seems that things are not as we thought. Nature is not permanent, not separate. The sanctuaries we set aside for nature are not large enough, and no distance is far enough for coexistence.

Science confirms that our metaphors were wrong. Ecologists, paleoecologists, climatologists, and forest and wildlife managers are finding that "natural succession," once interpreted as a preordained sequence toward a balanced state, may be a matter of chance. Nature's way may not be the flow of a river but the spin of a roulette wheel. Ethnobotanists and biologists are challenging our quintessentially American idea of pristine wilderness. They say that lands once thought of as untouched by human culture reveal patterns, often millennia old, of complex cultural-natural interactions. Humanity's disturbances are permanent; "stepping lightly" never was an option.

These revelations belie the metaphors we lived by and

believed in, creating a cataclysm in our most personal rev-
eries, in the silent poetry of our thoughts. Companionship
has turned against us.

The Algonquians, in the death throes of their tribes in
the seventeenth century, wracked by European diseases
spread by trade in metal, cloth, and furs, believed they
were dying from the wrath of the spirits of the beaver. Our
bewilderment is like theirs; we fear we have damaged a
companion. Perhaps we worshipped it in the wrong fashion. Perhaps it was a colossal misunderstanding. We are
haunted by its spectre.

These writings are an exploration of a changing culture's way of living with a changing nature, as found in the
literature of nature. They are a reflection of our own bewilderment, and of the effort each of us must make to reforge our bonds to nature. Like the writers represented
here, we are Prospero's people, cast ashore on a wilderness
that no one among us has seen before. We know we cannot
leave. So, we set about exploring, using all our faculties of
observation, imagination, and spirit, to make a relationship with this place—to find a home.

II

If the emergence of a new vision of nature was marked by
any single event, it might be the publication of René
Dubos's *The Wooing of Earth* in 1980. At a time when the
environmental movement was concentrating its greatest
political efforts on the preservation of unpeopled wilderness, Dubos proposed the idea that humanity and nature
were capable of productive collaborations.

Dubos, who enjoyed stirring people up, opened *The*

Wooing of Earth with the provocative remark: "Many people . . . will be disturbed by my statement that deforestation and erosion have produced some of the most admired landscapes." He went on to assert that, for instance, the Île-de-France was "visibly more diversified and emotionally richer than it was in its original forested state" and to talk about "the quality of blessedness that emerges from long association between human beings and nature." *The Wooing of Earth* was dismissed by many, while some found it disturbing enough to attack as a "sell-out" to land developers.

Although he died in 1982, before the publication of the second issue, Dubos was an early mentor to *Orion.* The magazine went on to become the forum in which many American writers have examined the implications of "humanized landscapes."

Orion's first aim was "to characterize conceptually and practically our responsibilities to the earth and all forms of life, and to explore the ethic of humane stewardship." Unlike many contemporary nature magazines, which are published in part as vehicles for the editorial statements of their national institutions and organizations, *Orion* was established and survives today as a journal devoted to the exploration of elusive ideas, not to the promotion of specific causes. In the magazine, and in this anthology, the exploration embraces art and literature, including both personal and scientific writing, in a mixture that is unusual in a "nature magazine," but essential in a colloquium created to discuss the relationship between humanity and nature—to probe our wooing of earth.

III

The reformulation of our cultural relationship to nature was spurred by what happened in the Amazon in the 1980s. Both scientific and popular views of nature were changed by the burning of the Amazon rain forest. Scientists were there and documented the environmental cataclysm going on around them; the rest of us watched it on public television.

The destruction of the Amazon rain forest became a symbol of a global environmental crisis: of a warming climate, acid rain, the oppression of the third world, and the avarice of the exploiters of natural resources. By the end of the eighties, environmental issues were matters of national and international dispute. The environment had become an anticipated issue in local and national elections from the United States to Southeast Asia and in the revolutions in Eastern Europe.

Ironically, efforts to save vanishing tropical forests—symbol for all that was wild—led almost accidentally to a discovery of a new vision of wilderness.

Before the destruction of the forests triggered a massive public education effort to inform and to rally public action, the Amazon was only dimly perceived, blurred by a haze of myth and presumption. The rain forest was known only as a trackless, uniform wilderness. The Amazon—the word rings with adventure—was the last bastion of true "nature," a dangerous, untouched, and unknown frontier. It teemed with poisonous snakes, plants, and insects; piranhas and alligators infested its waters. Steaming wilderness concealed birds and mammals that had never been discovered or described. The Amazon was a dream place,

5

somewhere near the heart of darkness, protected by an inner circle of fearsome cannibals and headhunters.

Colonial racist assumptions shrouded the people of the forest in a mythology even more impenetrable than that which concealed the forest. Native populations were thought to be inconsequentially small and widely dispersed, mostly in the interior. It was assumed they supported themselves by primitive means, were often nomadic, and were without cultural sophistication. Their hunting and gathering methods were believed to have as negligible an effect on the flora and fauna of the vast wilderness ecosystem as the browsing of deer, or the hunting of leopards.

As the smoke from burning jungles closed Brazilian airports, the heat of these fires appeared on satellite images like the lights of cities. Scientists rushed to the Amazon to learn secrets from its flora and fauna and from its indigenous peoples before they disappeared. Working just ahead of the road builders, forest burners, and mining companies, searching for plants that contained undiscovered cures for cancer, the scientists were engaged in a critical race to save a vast forest, to stop global warming, and to retrieve knowledge from nature before it was lost forever.

Their science became news, and the scientists became cultural heroes, working against a science fiction plot that had become a twentieth-century reality. Unfortunately, the scientists' work confirmed their worst fears: no inventory could outpace the destruction. But they also discovered something they had not expected to find: a new natural history of the Amazon, a glimpse of a "new" nature. They uncovered a story that was to become the new paradigm for our understanding of all American forests.

In the early seventies, a researcher became aware of "interesting distribution patterns of organisms in Amazonia." The jungle was not uniform, but contained areas of greater diversity of plants and animals. The researcher, an ornithologist named Haffer, first described these patterns in a paper entitled "The Speciation of Amazon Forest Birds," published in 1969. Speciation—creation of new species—often occurs within isolated (and therefore smaller and less stable) populations. A diversity of related bird species in areas within a forest that had been assumed to be uniform was evidence that these areas were older and once isolated. Haffer's work was followed by studies of lizards, in 1970, and of Heliconian butterflies, in 1972. Botanists went back to rain forest plant inventories and found that the distribution of shrubs, vines, and trees also reflected this uneven pattern. As Haffer had originally proposed, the patterns were quickly accepted by scientists as the remnants of "refuges," areas of the Amazon basin that had remained forested during the dry cold periods of the Ice Age, when most of the Amazon was covered with savanna. Plants and animals had been forced into the isolation of the refuges during this period and, while there, hybridized and "speciated." When the earth warmed and the savanna became a rain forest again, the former refuges remained as biological footprints, rich pockets of animal and plant diversity.

The connections between these areas of bio-diversity and the people of the Amazon were the second and more difficult idea to establish. The groundwork was laid in 1973 by B. T. Meggers's and C. Evans's research, followed in the 1980s by the work of numerous anthropologists who came to study the peoples of the forest. Their studies, which indicated that human societies had moved in a pattern similar to that of the spreading forests, supported the theory that the forests expanded outward from the refuges.

Then, anthropologists who had been living with the people of the forest began to describe what they had observed. The relationship between the people and the rain forest was more sophisticated than the term "hunter-gatherer" implies. Amazonian peoples were not passive consumers of the forest's bounty, but horticulturalists, orchardists, and forest and wildlife managers. The forest people were land managers, sometimes on massive scales. The earlier estimates of the native peoples' prehistoric populations were discovered to have been much too low: archaeologists found cities with networks of roads to gigantic suburban agricultural and food storage centers—all in a jungle where no agricultural production had been imagined possible. Areas of the forest assumed to be natural contained plants that had been collected and brought there by people. In these places the rain forest was not truly a "wild" untouched jungle but rather a living artifact, an abandoned garden.

In 1985, Darrell Addison Posey, whose "The Science of the Mebêngôkre" appears in this collection, wrote in a scientific paper, "the presence [in Amazonia] of extensively managed areas emphasizes the necessity for the reevaluation of concepts about the natural landscape. 'Naturalness' of ecological communities can never be assumed without investigating the human history of the area." This careful, understated observation has revolutionary implications that will change not only our vision of the Amazon, but our very concept of nature.

The news from the Amazon has subsided to a murmur

now. The worst of the fires are extinguished and the most destructive highways into the jungle have been halted, but millions of hectares have been lost—and are being lost—and thousands of Indians are dead from imported disease and the guns of settlers. The knowledge gained in the Amazon will not bring back the people or the forest, but there is hope in it.

The new story of the Amazon—perhaps of all American forests—begins fifteen thousand years ago at the end of the Ice Age. The land was a great savanna, the range of large mammals, and the home of people who managed the land to harvest its plants and supply of game. The grass plains were punctuated by islands of trees, which grew in the shelter of river valleys. The people made these forest islands their homes, which they managed and gardened. With the warming of the earth, the islands of garden and orchard forest began to spread from the valleys and rivers. People were part of this process, managing the land as it changed, influencing the evolutionary process with their burning, planting, and harvesting.

Perhaps we will never learn the extent to which human activity changed the history of the forests in the Amazon. But the significance of these studies lies not in what we know about the forests, but in what we can imagine of an ancient and interactive process between nature and humanity.

IV

In the summer of 1990, the Ecological Society of America, a sixty-year-old, respected, professional scientific organization, convened in Snowbird, Utah. The announced purpose of this conference was to explore the ramifications of two interlocking ideas: that nature's natural state is constant change; and that human participation in this process is natural and not necessarily destructive.

What coalesced at the Snowbird conference was the realization that these ideas are highly at odds with the view of nature current in popular culture. As the *New York Times* (July 31, 1990) reported in its coverage of the Snowbird conference: "Many scientists are forsaking one of the most deeply embedded concepts of ecology: the balance of nature. . . . textbooks will have to be rewritten and strategies of conservation and resource management rethought." Dr. Steward T. A. Pickett, a plant ecologist at the Institute of Ecosystem Studies of the New York Botanical Garden at Millbrook, New York, was quoted as saying: "The balance of nature concept . . . makes nice poetry, but it's not great science." The *Times* continued: "In this developing new perspective, humans are emerging as just one of many sources of ecological disturbance that keep nature in a perpetual state of uproar. . . . humans and their near-human ancestors have been doing so for eons, and ecological systems around the world bear their indelible imprint."

American nature educators and many organizations involved in the preservation of nature teach and rely upon the idea of a separate nature—a nature doing its own, natural, balanced thing—as the basis of their work and as the rationale for their fund-raising. The tenacity of this accepted explanation of how nature works is due only in part to the lag between research and textbook publication. The idea of nature-as-separate has its own staying power because it "fits" American culture. It is the bulwark of the methodology of the preservation movement and the raison d'être for our national parks system. As John Elder writes in "Wildness and Walls," "the American system of national parks . . . made a unique contribution to the stewardship of nature in the twentieth century. But it . . . also contributed in certain ways to the polarization of 'nature' and 'culture.' "

The idea of a separate nature is not an idea that America owns. But it found a new embodiment in the "discovery" of America, a myth absorbed into our culture. No matter that the "discovery" was an invention. The discovery myth sprang from the willingness to ignore the people who were already living on the land. It was a fiction of expediency, which, by ignoring husbandry, created real estate.

The notion of a separate nature is so profoundly entwined with American culture that it serves as the axiom upon which are founded *both sides* of the great American debate about nature.

In this debate, the preservationists of nature and the developers, dependable adversaries, are squared off in opposite corners. Americans have come to rely on the simplicity of these battle lines, and politicians thrive on them. Developers use the concepts of natural succession and climax forest, principles of progression to an undisturbed, "balanced" nature, to prove that, no matter what they do to the environment, nature heals itself. And preservationists argue that succession and climax prove that nature is a valuable heritage, a pristine treasure in need of sanctuary and protection from its unnatural enemy, humankind.

The debate rivets all attention and makes it difficult,

even seditious, to suggest to either side that a third, alternative idea might be available. The irony is that these two positions, so strongly held and hotly debated for two centuries, share a fundamental principle: nature and humanity are separate.

But, what if they are not separate? If the connections between culture and nature are to be made visible and real, textbooks and wildlife management guidelines must be rewritten; legislation, funding guidelines, and the goals of national conservation organizations must be rethought; the politics and policies of land use and management, of nature and wilderness, of agriculture and resources recovery must be reformulated; and even the relationship between the scientific and the spiritual must be scrutinized and challenged. The cultural ecology of a status quo is as complex and powerful as that of any rain forest.

V

In the American West a school of "new historians" is revising the accepted history of the region. These scholars question the history of the West as a process that unfolded at the "frontier" of European expansion and are reformulating it as the story of specific places shaped by the peoples who lived in them before "discovery and conquest." "In rethinking Western history," explains Patricia Nelson Limerick in *The Legacy of Conquest*, "we gain freedom to think of the West as a place—as many complicated environments occupied by natives who considered their homelands to be the center, not the edge."

Ethnobotanists working in the Southwest, among them Gary Nabhan, whose "A Child's Sense of Wildness" is included here, have documented domestic plants in land previously assumed to be "wild." And anthropologists in New England are weighing evidence of "interactive human-land relationships" that raise the possibility that the forests of New England, like those of the Amazon, might be derived in part from the management practices of thousands of years of Native American occupation.

But perhaps the strongest and most effective proponents of a new vision of land come not from the anthropologists, ethnobotanists, or professional historians, but from the ranks of Americans concerned with the preservation of historic and cultural landscapes. Organized at the grass-roots level, these advocates have formed a growing force of land trusts, historical societies, and conservancies with which to push for the preservation of "humanized" places on the land for the study and understanding of the biological and spiritual bond between culture and nature. These grassroots organizations understand that historic landscapes are more than the locations of historic events and see them as living artifacts, worthy of the status of national heritage. As a result of their activism, "viewshed" (which means a vantage point that offers a distant view) has been added to the vocabulary of environmental impact statements, tree cutting to restore an original landscape design on public parkland is becoming acceptable, and legislation is being drafted to confer landmark status on areas of land.

When Dubos wrote of the "emotional richness" of humanized landscapes, he was criticized for mixing science and poetry. A *sense of place* was an entirely abstract idea; it belonged to poetry or regional literature. Twenty years later, "place" is an accepted field of inquiry.

VI

The clamor of the debate and politics over a separate nature cannot make the new nature go away.

For its readers and its writers, *Orion* has become a place to try to make sense out of how we are to live with this changed nature. For the writers especially, it is not enough to assert that humanity and nature are bound in an inexorable, reciprocal relationship and have been since our ancestors appeared on the savannas of Africa two million years ago. It is not enough to "prove" that the forests of the Amazon, or those of the northern Appalachians, are the products of interaction between people and land. These are essentially facts about nature and do not say enough about *us*. We may attempt to treat them as science and keep them at objectivity's distance. But facts about nature are at the core of culture and integral to the construction of our most personal thoughts about who we are and how we should live.

Facts about nature have implications for our passions, politics, religion, and art. Science never was conceived as an instrument for investigating these aspects of being human. Science cannot say what we must do in order to settle up with a spirit we have wronged or to reforge the poetry that orders our lives. These are tasks that require all the faculties of our humanity.

The nature discussed in *Orion* is both the nature we observe—the nature of science—and the nature we believe. To explore both in search of a synthesis requires a mix of disciplines and epistemologies. The authors whose work appears in this anthology include ethnobotanists, historians, philosophers, writers, and artists, a student of interspecies communication, and a professional magician who used his craft to gain the confidence of shamans.

The five sections of the anthology are based on the lands and relationships they explore: home ground; geographies, near and distant; childhood; and metaphors.

In the first section, "Finding Home," four writers describe what happens when intimate relationships with places and nature are altered. Robert Finch and Wallace Kaufman write of the pain that bulldozers can inflict, as felt from different perspectives. David Ehrenfeld looks at the tenuous strands across distance and time that tie the nature of a place to its meaning, and how easily they may be severed. Brenda Peterson recalls a Nez Percé tradition in which intimacy is an expression of kinship.

"The Geographies of Home" and "Other Walls, Other Wildness" explore the interactions that occur as a culture transforms a wild place into a home, by altering the land and how the people see it. John R. Stilgoe traces changing attitudes and practices at the edge of the sea, on the uncomfortable margins of humanity's terrestrial range. J. Ronald Engel looks for sacred places on the margins where Western culture and nature meet, in landscapes that retain the power to reengage the bonds between humanity and the land. William R. Jordan III celebrates the reestablishment of these bonds through projects undertaken to restore damaged landscapes, and Barry Lopez decries the homogenization of American geographies, which makes these bonds difficult if not impossible to perceive, by trivializing the qualities of local relationships with the land.

In "Other Walls, Other Wildness," distant lands reveal the human origins of our concept of nature and invite reexaminations of our own metaphors and geographies. Darrell Addison Posey describes a people who dwell in the complexity of a rain forest's embrace and sees his own cultural constructs laid bare. John Elder contrasts the architecture of the walls around people, land, and nature in Japan and the United States and sees a common future. David Abram tells of a people deeply engaged with animate powers that reside beyond the human community. The intensity of these people's conviviality with the Others momentarily penetrates the veil that in the developed world separates people from nature. Susan Power Bratton travels back a thousand years, to the time of the weaving of that veil, and finds threads of harmony between people and the wilds of early Europe.

"A Child's Sense of Wildness" contains three accounts of the relationships between nature, land, and generations, as clarified in the epiphanies of childhood. In each of these moments, nature changes as it passes between generations. Terry Tempest Williams recalls sorting out her grandmother's explanation of how God and Congress made a refuge for birds. Scott Russell Sanders compares the land of his childhood with the tokens of mystery his son experiences beneath the muffling order of Boston. Gary Nabhan watches children dancing on a rock and learning wildness on a scale that will bind their lives to it.

"Metaphors of Desire" depicts how we achieve intimacy with nature when we refine the skills and methods of our perception. Ann Zwinger uses drawing to examine both how and what we see. Jim Nollman redraws events, and how we might see them, through science fiction. And Barbara Dean and Charles Bergman inspect close encounters that shape the metaphors we use to place ourselves in the world and to construct a way to live.

The new understanding of nature is both scientific and spiritual. It is not only a matter of figuring out what to do with misplaced hydrocarbons or rising sea water and mountains of trash. It is figuring out what we see when we look into a still pool, a mountain range, the country of another people, or the mysteries of childhood, and how these visions may help us to formulate a future—to find home.

PETER SAUER

PART ONE

✳

Finding Home

The Once and Future Cape

✳

ROBERT FINCH

S A NATURE WRITER, I HAVE always felt that my primary purpose was to celebrate the natural world— "celebrate" not only in the familiar sense of extolling and publicizing the delights of local environments, but also in the religious sense of performing ritual observances, and perhaps even more in the oldest etymological sense: that of simply being acquainted with a place or thing (from the Latin *celebrare*, "to frequent").

I began doing so, publicly, in 1975 in a series of weekly columns that ran in local Cape Cod newspapers. These were not so much "nature columns" as personal essays describing my own adventures with the land. Thanks to tolerant editors and sympathetic readers, I eventually wrote myself into an off-Cape audience, then off-Cape publications, then a book, and finally out of the local papers altogether.

But I continued to think of myself primarily as a celebrant of the natural world, preferring to keep whatever environmental debates or activities I was involved in out of my "real work," or at least to allude to them only indirectly. Celebration, I believed, was the most important way to change people's thinking about nature, by conveying its possibilities in a way that could be felt, rather than argued. One reviewer of my first book even commented, "It's so good to find an *unburdened* nature writer." It was, apparently, a successful fiction.

Lately, however, I seem to be seeing myself more and more not as a celebrant of living nature, but a eulogizer, a writer of epitaphs for moribund places and creatures, one who speaks well of the dead, or dying. Leafing through my old columns I am depressed to see how many of them celebrate things that no longer are, or have become distorted out of all recognition.

One of my earliest pieces described a tract of typical scrubby pine-oak woods across the street from where I used to live as "vintage Cape Cod woodland, impossible to improve, beyond improvement, unique only in its dwindling representativeness of a native landscape almost unrecognized because so characteristic, speaking mutely to us, asking only, like us, to fulfill itself." Today that patch of woodland has fulfilled, not itself, but some developer's ambition, has been "improved" now into final unrecognizability with paved roads, houses, cars, lawns, dogs, cable TV—not, it must always be said, that these things are bad or undesirable in themselves, but spreading as they have so relentlessly across a native landscape, they leave no room for any presence other than the human one.

I wrote once of a small landing at one of the herring ponds in our town, an unaltered piece of low shoreline that had for generations been used informally by fishermen and now served as a private beach for a nearby subdivision. I praised "its extraordinary plant and animal diversity which flourishes in unredeemed heathen health; its cup of life runneth rank and over. Here, on its shores, a man may still stand and put the electric human summer at a distance, the spirit may go out and claim such pools of peace for its own." Recently I stopped at that landing and saw that it had deteriorated sadly within the last year. Erosion at the end of the subdivision road has gotten so bad that soil runoff has covered most of the low beach vegetation and is now silting into the pond itself. With such natural degradation, license for human abuse seems to have increased. Tires, plastic buckets, and other refuse litter the shore and shallows. The landing has become, in essence, a slum, ugly and insulted, and I realized that I wanted nothing more to do with it. A few yards offshore a rusty oil drum, remnant of a homemade raft that has deteriorated, rested half-submerged in the water. Two boys, twelve or thirteen, rode their bikes down the eroded cartway and out into the pond, beating on the drum to scare frogs.

I have always regarded the extensive clam flats in our town as not only a source of chowder and tasty hors d'oeuvres, but also a kind of spiritual sanctuary, a refuge from the burgeoning human presence. "Out here," I wrote several years ago, "there is still space enough for all of us. How well used these long, low flats have been! And how remarkably unscathed they have remained, even today, despite the increasing intensity of human activity." How naive these words sound now, as each week seems to bring notices of more closings of swimming beaches and shellfish beds due to pollution, more evidence that we are poisoning with our own excrement, in insidious and often untraceable ways, the generous bounty of the ocean.

One would like to think that the ocean beach, at least that portion protected by the Cape Cod National Seashore, would be exempt from such debilitating change. Last

March, in a bracing northeaster, I walked for the first time in months along the Outer Beach in Truro. I did not see another soul during the entire afternoon, yet the beach itself was slathered with an appalling amount of plastic debris—bottles, jars, fence sections, tampon containers, whole rafts of plastic milk cartons tied together with plastic twine—an endless wrackline of enduring junk, so that at high tide I had constantly to watch my steps to keep from tripping over some half-buried piece, and was more aware of the smothering presence of human consumption and waste than if the entire beach had been plastered with the bodies of summer sunbathers.

In fact, as I look back upon the local places I have described over the past decade, about the only one that has remained essentially unchanged is the little cemetery next door, a place for burying things.

Change in itself, of course, is not bad. It is, as I have asserted many times, one of the chief attractions about a place like Cape Cod. "Change is the coin of this sandy realm," I wrote at the beginning of my second book. What is destructive is change that bears no relationship to its setting, change that is merely directionless, visionless exploitation. What scares me is the way we seem increasingly to accept such change as normal, or at least unavoidable. Last winter, in a neighboring town, a twelve-acre tract of pine woodland simply disappeared overnight, topsoil and all, creating an instant and utter wasteland of denuded, blowing sand—the site of yet another mammoth shopping center. In the aftermath there was no general outcry of rage at the arrogance, the total disengagement from the environment that such an action, however legal, implies—merely some complaints from nearby businessmen about the effect of the resultant dust storms on new autos and motel windows.

What I fear now is perhaps the most dangerous change of all, a change in our own regard, or sensibilities, for the land we have defiled. There is a point, a very definite and noticeable point in our relationship with the land, when, in spite of ourselves, we realize that we do not care so much anymore, when we begin to be convinced, against our very wills, that our neighborhood, our town, or the land as a whole is already lost, that what is left is not some injured yet still viable and salvageable entity, but merely a collection of remnants no longer worth saving. It is the point at which the local landscape is no longer perceived as a vital *other*, a living, breathing, healthful counterpart to human existence, but something that has suffered irreversible brain death. It may still be kept technically alive—with sewage treatment plants, water purification plants, "compensatory" wetlands, shellfish reseeding programs, lime treatments for acidified ponds, herbicides for hypereutrophied ponds, beach nourishment programs, fenced-off bird sanctuaries, and designated "green areas"—but it no longer *moves*, or if it does, not with a will of its own. Many of our Cape Cod towns have already passed that point; the rest are fast approaching it.

It was not that I was innocent, even at the beginning, about the magnitude of the forces threatening this once-lovely peninsula. In an early column I wrote, "The capacity for human change now rivals, and on the surface surpasses, natural process itself, so that the earth seems to shift under our feet. Land itself becomes little more than abstract patterns on a developer's plans or the assessor's map, coordinates for profit or taxes."

No, I was not innocent, but I may have been proud. Perhaps I thought too much could be done by writing, believed that language really did have some magical, incantatory power, so that what was captured in words good and true would somehow be protected from the forces of greed and indifference. If I ever thought so, I have been disillusioned once and for all.

In the end, what hits hardest is what hits closest to home. Nothing has shown me so clearly the direction the winds of change are blowing over this unsheltered land as the slow but steady demise of the dirt road I live on.

When I first wrote of it, some ten years ago, it was a soft, winding, country road, overarched by the bordering oaks, lined with banks rich with tapestries of lichens, mosses, and small native wildflowers. I loved it for the way it discouraged speed and encouraged observation, for its close relationship with the surrounding landscape. Birds' nests could be found in the bordering shrubs, and tree seedlings, flowers, ant and wasp nests would occasionally show up in its surface. I loved the way its soft and yielding surface recorded the passing of the seasons and the passing of local wildlife, the way it offered unexpected encounters with animals: a glimpse of a deer or fox, the slow peregrination of a box turtle, a hawk pouncing on some unlucky vole or chipmunk, a woodcock performing its mad vernal dances and songs in a locust clearing just off the roadside.

Gradually all that has changed. For several years now the local highway department has been grading and "improving" the road, spreading a thickening layer of gray gravel and stone dust on its sandy surface. Though the original road could become an inconvenient muddy mire during wet times of the year, it generally maintained itself pretty well, following as it did the natural contours of the land, using natural drainage, and requiring grading only twice a year. With the new surfacing, and increased traffic from a new subdivision at the other end, a typical pattern of "washboarding" has developed, chronic pot-holes and ruts that have required more and more frequent grading, more and more loads of hardening, which in turn create more and more gullies, bumps, and holes, which in turn . . .

One portion of the road, a wide curve around a natural depression, was straightened out a few years ago because it lay off the official town road layout and, in this modern world of economic paradoxes, the town engineer found it cheaper to move the road physically than to relocate it on the paper layout. Consequently the hollow, where scarlet tanagers used to nest in an old cherry tree, was filled in, the woodcock courting ground was wiped out, and a constant runoff of gray slurry onto a small piece of conservation land was set in motion.

Then, two years ago, partially to correct some of the drainage problems created by the straightening, and partially at the request of the subdivision residents at the far end, one half of the road was paved—a full-fledged high-way with twenty-two feet of asphalt and ten feet of scraped, denuded shoulder on either side. After it was put in, some of the residents commented, "We didn't know it would look like that."

And, just recently, the owner of the woods on the remaining unpaved portion of the road died. Her family had owned the land for almost two hundred years, sharing it with deer, grouse, box turtles, and whippoorwills, all species that disappear with even modest development. Now the land has been surveyed and subdivided by her heirs, the first of the lots has already been sold, and houses will soon come, and I am sure the request to widen, pave, and straighten the rest of the road, in the name of safety and convenience, will not be far behind.

Already the traffic has increased noticeably. For a while I tried to hold the road's beleaguered rurality intact in my mind, denying the changes that appeared, making excuses for each new vehicle I saw, as if each were only some temporary or special user. But they are too many for me now. The old dirt road, though not completely altered or built up yet, is no more; what was a back road is now an artery, and the twentieth century has at last arrived on my doorstep.

Even though our end of the road still retains more semblance of what it was like when I first moved here, I am reluctant to walk down it these days. It is too much like cataloging what will soon be gone. The actual trees, shrubs, rocks, birds, and other presences at times seem already indistinct, less than real, while the as-yet unbuilt houses, driveways, swimming pools, and outer accoutrements of suburbia loom with the intensity of the inevitable.

But one night this spring, at dusk, after cleaning some fish, I walked outside and found the evening air so soft and the dying light so sweet that I could not resist their call. I set off down the road in a light sprinkle and gathering dark to see if, perhaps, the woodcock had returned this year, though he has been gone for three seasons now. Once again the magic, the soft solitude of this road in early spring, engulfed me, full of unexpected possibility as of old, cruelly mixing knowledge and desire. In spite of myself my spirit went out into its still leafless hollows and slopes, like pond ripples expanding into hidden coves. I suddenly knew that it would not be possible for any car to appear along the road that evening. None did. Where a pair of old cartways veer off into the woods to the east, I heard what I first thought was an early wood thrush, but it proved to be the song of a hermit thrush—a clear, single, initial note followed by short, rising trills that vanished upward into ethereality. It is such a fragile, vulnerable, beautiful, and intricate song that the heart contracts with its poignancy. I turned off the road onto one of the cartways and followed the faint notes for several minutes, not actually hoping to see the bird itself, but simply to follow it and let the song etch itself permanently into my memory: *Once here, on this road, in late April, a hermit thrush sang out of the darkness*—a gift that asked nothing in return but attention.

A little further down the road, just before the paved section begins, behind an old homestead that is now part of the new subdivision, I heard a whippoorwill, tentative at first, but then, like a balky motor coughing and settling into a steady run, confident and regular, the bird song opposite of the thrush's shy, tender aria, yet complementary. I stood listening in what was now true darkness, as the bird ranged wide with its song over the oak woods, loving and requiring its solitude as well.

Whippoorwills and hermit thrushes, songs heard on a spring night, what are they against the tides of money and self-interest that wash ever more insistently at our land, changing it, despite our best efforts, into something poor and undistinguished?

Yet in spite of what I know is good for me, in spite of the all-too-real and palpable risk in loving something so vulnerable, I know that I will continue to walk out along this road, along this land, as I know the birds will continue to sing, undampened and undefeated, until the bulldozers arrive. After that, well . . .

We all have to adapt to change. Some of us do it by changing our manner of living, reducing expectations, others by changing location, migrating; some simply disappear. Oaks shade out pines, house finches replace purple finches, starlings and English sparrows evict bluebirds, gulls push out terns, houses dispossess meadowlarks and screech owls. It is called succession. Some of it is natural, some of it is not. But if I have learned anything as a writer, as a chronicler of this extraordinary, doomed place, it is this: There is only so much fascination in watching something beautiful die.

Places

※

DAVID EHRENFELD

I BECAME A CONSERVATIONIST gradually, as a result of getting to know a place worth saving. There are other ways of becoming a conservationist, through books or television for example, but getting to know a place is the surest and most pleasurable way. It's also the most time-consuming. What's more, a feeling for places doesn't always come naturally. In my case, it was definitely an acquired trait. The place was Tortuguero, in Costa Rica. I had gone there as a graduate student, sent by my major professor, the late Archie Carr. He was, I believe, the greatest conservationist of our time, but he didn't teach conservation by any formal process of instruction. He was too smart for that. He had a better way.

The beginning of my introduction to places was not in Tortuguero at all, but in Gainesville, Florida, where I had come to study zoology with Dr. Carr. It was my first day there, and it was summer, hot and humid. My new medical diploma from Harvard was in my suitcase and I was wearing a tie and jacket. I was terribly out of place, the way only a person who doesn't have a good feeling for places can be.

Archie greeted me as if he had been waiting eagerly for my arrival for years. (Even after I had been around long enough to learn that he greeted everybody that way, those greetings still made me feel good.) When the formalities were over, a matter of maybe a minute, he said:

"Ehrenfeld, have you ever seen an alligator nest?"

I hadn't. There weren't any in Boston. Nor in northern New Jersey, where I grew up.

In five minutes we were plunging through the vegetation along the shore of Lake Alice, at the southern end of the University of Florida's campus. I was still wearing my jacket and tie. The alligator nest, when we reached it, looked like a haphazard pile of mud and sticks. I don't remember whether Archie uncovered any of the elongated white eggs to show me; probably he did. What I do remember is that he pointed out the mother alligator floating about fifty feet offshore and told me to watch her. Then, while I watched, he began to make a soft, croaking, chuckling, grunting noise.

Soon, the alligator swung around toward us and moved closer to shore.

"That's the noise alligator hatchlings make," said Archie. "When they hatch out, the mother hears them and comes to release them from the nest and protect them. They stay with her a year or two. Old E. A. McIlhenny, the Louisiana tabasco sauce king, was the first person to write about the fierce maternal behavior of alligators, back in 1935. He wasn't a trained zoologist. Nobody believed him. Reptiles weren't supposed to be maternal. But everything he said was right."

He resumed croaking. The alligator came a little closer and then stopped. Apparently she was getting used to Professor Carr's impersonations and was no longer impressed. After a while, we left.

That night, as I was dropping off to sleep, I wondered why Archie had taken me to look at an alligator nest before introducing me to his colleagues or showing me around the lab. I couldn't figure it out. Only years later did it occur to me that this was a proper introduction to a place—visiting a typical part of the landscape and meeting its oldest inhabitants. Alligators, after all, are just an advanced kind of dinosaur. And knowing Archie and his delight in the comic, he probably also wanted to see me in my tie and jacket up against that alligator nest. But at the time I wasn't aware of these things. It took another kind of reptile to teach me about places and conservation.

It was Archie's intention, and mine, that I would do my doctoral research on the orientation and navigation of sea turtles, the so-called green turtle (*Chelonia mydas*), at Tortuguero, the great nesting beach along Costa Rica's Caribbean coast. Archie's research had proved that green turtles are philopatric nesters, that is, they return to the same place to nest every two, three, or four years, often swimming many hundreds of miles to get there. Any turtle we found nesting at Tortuguero we measured, described, and marked with a numbered metal tag attached to a front flipper and bearing Archie's address and an offer of a reward for its return. That way we recognized turtles who had been on the beach before, and the tag returns from turtle fishermen told us where the turtles went after they left Tortuguero.

Because the turtles come out to nest after dark, much of my work was done at night. There was a great deal of waiting between turtles, plenty of time to sit on a driftwood log and think. In the first years of my research I was often the only one on the beach for miles. After ten or twenty minutes of sitting without using my flashlight, my eyes adapted to the dark and I could make out forms against the brown-black sand: the beach plum and coconut palm silhouettes in back, the flicker of the surf in front, sometimes even the shadowy outline of a trailing railroad vine or the scurry of a ghost crab at my feet. The air was heavy and damp with a distinctive primal smell that I can remember but not describe. The rhythmic roar of the surf a few feet away never ceased—my favorite sound. I hear it as I write in my landlocked office in New Jersey. And then, with ponderous, dramatic slowness, a giant turtle would emerge from the sea.

Usually I would see the track first, a vivid black line standing out against the lesser blackness, like the swath of a bulldozer. If I was closer, I could hear the animal's deep hiss of breath and the sounds of her undershell scraping over logs. If there was a moon, I might see the light glistening off the parabolic curve of the still wet shell. Size at night is hard to determine: even the sprightly 180-pounders, probably nesting for the first time, looked big when nearby, but the 400-pound ancients, with shells nearly four feet long, were colossal in the darkness. Then when the excavations of the body pit and egg cavity were done, if I slowly parted the hind flippers of the now-oblivious turtle, I could watch the perfect white spheres falling and falling into the flask-shaped pit scooped in the soft sand.

Falling as they have fallen for a hundred million years, with the same slow cadence, always shielded from the rain or stars by the same massive bulk with the beaked head and the same large, myopic eyes rimmed with crusts of sand washed out by tears. Minutes and hours, days and months dissolve into eons. I am on an Oligocene beach, an Eocene beach, a Cretaceous beach—the scene is the same. It is night, the turtles are coming back, always back; I hear a deep hiss of breath and catch a glint of wet shell as the continents slide and crash, the oceans form and grow. The turtles were coming here before here was here. At Tortuguero I learned the meaning of place and began to understand how it is bound up with time.

I also learned what it means to have to stand by while a place is damaged. What it means to watch while the forest behind the beach is exploited by ignorant opportunists with foreign capital. What it means to watch while a tagged turtle, one we have found nesting at the same spot three times in a decade, crawls slowly down the beach back to the water, where a dozen turtle fishing boats are waiting just beyond the surf.

Although my awareness of the need for conservation came slowly as a result of many experiences, I associate it especially with one night at Tortuguero. There were four or five of us walking the beach, including Archie and Jose Figueres, better known as "Don Pepe," the leader of the revolution, liberator of Costa Rica, and first president of the only nonmilitarized democracy of any size on the planet. There was no guard; none was needed.

It was Don Pepe's first visit to the legendary Tortuguero—we had been watching a green turtle nest, also a first for him. El Presidente, a short, Napoleonic man with boundless energy, was enjoying himself enormously. Both he and Archie were truly charismatic people, and they liked and respected one another. The rest of us went along quietly, enjoying the show. As we walked up the beach toward the boca, where the Rio Tortuguero meets the sea,

Don Pepe questioned Dr. Carr about the green turtles and their need for conservation. How important was it to make Tortuguero a sanctuary? Just then, a flashlight picked out a strange sight up ahead.

A turtle was on the beach, near the waterline, trailing something. And behind her was a line of eggs which, for some reason, she was depositing on the bare, unprotected sand. We hurried to see what the problem was.

When we got close, it was all too apparent. The entire undershell of the turtle had been cut away by poachers who were after calipee, or cartilage, to dry and sell to the European turtle soup manufacturers. Not interested in the meat or eggs, they had evidently then flipped her back on her belly for sport, to see where she would crawl. What she was trailing was her intestines. The poachers had probably been frightened away by our lights only minutes before.

Dr. Carr, who knew sea turtles better than any human being on earth and who had devoted much of his life to their protection, said nothing. He looked at Don Pepe, and so did I. It was a moment of revelation. Don Pepe was very, very angry, trembling with rage. This was his country, his place. He had risked his life for it fighting in the Cerro de la Muerte. The turtles were part of this place, even part of its name, Tortuguero; they had been coming here long before people existed in Central America. He understood that, just as he understood the profound significance of the useless, round, white eggs swept by the retreating wavelets down the packed sand into the surf beyond. No green turtle born at Tortuguero will ever lay her eggs anywhere else. She was home, laying her eggs for the last time.

Today there are far more green turtles at Tortuguero than there were when Don Pepe made his first visit, thanks to him, to other enlightened citizens of his remarkable country, and above all to Archie Carr. I haven't been back since 1983. No time, the cost of flying a family of six to San José—these are the sorts of excuses I make. But the real reason is more selfish. How will Tortuguero be with electricity and vacation cabins, with a road to Tortuguero Village, without Archie or Sheftan Martinez or Bertie Downs or Miss Sibella, and with all those eager new conservationists crowding the black beach at night? Will it be the same place? Will I enjoy being there?

Of course I know the answer is yes. Places can be destroyed, that is, they can have their nature and meaning irrevocably changed and their connection with the past severed. All conservationists are aware of that. This hasn't happened at Tortuguero. It has changed, but it is still the same place. When I do go back, as I must because places get in your blood, I know I will still be able to find a log on the beach to sit on alone in the darkness, and with luck will see a dim, rounded form heaving itself out of the nearby sea.

Confessions of a Developer

✳

WALLACE KAUFMAN

I AM A MEMBER OF A PERSE-cuted minority. It's one whose story you haven't heard. Nobody has written poignantly about the daily personal abuse, the exile within society, the injustices we suffer. We haven't been eloquent in our own behalf either. A literary tradition has not emerged yet among developers.

I try not to be ashamed of who I am, but that is hard when I go to meetings with my friends in the environmental community. I often feel as if I were Italian and through the whole meeting people have been talking about the Mafia; I feel as if I were black and the talk is about nothing but crime and drugs and Willie Horton. Developers, too, are victims of stereotypes.

Like most minorities I can point to the past and say, "See, I come from a people with a rich history. Look how we raised ancient Sumer in the desert. How about that 'rose-red city half as old as time' in Egypt? What about the road we built over the scenic peaks of the Andes—the Inca trail—and the great market squares and shopping centers our Mayans built in the rain forest of Yucatán?"

People look, but they still don't see. Revisionists have already eliminated my forerunners from history. Sumer,

38

Alexandria, Chichén Itzá, the Inca Trail, Venice—these are celebrated as triumphs in the life of civilization, but no one celebrates their developers. America is awash in monuments to soldiers, politicians, musicians, poets, civil rights leaders, teachers, conservationists, athletes, Indian chiefs, dinosaurs, and dogs, but how many monuments do you see to a real estate developer?

Who has raised a statue to Elmer Harmon, who in 1887 created the first planned suburb, which indeed was "the best chance ever offered in America for a poor man to acquire good property"? Harry Black brought skyscrapers like the Flatiron Building to Manhattan, and millions of Americans send postcards celebrating the skyline he inspired, but not even a stubby obelisk bears his name. Why is there no monument to Bill Levitt, whose housing innovations after World War II provided homes for tens of thousands of struggling veterans?

The truth is Americans associate real estate development more with wealth than courage or genius. Despite a reputation for materialism, Americans keep a cautious distance from people whose fame is inseparable from cutting trees, paving, wrecking, laying sewage discharge pipes, and spending large sums of money. It is not the money that is feared. It is the power. Those large sums endow the user with the power to change the face of the earth, the character of a city.

In the mind of an America that loves convenience, cars, technology, comfort, farms, parks, and wilderness, developers occupy a secure but lonely corner. We are what Jewish moneylenders were in the mind of medieval Europe, which craved and hated interest-bearing loans. Development is to the course of civilization what libido is to courtship.

I understand how people feel about development. Give me five minutes and I'll prove it faster than a bulldozer flattens a dogwood. In me parts of humanity are at war with each other. I am a developer and a conservationist. I love bulldozers, and I've never met a tree I didn't like. I would rather walk around a farm than a shopping center, but I believe that in many communities, shopping centers are a good substitute for a "downtown."

I am not so different from most Americans. All of us are by nature developers. When I visit a day-care center I don't see two kinds of kids—one growing plants and feeding fish while the other piles up blocks and pushes model trucks and bulldozers around the sandbox. (Neither toy manufacturers nor the Sierra Club offers a wilderness kit alternative.) Almost all the kids are making skyscrapers, building railroads, making Lego mansions. There we are, the developer animals.

Most kids never grow up to develop anything beyond the living room rug or the sandbox. Perhaps in some of us the developer perspective becomes dominant, while a nature preference prevails in others. Maybe some day someone will locate the development and nature preferences on opposite sides of the brain. In any case, a few people accept the development imperative and learn to build subdivisions, roads, shopping centers, and cities. Along the way they have to learn to destroy woods and prairies, orchards and farms, marshes and meadows.

I propose that if we understand and accept the development urge, we will come closer to solving our land-use problems. We should no more repress the development part of our psyche because some developers pillage nature than we should repress our sexuality because some men and women are pornographers and prostitutes.

I became a developer because I didn't like developers. I thought I could do it better. In 1966 there were five of us young English professors at the University of North Carolina at Chapel Hill who wanted to live in the country and have a little land.

I found an eighty-acre "mountain" overlooking the town water supply. We could have four or five acres each for a grand total of $5,000. For months we talked about what we would do. Finally, time came to buy in or drop out. "Too far out," said the James Joyce scholar. "What about snakes?" asked the man who taught about the courage of hunters in Faulkner's fiction. "Can we get a road in there?" wondered the Dos Passos biographer. The whole thing became an excursion into pastoral fantasy. I even said to myself, "Well, maybe the mountain is better off just the way it is."

I was learning my first important lesson in development: no development in the world can pass all the safety tests that concern even a small number of people. Certainly if we lived on the outskirts of Eden and Moses proposed the modest city of Jerusalem, he could not have written a satisfactory environmental impact statement. We certainly couldn't have done it for the irrigation projects of the Nile, or the Tigris and Euphrates. Most people would rather analyze risks than take them. There is no risk-free development. Development is the process of taking risks—financial, environmental, social, and personal.

As an academic myself, I should have known that scholars are not trained to take risks. I came, though, from a blue-collar family where new ideas were few but firmly attached to action. What I had started to do for myself and my colleagues in the English department, I now decided to do on speculation—for all those people who wanted to live in the country in peace with nature. With the help of a graduate student friend whose only expertise was an exhaustive study of the Icelandic Eddas, I put a small down payment on 330 acres of trees that had taken over abandoned farms or grew in untillable valleys and rocky soil.

I was moving too fast to think about what I was doing and why, but I know now. My idea may have been different from other developments, but my inspiration was all-American. The concept had come in a straight line out of the tin double bed in a poor section of Queens where my brother and I used to lie awake at night telling each other how we would get out of the city and live on a jungle farm where we would tame panthers and boa constrictors and the only domestic animal would be a coal-black stallion. This was a child's version of what we often call "The American Dream," the place where we really want to live. Americans have been searching for it for four hundred years. Some Americans, call them developers, have been building places they hope will satisfy the searchers.

Like every other developer I offered my development as one of those places. I said to myself (and probably to a few others), I can provide homes for people without messing up the landscape the way other developers do. What's more I can do it cheaper and give people several acres where they can really appreciate what goes on in nature. While this wasn't a panther farm in the Colombian jungle, it was to be a Peaceable Kingdom of the Piedmont.

What I planned and began to advertise didn't seem like development but the realization of my environmental and social ideals. The principles were simple: (1) make home-sites five acres or larger where one person's way of life wouldn't interfere with a neighbor's; (2) write covenants to prevent people from cutting too many trees, polluting the streams, and leaving junk in the woods; (3) keep costs low by bypassing the realtors and paying for development from sales instead of debt; (4) finance the lots so that anyone with a steady job in the local mill could afford to buy.

Realtors assured me the idea was nice, but people really wouldn't want to live in the woods thirteen miles away from town. My friend who read the Eddas nevertheless believed in me. "Don't pay any attention to them," he said, and went on to finish his thesis on Mohammed in medieval literature. The month after we signed the mortgage, he expressed his regrets and moved to the Bronx to explain the terrible justice of Iceland's Snorri to slum kids.

In a way my critics were right. For a year and a half I guided prospective buyers down the little logging road into the property. I thought people would like the design-your-own-lot approach. They could choose how long and how wide the lot would be and what hills and trees might be on it. But even trail-seasoned country lovers arrived expecting to see some kind of development. All they saw was woods. There were no roads cleared, no lots laid out. Sometimes I would meet people on the public road. If I arrived late, they would be standing by our little wooden sign as if it offered some necessary anchor in the wilderness. Some people showed up in dresses and ties, sandals and shorts; some with babies barely able to walk and too big to carry far. They went back to town and talked about their crazy afternoon in the wilds. They didn't buy anything.

I was learning development lessons two and three. People buy a sense of place. They want a recognizable order, a road that leads somewhere, driveways that tell where a house might go. They want electricity. Perhaps they have their ideas of an ideal lot and home, but most people want developers to go ahead and give them something about which they can say yea or nay.

I also learned that satisfying this desire for a sense of place and security means investing a lot of money before answering the first inquiry. This front money means more risk. That means investors expect more profit. It also means more interest expense. In sum, it means more expensive development.

Developers are willing to take risks, but they don't take many. One of the axioms of real estate economics is that success breeds competition. Developers try to minimize their risks by copying other successful developments. We can call developers timid, but many are risking not only their own money but family money, or their friends' money. If they are risking money put up by stockholders or banks, the law, not to mention a bunch of nervous strangers, is always looking over their shoulder.

I was lucky. America celebrated the first Earth Day in 1970. It reaffirmed the intuition that "out in the country" was a good place to live. In many minds the forest became the place where nature could exert its most healing powers. Thirty-three lots and 330 acres sold out by 1972, and our little company had made enough money to put aside some

45 acres of stream valley as common land.

As I said, my buyers were not ready to blaze any trails. I had to build a road. That was the end of my environmental virginity. I rented a little chain saw from the Rent All. I wasn't going to have any bulldozer pushing over my trees and piling them up. I'd carefully select a road line that avoided the big trees. What I had to cut, I would cut so someone could use the logs.

The rented saw was little because I only wanted to do a little damage. But no matter which way I tried to run the road, big trees stood in my way. There were a lot more than I had imagined. It was like trying to shovel a blizzard with a teaspoon. The next day I took a company check and went to town and bought a big Stihl 041 with a twenty-one-inch bar. I intended to execute each and every oak and hickory, holly, and loblolly pine myself. Why let some anonymous bulldozer be my surrogate? If I were going to build a road, I'd take the emotional responsibility as well as the legal.

I managed to curve the road around a few special trees, but I cut dozens that had been standing in place for 150 or 200 years. I rubbed my nose in the damage. I counted rings, learned the marks left by weather and animals and the fall of other trees. I severed grapevines as thick as my arms, and returning the next day saw their watery sap still bleeding from the stubs. I learned the licorice smell of a pine stump, the acid smell of red oak, and the musky tannin of white oak. It was a little like killing and dressing your own meat.

Within a week I had cleared the first half mile. Not too bad, I told myself. The canopy would soon grow back over the road and it would be a shady country lane. Buddy the bulldozer operator laughed when he came to grub the stumps. "Hell, I can't even turn around in that space."

I learned that a road fit for service according to the state of North Carolina has the following characteristics:

The roadbed must be twenty feet wide and paved.

Then there are shoulders. These may be soft. Add four feet on each side.

The shoulders must not be soggy, however, so they are accompanied by ditches. Add six feet each side.

The slopes on the ditches and the embankments must be gradual enough so grass will not fall off or the soil erode. If you have any embankment beyond the ditch add five or ten more feet.

Accommodating all of this kindness to man and nature requires cutting a swath through the forest that is fifty to sixty feet wide. This was no job for one man and a chain saw.

In one day the D-8 Caterpillar had piled up all the trees I had cut and a lot more in three big mounds that looked as though a giant beaver expected someone to turn a river down that roadway. In three or four places I had left an especially large tree near the edge of the road, something like Frost's "Tuft of Flowers" left by the mower. Life, however, happens differently than poems, and most of the trees had to go or have their roots cut: you can't run a road ditch around a tree. The dozer simply lifted its blade eight or ten feet up the trunk of a two-foot-thick oak and pushed until the tree's own whiplashing top helped break the roots' hold in the earth.

One weekend, while the piles were drying, I climbed over them looking for good logs and crotches to salvage for future woodworking. Everything was pinned at some point under something else. I did find a large hollow gum tree which I sectioned and split, intending to use the curved pieces for benches. When I scraped and pried the rot from inside the log, thousands of carpenter ants, beetles, and millipedes fell out and scattered in chaos on the ground. In that insignificant and dying tree a whole community of life had been carrying on confidently through years of darkness. By comparison the light-drenched roadbed was simple and lifeless.

On Monday Buddy arrived with a pickup load of old tires. We threw them on the piles, and he doused the pyres with gasoline. By evening the charred piles smouldered, not a tree or stump recognizable as oak, hickory, gum, or anything else. The next day the ashes were buried, and the road was clear—a red avenue of clay with big trees seeming to stand at numb attention on both sides. The dozer cut through the tops of hills until the roadbed had an acceptable incline. A pan roared up and down the road carrying the cutout earth to fill the low spots. The hills and valleys were being averaged into conformity.

Two days later, after scraping and graveling and grading, a car could drive from one end to the other at fifty miles per hour. Everything was slick and smooth.

I used to stand in that roadway, looking up and down and thinking, "God help me, did I do this?" I was like a man returning time and again to the scene of a hit-and-run accident. But there was no one to report to and not even a corpse to bury.

About that time Carolina Power and Light came along. They could not put their poles in the road right-of-way, so they cleared another fifteen feet alongside the road, felling trees, hacking away brush, and planting their poles.

Now people drove in with their Volkswagen bugs and Saabs and vans, and they began to buy. Nobody lamented the trees that had been cut and burned any more than cried about the destroyed forests of Manhattan Island.

Although each of them came praising the covenants that promised a peaceable and unpolluted kingdom, they approached their homes in the woods with a variety of styles that matched their paths through life. How did they love nature? Let me count the ways.

A young woman with milk goats and chickens allowed them to roam the woods, tearing up the forest floor and eating gardens as well as wildflowers. An insurance man with two Saint Bernards was happy his dogs had lots of room even though they walked through screen doors and knocked down a neighbor's eighty-year-old mother. Lou and Tammy's pack of hounds kept the ex-Marine next door awake. A dentist started a forest fire throwing out his wood stove ashes. The ex-Marine cherished his privacy so much he wouldn't build a drive to his house and carried all his lumber in by hand; but he cleared part of the wildlife buffer for his garden. A stone mason who laid his stone in imitation of natural deposits drained his bathtub, sink, and washing machine into the woods near the creek. An Episcopal minister who built a log house to blend into the woods objected to the width of our roads that didn't blend in, but he controlled beetles in his natural house by periodically treating it with a toxic preservative.

I, the developer, had made a place bound to attract people who were sentimental about nature. They taught me lesson number four, a lesson that ought to be one of the Ten Commandments of the environmental movement:

sentimentality applied is just another form of development.

If I am going to be vilified as a polluter and destroyer, I want the judgment to be applied impartially. I don't want someone spared because he wears hiking boots, reads poetry, or milks cows.

For an example of nature sentimentality at its worst, look at our attitudes toward farming. The notion that by preserving farmland we have fortified ourselves against development and struck a blow for nature is nonsense. From nature's point of view most farms are hugely destructive. What other form of development routinely poisons its soils and devastates such vast areas, exclusively to serve people? A farm murders natural diversity and extracts the life force from nature's carcass to sell for profit. Most farming is voodoo ecology that makes a walking zombie out of nature. So why do we celebrate America's farmers with such a soft heart? Why do we find beauty in the farmscape but not in the well-landscaped shopping mall or subdivision? It's sentimentality.

When I did my first development back in 1968 I was fortunate to be free from laws and regulations. I made my own decisions about erosion control, lot size, water, sewers, curbs, gutters, electricity, open space, setbacks, traffic flow, curb cuts, and who could do what on their land. In most high-growth areas, including the Research Triangle area of North Carolina where I operate, all these things are now subject to approval by state, county, and city governments.

As a citizen and conservationist I favor controls. I have

stood up in countless hearings and asked the planning board or county commissioners to tighten regulations, to require more open space in a subdivision, or to deny a permit for a shopping center. When Congress first considered a bill that would prohibit development on some of our ocean beaches I went to Washington and sat next to the head of the most powerful Political Action Committee in the country, the Realtors PAC, and testified that my leader's position was short-sighted, uninformed, and motivated by greed.

Developers, however, are just like a lot of writers, teachers, farmers, and dancers. We think we can learn the business on our own, asking for help when we think we need it and from the people who make us comfortable. Although I see a legitimate role for the public in my development plans, I still feel the way you do when someone looks over your shoulder as you write a letter or knocks on your door when you're making love.

The public, of course, thinks developers need more attention than it gives to people who merely create culture. There are several reasons for this. First, development is an assault on our sensibilities. It's noisy and it's dirty, and it changes our surroundings right before our eyes. Second, development destroys things we care about deeply—streams, trees, hills, animals. Finally, and most important, development brings out greed.

My attempt to deal with greed taught me my fifth important lesson as a developer. The public is right that development tempts developers to do things they know are not right. It tempts everyone. Almost everyone has a price. In my first development, I began to see sellers who had gotten a good deal from us charging what the market would bear when they resold their lots. The kind of family I grew up in couldn't afford them anymore.

When I did my second development I wanted to protect everyone from greed. Into the covenants for this 225-acre community I wrote a clause that controlled resales. A seller could get the original purchase price of the land plus an amount equal to general inflation. For the house he could get the cost of replacing it. Half of anything over these figures had to be put in a landowners' trust fund to help lower-income people buy land.

Lawyers who undertook a closing on a resale here would call me up as if they could not read. They could read, but they couldn't believe what they were reading. Sometimes my covenant worked and owners sold at the formula price. Others got their neighbors to waive the profit restriction.

When it comes to money, I learned, there is no such thing as a liberal or a conservative. At the extremes are a few saints and Midases. Everybody else wants as much as he or she can get. I once designed a small subdivision of a farm bought by a professor who specialized in Latin American land reform, a champion of redistributing wealth. He looked at the lot prices I proposed and said, "Aren't these very low? Can't we get much more than this?" I pointed out that after the road and survey costs, he would be doubling his money. And didn't he want as many people as possible to be able to afford his land? No, he wanted the same kind of money everybody else made on real estate.

When it comes to buying and selling real estate I've decided I too might as well make everything I can. If I forgo some profit someone else will grab it. They could be one of James Watt's Sagebrush Rebels or one of my allies in conservation.

I made enough to free my house and land from mortgages and to devote more time to proving that the pen was mightier than the bulldozer. I dropped out of development for five or six years. Then at a conference on land use I ran into a conservative big-time realtor and developer who had grown wealthy on the Research Triangle's land boom. Some years earlier he and other investors had agreed to sell a seven-hundred-acre tract to a land trust that wanted to build a solar village on its south slopes overlooking the softly muscled waters of the Haw River. I had been president of the trust then, and we had failed to raise the money for a bargain price.

The price was higher now, but still a bargain. I sold new stock in my shrunken but still existing company, and we bought. I was back in business. Here were 720 acres full of beautiful beech and oak forests, silent stone chimneys surrounded by walnut and giant oaks, old fields once worked savagely by desperate family farmers and now lying quiet under a blanket of pine needles in the deep shade of big loblollies. The site was big enough to contain both the source and the mouth of several small creeks that ran clear. Wherever there was a soft stream bank or mud puddle, deer, raccoons, possums left their tracks. Turkeys thrived on the acorns and grubs in the leaf mold. It was a place that should have been preserved as a wilderness.

There was no one to preserve it, however, and the market was full of people more than willing to spoil it. If I had had a million dollars I would have bought it and left it for the animals and trees. It would have been the most natural and best-protected place left in this new Silicon Valley. I didn't have enough money for a new pickup truck, much less the funds to pick up seven hundred acres of land. I knew I was once again going to go to war with myself.

I immediately began to write a peace treaty. Like most, it is full of compromises. I drafted a long set of covenants that reflected my accumulated frustrations with the way people use land as well as everything I know about how to protect wildlife, water, and air from people.

The building boom has begun. People have been moving in. Already I have problems. Owners don't want to keep their dogs and cats under control when the poor things could be enjoying such happy freedom of the woods. So there is now a little pack chasing deer and baying raccoons into the trees. I see an occasional cat prowling the roadside for rabbits, birds, lizards, mice, and voles.

There are days when I am ready to plough up the roads I've built and tear down the houses. I'm not alone in my regrets. In a recent issue of *North Carolina Wildlife*, a local conservationist and hunter lamented the changes development had brought to this place. Yet until I came along no one else had made a move to protect this land from the gathering forces of the market. No environmental group had even explored it, although it was one of the few big tracts left in the river valley.

Antidevelopers are fond of printing on their banners and posters Thoreau's declaration, "In wildness is the preservation of the world." History and my own experience suggest the opposite: "In civilization is the preservation of wildness."

Real estate development doesn't pretend to be natural, but in the big picture it is kinder in quantity and often gentler in quality than other land uses. My road building has contributed its share of sediment to local streams and rivers, but not a fraction as much as the nearby dairy farmer's creekside feedlot. Acre for acre fewer toxic chemicals run into our rivers and streams from a subdivision or even a shopping center than from a farm.

Yet Americans are prejudiced for farmers and against developers. We are prejudiced for furry animals and against machines, for green plants and against concrete. The bias against developers and development finds many worthy targets, but like all prejudice, its driving force is irrational fear. We project onto others what we fear within ourselves.

Developers and environmentalists feel betrayed by each other. Betrayal, however, is possible only among people who share common values and commitments. Our dilemma is that as individuals and collectively as a society we have chosen both nature and development.

Almost anyone who drives a car, goes shopping, uses an airport, attends a school, wears factory-made clothing, or owns a musical instrument supports development somewhere. The real way to combat bad development is the same as the way to combat drugs. The users have got to say NO. I wouldn't have trundled my chain saw out to my first development if I had thought no one wanted to live there.

Development is not "unnatural." Nature made us the animal that imagines worlds more enjoyable than the world we were given. Then we develop that world. What human beings do to the planet is as much a part of nature as Yosemite Valley.

Knowing that won't help me the next time I set a bulldozer to work in a forest or channel a sparkling stream into a length of dark culvert. Just as we are the animal that imagines how things might be, we are also the one that re-members how things were. It is embarrassing and frustrat-ing. Writing about it has helped me draw yet one more les-son from my life as a developer: none of us will succeed as either developers or environmentalists until we accept that we are both.

Killing Our Elders

✳

BRENDA PETERSON

S A SMALL CHILD GROWING UP near the Oregon border on a Forest Service lookout station in the high Sierras, I believed the encircling tribe of trees were silent neighbors who protectively held the sky up over our rough cabins. The Standing People, I heard them called—but that was later, when I could almost understand the rapid-fire noises people aimed toward one another like so much scattershot. Because the trees were taller and older than grown-ups and because all of us—from snake to squirrel to people—were obviously related, I assumed that the trees were our ancestors. They were here before us. We were their children.

For all their soaring, deep stillness, the ponderosa pines and giant Douglas firs often made noises in the night, a language of whispers and soft whistles that sang through the cabin's walls made of their lying-down pine kinfolk. I first memorized the forest with my hands, crawling on all fours across prickly pine needles. Like a blind girl reading braille, my stubby fingers traced sworls of pine bark, searching for congealed sap. I'd chew the fragrant pine gum, more flavorful than any bland baby food. The snap of pine sap against my tongue woke up my nose and brain; I'd wriggle my face in delight, which earned me the nickname "gopher."

Toddlers didn't have to be human up there in the forest. Adults called us animal or vegetable names like "coon" or "pumpkin-head" or "skunk." And the trees didn't have to be not-alive, or dead timber. Forty years ago when I was born in that Pacific Northwest forest, the old trees stood in abundance. Forty years ago, my ancestors still stood watch over me, over us all.

Late last August I drove through those high Sierra and Cascade forests again on a road trip from Los Angeles to my home in Seattle. In the four-hour drive between the old mining town of Yreka in northern California and Eugene, Oregon, we counted fifty logging trucks, roughly a truck every four minutes. Many of the flatbeds were loaded with only one or two huge trees. I don't know when I started crying. Maybe it was when we called on our friend in his cabin on Oregon's Snake River, outside of Merced, and he told us that every day from dawn to dark a logging truck had gone by every five minutes. "It's like a funeral procession out of the forest," my friend Joe said.

As I drove through those once lush mountains, I noticed my fingers went angry white from clenching the steering wheel every time a logging truck passed by. I wondered about the loggers. They, too, had grown up in the forest, their small hands also had learned that bark was another kind of skin. Among these generations of logging families there is a symbiotic love for the trees. Why then this desperate slashing of their own old-growth elders?

Our pagan ancestors believed trees were more important

than people because the old forests survived and contributed to the whole for many more than one human lifetime. Cutting down a sacred oak, for example, meant the severest punishment: the offender was gutted at the navel, his intestines wrapped around the tree stump so tree and man died together. When we recognized that our fate was directly linked to the land, trees were holy.

Two years ago this winter, my grandfather died. An Ozarkian hard-times farmer and former sheriff, Grandaddy was larger than life to the gaggle of grandchildren who gathered at his farm almost every summer vacation. Speaking in a dialect so deep it would need subtitles today, he'd rail against the "blackguards" (*blaggarts*) and "scoundrels" (*scundrills*) he sought to jail for crimes from moonshining to murder. One of my earliest memories is playing checkers with a minor scoundrel in Grandaddy's jail. Another is of bouncing in the back of his pickup as he campaigned for reelection, honking his horn at every speakeasy and shouting out, "I'll shut ya down, I will, quickern' Christ comin' like a thief in the night!" I also remember Grandaddy sobbing his eyes out over his old hound's death. "It's just that he won't never be alongside me no more," Grandaddy explained to us. Somebody gave him a young hound pup, but Grandad was offended. "You can't replace all that knowin' of an old hound with this pup. That hound, he took care of me. Now, I gotta take care of this young'un."

My Grandaddy's funeral was the first time I'd ever seen all my kinfolk cry together. Without reserve, some thirty-odd people in a small backwoods church sobbed—bodies bent double, their breathing ragged. It was a grief distinct from the despair I'd heard at the death of an infant or a contemporary. At my Grandaddy's funeral, we all, no matter what age, cried like lost children. We were not so much sad as lonely. We were not so much bereft as abandoned. Who would tell us stories of our people? Who would offer us the wisdom of the longtime survivor? Our grandfather, this most beloved elder, was no longer alongside us.

When I returned home from the funeral, someone asked me, "How old was he?" When I replied eighty-six, this person visibly lightened. He actually made a small shrug of his shoulders, "Oh, well, then." I wondered if he were going to suggest I get myself a new hound puppy.

In a preindustrial or agrarian society, the death of an elder was cause for great sorrow and ceremony. In our modern-day arrogance, we equate youth with value.

If my Grandaddy were one of those old Douglas firs I saw being trucked out of the forest, would he really be equalled by a tiny sapling? Old trees like old people survive the ravages of middle-age competition for light, or limelight; they give back to their generations more oxygen, more stories; they are tall and farsighted enough to see the future because they are so firmly rooted in the past. Old-growth trees or persons are nurturers; the young saplings planted to replace them need nurturing.

A Nez Percé Indian woman from Oregon recently told me that in her tradition there was a time when the ancient trees were living burial tombs for her people. Upon the death of a tribal elder, a great tree was scooped out enough to hold the folded, fetuslike body. Then the bark was laid back to grow over the small bones like a rough-hewn skin graft.

"The old trees held our old people for thousands of years," she said softly. "If you cut those ancient trees, you lose all your own ancestors, everyone who came before you. Such loneliness is unbearable."

Without our elders, our tribe will soon be lost. We will forget who we are and wander like lost children, all.

I will always be lonely for my grandfather; the child in me will always long for my first tribe of Standing People who watched over me, who even lent their skin for my cradle. On some spiritual level our human entrails are still wrapped around the trees, like an umbilical cord. And every time a great tree is cut, our kind die, too—lonely and longing for what we do not recognize as ourselves.

PART TWO

✳

The Geographies
of Home

Bikinis, Beaches, and Bombs

HUMAN NATURE ON THE SAND

✳

JOHN R. STILGOE

*IKINI.* NO OTHER WORD MORE accurately connotes the intricate web of meaning infusing modern ocean recreation. *Bikini* suggests sun, tanning lotion, surf, and swimming, all mingled with a zesty vivacity, sexuality, and vague wantonness. It evokes California rock-and-roll music, a series of 1960s beach movies, and echoes of the long feminist struggle for abbreviated beach attire. And only rarely do contemporary Americans recall the other meaning of the word, as the name of the tropical island reduced to ashes in repeated atomic bomb tests. Sexuality and death, bronzed health and charred wreckage—do any more troubling dichotomies thrive in a single word? Do such searing dualities explain the American unwillingness to link the bikini with Bikini Atoll, to link natural vitality with thermonuclear fire?

Margin

✳

Every beach is marginal; ocean beaches are more marginal than most. By definition, a margin is something like a boundary, something like an edge; but a margin is not a boundary, not an edge. It is a zone, a space, an empty area, in typographical terms usually thought of as the blank space separating the ends of lines from the edges of pages. By definition, everything within a margin is marginal, somehow on the edge, somehow hovering between proper and improper, between acceptable and unacceptable, between place within the text and no place at all. The word derives from the Latin *margo*, a word that sixteenth-century English men and women knew as *marge* and used to designate what ecologists now call the littoral or coastal zone. In 1907, the Canadian poet Robert Service resurrected the anachronism in "The Cremation of Sam McGee," describing "the marge of Lake LeBarge" where the poetic narrator "cremated Sam McGee." Service perceived the continuing connotation of marginality intimately associated with any beach; where else could something as utterly marginal as the cremation of a living man more properly occur?

For centuries, mariners and landsmen alike distrusted the marginal zone as a place neither land nor sea, a zone of shipwreck, drowning, quicksand, and surf, the very lair of sea serpents, rocky hazards, and undertow. Mariners shunned the ledges and reefs they named "woes," and kept far offshore; farmers scorned the infertile sand and the fickle dune grass soon destroyed by grazing livestock. Throughout the American colonial era, indeed well into the middle of the nineteenth century, visitors to marginal zones saw only drifting sand, hazardous rocks, and an eerie barrenness. "Strewn with crabs, horseshoes, and razorclams, and whatever the sea casts up,—a vast *morgue*, where famished dogs may range in packs, and crows come daily to glean the pittance which the tide leaves them," and where "the carcasses of men and beasts together lie stately up upon its shelf, rotting and bleaching in the sun and waves," the unvisited ocean beach haunts Thoreau's 1865 travelog, *Cape Cod*. Thoreau saw only the grasping waves gnawing at the blowing, eroding dunes, felt only the suck of the surf, the sting of salt and sand. Nowhere in *Cape Cod* does the contemporary reader find the delicate love of nature that suffuses *Walden*. To the visitor from inland Concord, the great barrier beaches evoked only fascination tempered by distrust.

Not for decades would American attitudes change. The national apprehension of the marge was reshaped gradually by a developing love of tropical scenery and lifestyle. As early as 1776, in "The Beauties of Santa Cruz," Philip Freneau extolled the voluptuous landscape of the island known now as St. Croix, a setting for a life of perfect ease. But Freneau explicitly omitted the island beaches from his catalog of beauties, noting that "the threatening waters roar on every side," and that "sharp craggy rocks repel the surging brine." Only inland, away from the marge, does he find scenery worthy of paradise; the littoral he dismisses as dangerous and barren. Fifty years later, when Charles S. Stewart published his Hawaiian adventures in *Journal of a Residence in the Sandwich Islands*, the traditional attitude still shaped scenery assessment. Stewart described the entrance into the bay of Waikiki, the panoramic view of the south side of Oahu, the groves of coconut trees, the plain and hills beyond—and said not a word about the beach separating ocean from groves of trees. For Stewart, the beach existed as a mere threshold, sometimes dangerous, always unworthy of attention; only the lush inland scenery deserved remark.

Herman Melville heralded a shift in popular attitudes when he published his first two novels, *Typee* and *Omoo*, in the late 1840s. Melville appreciated more than the South Seas landscape. Unlike missionaries and explorers, he praised the ways of the natives, noting that "to many of them, indeed, life is little else than an often interrupted and luxurious nap," a lifestyle perfectly fitted to a luxuriant landscape. As a beached sailor, a deserter from his whaling ship, Melville lived among the natives, enjoying their idle, idyllic life, learning to mock the attempts of American missionaries to civilize the Marquesans. His books brought him success fired by scandal; conservative critics attacked his thinking on nearly every subject. According to their arguments, Melville had gone native and deserted the values of Western, genteel civilization as surely as he had deserted his ship.

Melville rejoiced in discovering a prelapsarian society, a society in which men and women lived more naturally than at home. His descriptions of people swimming scandalized and titillated his readers, because they explicitly legitimized nakedness. "The ease and grace with which the maidens of the valley propelled themselves through the water, and their familiarity with the element, were truly astonishing," he marveled. He tells how, on one occasion, he plunged in among them, "and counting vainly upon my superior strength, sought to drag some of them under the water, but I quickly repented my temerity." His readers learned quickly enough that the women swam nude; Melville describes one "beauteous nymph" who "for the most part clung to the primitive and summer garb of Eden. But how becoming the costume! It showed her fine figure to the best possible advantage." In Melville's books, the South Sea islands became the very paradisal place about which some readers dreamed, a place beyond social inhibition, a place beyond ill health, a place beyond work. To be sure, few Americans voiced their agreement with Melville, but the books kept on selling even as more missionaries sallied forth to terminate the wickedness he so enjoyed.

Despite the success of *Typee* and *Omoo*, an uneasiness born of prudery continued to shape American attitudes toward the South Seas margin. Victorian sensibility cowed even Mark Twain, whose 1872 *Roughing It* reveals its author's difficulties on Hawaiian beaches. As he approached the islands, Twain no more noticed Waikiki Beach than did Stewart; only later during his stay, when he tired of the luxuriant inland scenery, did he explore the margin. "At noon I observed a bevy of nude native young ladies bathing in the sea, and went and sat down on their clothes to keep them from being stolen," he remarks in the dry humor for which he was already known. "I begged them to come out, for the sea was rising, and I was satisfied that they were running some risk." But a closer reading of the final chapters reveals his profound discomfort with such local customs as "the lascivious hula-hula." He shied away from the innocent unclad native women he met with everywhere along the shore. In the Hawaiian marginal zone, even the iconoclastic Twain encountered a lifestyle of such unrestrained vigor that retreat became the only solution.

Until the beginning of the twentieth century, the South Seas marginal lifestyle remained the bane of missionary efforts and the secret delight of American men and women frustrated by the tightening strictures of Victorianism. Then slowly, but as certainly as the incoming tide, Americans discovered their own beaches. Books like *Typee* and *Omoo* may have predisposed some people toward beach-going, but other forces account for the throngs that soon wandered along the sand.

Discovery

✳

Fear drove many Americans to the seashore. Urban families found that summertime diseases were rampant in the burgeoning cities—diseases born of filthy streets, contaminated food, and unsanitary plumbing, diseases spread by overcrowding, foul air, and lack of exercise. Well-to-do families had long ago deserted the summer city for the healthful environment of rural villages, mountain hotels, and seashore inns, but by the 1890s, thousands of middle-class families had also begun taking out-of-city holidays, and even working-class families enjoyed day trips beyond suburban limits. Most frequently, wives and children abandoned cities for weeks or months on end, leaving husbands behind to endure the summer torment. Fortunate men visited their families on weekends, in the strange way William Dean Howells described in 1885 in *The Rise of Silas Lapham*. Families sacrificed togetherness for the seashore vacation in particular, for they believed that in the marginal zone lay the chance for health and longevity.

Many health experts drove home the near-miraculous advantages of beach life. In *Sea-Air and Sea-Bathing*, an 1880 guide to health and vigor, John Packard argued that the coastal zone offered dozens of advantages to the frail or sickly urban resident. Fresh, clean air refreshed the lungs and stimulated the appetite; sunshine warmed the blood and eased muscle strain; and—most importantly—salt-water bathing refreshed the entire body. According to Packard and other authorities, bathing in fresh water leached precious salts out of the body, while splashing in salt water strengthened the saline concentrations. That medical advice alone sent millions to ocean beaches, prompted the donning of "bathing suits," and led to grown men and women jumping up and down in breakers. And it led to children being cajoled or dragged into the waves too.

Families eagerly embraced medical notions that beach play prevented childhood illness; in an age of high infant and child mortality, parents grasped at any theory, but the beach-life theory made common sense: sun, exercise, and salt water together would give old-fashioned vitality, the vitality of the farm of generations past. "A cleaner or more healthy occupation can scarcely be imagined," Packard argued, "and the only caution needful is the obvious one as to the mid-day heat." But other, deeper currents prompted parents to bring children to ocean beaches. Slowly, almost incredibly, considering the ongoing racism directed against blacks and Indians, there developed the argument that sun, sand, and surf engendered the vitality usually associated by Caucasians with people of color. "Children of tender years, barefoot and with streaming hair, play for hours upon the beaches, now in and now out of the water with perfect immunity from colds," announced an 1896 Maine Central Railroad Company brochure advertising Casco Bay summer vacations. "Youngsters, after a season of such sports, look like young Indians; moreover they fare like Indians, at least three times a day." Sea-bathing, coupled with seashore exercise, consequently produced not only good health and good appetite, but an extraordinary vitality associated with sunburnt skin, or with the skin of races more vital than the white.

At first, only children enjoyed the luxury of sunburn and tanned skin; adults, particularly women, shunned the glare. "It is hard to picture nowadays the shell-like transparence, the luminous red-and-white, of those young cheeks untouched by paint or powder," recalled Edith Wharton in 1934, in her autobiography, *A Backward Glance*. "Beauty was unthinkable without 'a complexion,' and to defend that treasure against sun and wind, and the archenemy, sea air, veils as thick as curtains were habitually worn" by women summering in Newport in the 1870s. As late as 1901, in fact, *Collier's* and other magazines still published advertisements for Anita Cream and similar skin lighteners, although by then fashion too dictated change. For as long as Americans remained an agricultural people, upper-class women prized pale skin—"a complexion"—as proof of freedom from outdoor farm work; as the nation industrialized, pale skin began to suggest the pallor associated with factory labor, and men and women of leisure slowly embraced a tanned or "bronzed" skin as a sign of status, a sign announcing their ability to summer outdoors, usually along the seashore. Period paintings and photographs clearly reveal the change; in the 1860s, young women carry parasols above their hats and veils; by 1880 they wear only hats, and by 1905 they are hatless and sometimes with streaming hair. Feminists championed the changes, for they argued that the abbreviation of beach attire announced a new value placed on health, not simple devotion to clothing fashions.

More than any other feminist, perhaps more than any other American, novelist Kate Chopin deciphered the changing attitude toward the sea. In *The Awakening*, a novel of 1899, Chopin details the summer life of a young mother visiting the seashore, wandering along the beach with parasol and long dress to defend her skin against tanning, and trying to learn how to swim while wearing a voluminous woolen suit intended for bathing, not swimming. "A certain ungovernable dread hung about her when in the water, unless there was a hand near by that might reach out and reassure her," Chopin writes of the woman she calls Mrs. Pontellier. As the summer passes, however, the woman begins to "loosen a little the mantle of reserve that had always enveloped her," and suddenly learns to swim. "She could have shouted for joy. She did shout for joy, as with a sweeping stroke or two she lifted her body to the surface of the water," writes Chopin at the climax of the novel. "She wanted to swim far out, where no woman had swum before. She would not join the groups in their sports and bouts, but intoxicated with her newly conquered power, she swam out alone." From that moment on, the woman becomes a different person; she casts off her parasol and becomes so sunburnt that her husband, arriving for a weekend visit, grows annoyed; she rebels against her role as a housewife; and eventually she moves away from her husband, leaves society, and commits suicide. "She cast the unpleasant, pricking garments from her, and for the first time in her life, she stood naked in the open air, at the mercy of the sun, the breeze that beat upon her, and the waves that invited her," writes Chopin of the woman now called Edna. "How strange and awful it seemed to stand naked under the sky! How delicious! She

felt like some new-born creature, opening its eyes in a familiar world that it had never known." No longer does the
sea terrify her. Bereft of woolen bathing suit, alone on the
white beach, she strikes off into the waves and deliberately
drowns, finally free of her conventional lifestyle.

Swimming marked the height of the discovery period.
After the Australian crawl entered American consciousness
in the first years of the new century, men and women
learned that exercise and bathing might be combined.
And they learned too that in the water the sexes are equal
in physical capacity, something that stunned men accustomed to dominating women. *The Awakening* shocked
readers more than *Typee* and *Omoo* had a half century before, and the novel disappeared from bookstores; but Chopin had perceived the awe-inspiring significance of beach
life. On the seacoast women achieved more than the vigor
acquired by children and men—they reaped a new understanding of themselves, an understanding laced with
South Seas energy. In the ocean surf they glimpsed the
physical prowess that had challenged Melville years before, when he swam among the lithe women of the tropics.

Exhilaration

✳

Despite the growing popularity of seashore recreation,
salt-water bathing and swimming disconcerted many conservative Americans. Not only did men and women wear
costumes considered abbreviated, but in the surf both
sexes tumbled together wildly, limb touching limb, body
touching body. In a turn-of-the-century essay, "The Beach

at Rockaway," novelist William Dean Howells described the "promiscuous bathing" as something disturbing even to watch. "It was indeed like one of those uncomfortable dreams where you are not dressed sufficiently for company, or perhaps at all, and yet are making a very public appearance," he mused. He concluded that "all was a damp and dreary decorum"—a curious finale to an essay depicting "swarms and heaps of people in all lolling and lying and wallowing shapes" sprawled on the sand or "slopping and shouting and shrieking" in the waves. Being among so many people doing so many scarcely decent things sent Howells back inland in his carriage. Along with others of his years, the novelist retreated before the beach play of the younger generation.

Even as the retreat turned to rout, conservatives attempted to control what they perceived as the lazy morality of the summer beach, usually by controlling clothing. As late as 1930, Chicago police officers measured the hemlines of women's bathing suits, making certain that none swayed more than four inches above knees. Many states and municipalities passed ordinances prohibiting dressing and undressing in automobiles, although automobile manufacturers persisted in equipping large cars with curtains. And in Atlantic City, a resort dedicated to boardwalk promenades and bracing sea air, city fathers forbade men to remove bathing suit tops long after Malibu and other California communities had regarded male chests with disinterest. Advertising and corporate retailing quickly surmounted the conservative restrictions, however, and freed men—if not women—from the dictates of yesteryear.

So long as men swam in suits with long sleeves and

pants, men drowned. Traditionally, boys and men had swum nude, enjoying the male-only conviviality of rural swimming holes, abandoned quarries and sandpits, or industrial waterfronts. Mixed bathing provided more freedom to women, but condemned men to paddling in heavy woolen suits almost as constricting as the female bathing dresses. By the early 1920s, however, men had discarded ankle-length leggings and long sleeves; ten years later, they swam in sleeveless tops. Underwear manufacturers anxious to broaden their markets recruited swimming champions like Johnny Weissmuller to advertise ever more abbreviated suits intended for competitive sport. They understood the tremendous potential implicit in making swimming truly enjoyable.

Manufacturers of women's clothing knew the potential too and vaguely discerned another. If bathing suit styles changed from year to year, fashion-conscious women would buy the latest design each spring, thus ensuring a steady market for clothes that might otherwise last many seasons. Consequently, the Jantzen Company and other firms began styling women's suits—for swimming now, not for bathing. The Jantzen Company precipitated an uproar when, in 1924, it distributed millions of decals depicting a young woman in a sleeveless, nearly legless red suit and suggested that motorists attach the logo to automobile windshields. In one of the first coups in modern advertising, four million motorists did, for unrecorded reasons; only in Massachusetts did motorists forgo the pleasure, for the state legislature, fearful of collisions resulting from male drivers mesmerized by the young woman's form, outlawed the decal at once. In 1920, the Jantzen Company sold 26,832 women's bathing suits; ten years later, in one season it sold 1,587,338, a merchandizing victory resulting from advertising, planned obsolescence, and an unanticipated cultural push.

Women adored the brief, one-piece suits that permitted genuine, effortless swimming. Exactly as Chopin had predicted, women delighted in enjoying water sports as equals with men. Charles Dana Gibson, the creator of the "Gibson Girl," caught the new enthusiasm early in the century, when he drew young women wearing not only ever briefer bathing dresses, but ever more arch expressions. Early Hollywood filmmakers, particularly Mack Sennet, caught the mood in a number of "bathing beauty" films. But most important, Gertrude Ederle both caught and nurtured the love when she swam the English Channel in 1926, breaking the records set by the five previous swimmers, all men. Clad in trunks, brassiere, and axle grease, Ederle became a heroine overnight, proof of a new level of feminine physical competence. And her two-piece suit prompted more women to demand briefer one-piece garments.

A national swimming craze forced park commissions everywhere to build pools, level beaches, and confront the horrors of water-borne disease. Packed urban beaches—on some summer days in the late 1920s, Chicago authorities reported a half million citizens splashing in Lake Michigan—proved less healthful by the year. Health departments tried chlorinating water, building swimming pools (New York City built the first in 1901) and wading pools, or directing would-be beachgoers to distant beaches. New York City opened Jones Beach, some thirty-three miles from Manhattan, largely to draw unprecedented crowds away from polluted harbor water. On summer days more than 100,000 people crowded Jones Beach, partaking of a novel social experience in which sun, sand, and water seemed secondary, yet absolutely essential.

In the years just before the Second World War, Americans finally and fully accepted the active beach vacation, or the active day-at-the-beach. No longer did most visitors content themselves with a quiet stroll, or a lazy afternoon of sitting on a blanket reading magazines. Instead the typical beach visitor engaged the environment; he or she ran along the wet sand, climbed dunes, lay in the sun smothered with tanning oil, and—above all—swam. Sometime in the 1930s, being unable to swim became unacceptable, an embarrassing ignorance; being untanned in summer became unfashionable; and being too skinny or too plump became a summertime nightmare for millions bombarded with bathing suit advertisements featuring perfect-bodied, bronzed swimmers. Wartime slowed but scarcely stopped the drift toward abbreviated beach attire—Hollywood dispatched tens of thousands of "bathing beauty" photographs to servicemen, most of whom still recall Betty Grable posing in a risqué one-piece suit—and accelerated the active use of beaches. Swimming, as Depression-era experts had pointed out, cost almost nothing; in the early 1940s, many Americans found that the ocean offered cheap, unrationed enjoyment.

Bikini
※

According to magazine articles from 1946 and 1947, a French fashion designer created the bikini bathing suit "to lift the spirits" of a country shattered by war. No Paris model would wear the garment for photographers; the design firm hired a showgirl. The name came from Bikini Atoll, a hitherto unknown Pacific isle that was the site of atomic tests in 1946. Just as the bomb represented an "absolute," said the designer, so the bikini bathing suit represented an absolute of brevity.

While American men had shed their swimsuit tops by the late 1930s, emboldened largely by Tarzan films and the examples of advertising, American women embraced the two-piece suit more slowly, at least in public. Between 1945 and 1960, however, the ocean beach changed character once again as millions visited the seashore not to swim, but to sunbathe.

Despite the warnings of dermatologists, American women enthusiastically embarked on "the perfect tan," a deep, coppery or bronze tan produced partly by tanning creams or oil, largely by lying for hours in bright sunlight. Women sunbathed in backyards, on apartment house roofs, and on the beach; the beach provided more sunlight, reflected from water and sand, and thus a greater degree of tan achieved within a few hours. The bathing suit became a sunbathing suit, becoming briefer, and less suited to swimming; women chose strapless suits to eliminate the lines that marred the effect of off-shoulder dresses. California women led the march toward even briefer suits, toward the bikini that became popular in the late 1960s.

On the beach in the 1960s, young Americans confronted the medieval four elements almost directly. Sea air, sunlight, sand, and salt water—air, fire, earth, and water in the language of alchemists—touched skin scarcely encumbered by cloth. The ocean beach became the first environment encountered by all senses; it became a very proving ground of sensory experience.

As adults and children shed most of their clothing, they shed social inhibitions too. On the beach, men and women lay crowded together, grooming their near-naked bodies with lotions and oils, sleeping within touching distance of total strangers. Conversation began more easily on the beach; neighborliness found expression in the sharing of pepper, child care, and radios. Strangers united in sports ranging from touch football to volleyball and gathered around cooking fires. Most of the subtle nuances of social rank and privilege vanished; a deep tan, trim physique, and accurate physical coordination mattered more than an expensive swimsuit or beach umbrella.

The "Bikini Beach" films of the late 1960s popularized the emerging image of the California beach as precursor to a better world. Nearly plotless, always zany, the feature films depicting scarcely clad teenagers surfing, singing, and flirting on broad sandy beaches nevertheless offer insights into a changing American culture—and changing attitudes toward seashore environments. The beach kids wage a ceaseless struggle against middle-aged prudes convinced that near-nakedness engenders depravity; they struggle also against young men and women of their own age committed to a 1950s love of industrialism—the motorcycle gang attired in black leather jackets. Honest, friendly, open to natural living, the beach kids lead totally marginal lives beset by opponents invariably depicted as ignoble. *Bikini Beach*, *Beach Blanket Bingo*, *How to Stuff a Wild Bikini*, and the others present a teenage generation poised between the restrictions of the past and the uncertainties of the future. Indeed the films say nothing about the antecedents of the characters—or about their plans and dreams. The beach kids are simply "on the beach," enjoying a nearly natural life free of the developing problems that culminated in the student revolts of the late 1960s.

To watch the films twenty years later is to understand the marginality of the beach culture. The beach kids now seem to be waiting for something, seeking some mission or direction, and receiving no guidance from inland. Where did they go, the bronzed young men and bikinied women? The men went to Vietnam.

In the "Bikini Beach" films, the beach is truly a liminal zone, an uncertain, momentary refuge between childhood and adult turmoil. On the beach blossoms a momentary awareness of pure nature that produces a carefree, loving existence threatened only by outsiders. The films spoke to a generation of teenagers already forgetting the Korean conflict, wary of the Cuban missile crisis, as yet unaware of Southeast Asia. They spoke to a generation aware of the atomic bomb, of the potential for a world of cinders and dry bones.

Consequently the films, and the actual life of the ocean beach that caught up children and adults as well as teenagers, embrace the youthful vitality that temporarily succeeds in blocking the specter of the bomb. More than a half century after *The Awakening*, Americans awakened to the wisdom of its author. "The voice of the sea is seductive; never ceasing, whispering, clamoring, murmuring, inviting the soul to wander for a spell in abysses of solitude; to lose itself in mazes of inward contemplation," wrote Chopin. "The voice of the sea speaks to the soul. The touch of the sea is sensuous, enfolding the body in its soft, close embrace." On the ocean beach, in the late 1960s, Americans fully embraced not only the four elements, but conflicting visions of the future. On the one hand, they glimpsed the future grounded in intimacy with nature, in equality of the sexes, in spontaneous friendship, sharing, and dreaming; on the other, they spied the future of the island paradise charred, the future of no future at all. In the rich mix of sun, sand, and surf, Americans rediscovered the long-lost vitality of the South Seas islanders. Literally turning their backs on inland civilization, they sojourned momentarily in an environment of possibility, in the marginal zone scorned by nineteenth-century critics. Wearing scarcely more than skin and sunglasses, they reveled in the magic of the littoral, thinking away the mushroom cloud hovering over Bikini Atoll.

And still today they dream, caring little for warnings about ozone layers and skin cancer, luxuriating in flesh alive to the elements, clad in bikinis far briefer than the postwar absolute. On the ocean beach, between land and sea, young Americans search for the paradise of innocence, the Eden found long ago by Melville, the Eden discerned by Chopin, the Eden of human life intimate with nature.

Renewing the Bond of Mankind and Nature

BIOSPHERE RESERVES AS SACRED SPACE

✳

J. RONALD ENGEL

In order to continue his astonishing adventure on Earth, Man must continue to balance two basic imperatives—the need to innovate constantly in order to meet the growing challenges of development and progress, and the need to preserve carefully his cultural and natural heritage upon which he depends for his spiritual and biological survival. Perhaps the greatest merit of the biosphere reserve concept lies in its combining these two imperatives through its innovative function in the domain of conservation.

Michel Batisse, Deputy Assistant Director-General
for Science, UNESCO

✳

This insane human adventure, called the technological society, needs to take pause, become wiser, and reconsider its direction. We must be able to leave the consumer society behind and go to places where the natural and human heritage looms large—offering us models of equilibrium and lessons on how to live. And then perhaps it may be possible for us to imagine another kind of time, a slower time . . . when, having learned how to live with our cultural and natural environment, taking it into account in our everyday life, and in our projects of technological development, it will not be necessary to legislate the setting aside of parks and protected areas. These measures exist only because the heritage of the past—our heritage—is neglected or poorly loved.

Girard Collin, Curator of Écomusée of Mont Lozère,
National Park of the Cévennes, France

✳

Spring in the Cévennes

✳

On December 8, 1984, Parc National des Cévennes in southern France was officially declared a biosphere reserve by UNESCO, as part of its Man and the Biosphere program (MAB).

On a warm afternoon the spring before, my wife and I had begun the ascent from Nîmes through the Corniche de Cévennes to the highlands of Florac, headquarters of the park. A delicate green was brushing the slopes of the steep ravines and terraced hillsides that abutted the winding road, crocuses were blooming, and the purple-orange of the jagged sierras above us shone brightly in the soft spring light. The weathered stone buildings scattered over the cliffs seemed to grow out of the landscape.

I remember wondering, as we drove from one spectacular prospect to another, whether my mission would be received by the staff of the Cévennes park in the same way it had been by MAB-related personnel in Washington, Nairobi, and Paris. I was not their typical academic visitor. My field of expertise lay neither in the natural sciences nor in park management, but in religion, ethics, and the humanities. Yet the aim of my sabbatical research—to test the hypothesis that biosphere reserves mark a new stage in the ethical and religious history of humankind—had been greeted by the MAB staff with a healthy mixture of skepticism, curiosity, and enthusiasm.

Such a reception was gratifying and was not necessarily to be expected—certainly not on the basis of a cursory reading of the mountains of technical papers that describe the biosphere reserves, for the project appears to be exclusively scientific and utilitarian. Yet, in this case as in others, the explicit text is not the whole story. There is also an implicit text, one written in the language of images and symbols, that tells about feelings, values, and commitments. Bits and snatches of this underlying text are visible even in the most technical of expositions about the biosphere reserves, for example, in occasional references to "evolutionary responsibility" and "partnership between Man and Nature." It is also apparent in the unstated presuppositions that inform the project. On such evidence my hypothesis was founded. And now I was on the threshold of examining the most important kind of evidence—the symbolism implicit not in the printed word, but in an actual (soon to be declared) biosphere reserve.

Parc National des Cévennes did not let us down. A more cordial reception would be hard to imagine. Nor did the advance billing of UNESCO, that the Cévennes was a singularly fine example of the meaning of a biosphere reserve in practice, fall short of the mark. We could see that the biosphere reserve idea, which the "father" of MAB, Michel Batisse, once described as arising "in a somewhat hazy manner," owes a great deal to the idea of the French regional parks. This is not to deny that every country participating in MAB has in some measure independently developed the biosphere reserve idea out of the unique circumstances of its own history. It is only to say that in the case of the Cévennes park, the designation as a biosphere reserve is peculiarly apt and should help the park move further and faster on the line of development it was already set upon.

The Cévennes Biosphere Reserve includes a large mountainous region of 800,000 acres and 41,500 people— 200,000 acres and 500 people in the highly protected central zone, 600,000 acres and 41,000 people in the buffer zone. Rock dominates the landscape—granite in the north, schist in the south and east, limestone on the great plateaus of the west. Each form of rock has given rise over millennia to a distinct flora and fauna and is associated with a distinct human culture, each of the latter marked by a distinctive use of rock in its architecture. The causse-dwellers who live on the limestone plateaus are chiefly pastoralists and 90 percent Catholic. Their limestone houses use a series of vertical vaults to support the enormously heavy stone roofs. The "Cévenols" dwell either on the high mountains and build their homes of white and rose granite, or live and die in the shade of the chestnut tree in the schist country and build their homes three or four stories high because flat places are so difficult to find; they are chiefly agriculturalists and 90 percent Protestant.

Ensconced in a small yellow Citroën, my wife and I (sometimes with eyes closed) were driven by the park interpreter, M. Collin, and the park botanist, M. Déjean, to and fro over the landscape—up mountainsides on roads with hairpin turns, no shoulders, and precipitous drops, over sweeping windblown plateaus, alongside rushing blue-green streams and meandering rivers, through gorges that seemed as large as the Grand Canyon, past picturesque hamlets cradled in valleys and folds of mountain slopes.

Against the baa of hundreds of sheep eager for spring pasture, we talked with a family of sheepherders on the Causse-Méjean and heard them complain about the regulations, yet grudgingly acknowledge that the park had helped restore the viability of their farm. We saw the dolmens (rock-covered mounds) and menhirs (rock pillars) of the neolithic hunters and gatherers who dwelt here five thousand years ago. We talked to the workers from a local commune who were restoring a farmhouse as a museum, and who ran *gîtes ruraux*, or family bed and breakfasts, for tourists in the summer.

On Mont Lozère, the highest mountain of the park (1700 m.), we learned how the park, in cooperation with the National Center for Scientific Research, was monitoring the chemical content of streams from various water-basins to determine what kind of vegetative covering was best for soil fertility. Nearby we visited the innovative Éco-musée of Mont Lozère, run jointly by the park and the Commune of Pont de Montvert as a multifaceted community center, exhibition center, and interpretive gateway to the special natural and cultural sites of the area. One morning I waited for long hours with red-bearded M. Bonnet, a park warden, for a glimpse of the great griffon vultures that have been successfully reintroduced into the park—we joined hands and danced for joy when a dozen or more soared in great spirals about our clifftop perch on the side of the Gorges du Tarn.

Sacred Spaces

In order to understand why, in my view, the biosphere reserves represent a new stage in the ethical and religious history of humankind, we must first make a brief digression and look at the nature and function of "sacred spaces" in human culture.

Sacred spaces are not necessarily associated with organized religion or with any given worldview. Historians of religion have shown that they are a universal human phenomenon. In every culture, East and West, ancient and modern, certain places are set aside as "special" or "sacred," as particularly worthy of respect and reverence. The French call such places the *hauts lieux* of civilization.

Examples of sacred places include the caves of Lascaux in France, and the monuments of Stonehenge in England; Mount Olympus in Greece, Mount Ararat in Turkey, and Mount Sinai in Egypt; St. Peter's in Rome, Notre Dame in Paris, and Westminster Abbey in London. Sacred spaces did not lose their meaning for people after the Middle Ages. In the modern world, however, the most powerful sacred spaces are often "secular" places that implicitly function in ways comparable to the explicitly religious places of the past: Red Square in Moscow, Arc de Triomphe in Paris, Gettysburg Battlefield in the United States. Today, for many people the world over, national parks are sacred spaces.

All these places have a common role in providing a fixed point of orientation in an otherwise chaotic world. By means of sacred places, societies come to hold a unified view of their own place in the cosmos and a shared interpretation of the ultimate meaning of existence.

Sacred spaces are perceived to be centers of extraordinary power and reality. Such a space is not mere space, but fully *a place*, imbued with a "sense of place." For some, they are places where one feels the Other, the Holy. For others, they are simply places of particular qualitative richness, of unique beauty or historical importance. In either case, they evoke a depth of experience that is more than ordinary. This experience is often expressed in the feeling of nostalgia for a more perfect world behind or beyond "this" world.

The spatial and temporal symbolism associated with sacred spaces is remarkably uniform. They are perceived as ideal. Written in their landscapes and in the design of their artifacts are not only how things are, but how things ought to be. One sees in sacred space the true pattern of the cosmos, a part that uniquely symbolizes the whole. To enter the sacred space is therefore to make a pilgrimage to the center of existence, and for this reason sacred spaces are typically conceived as centers of universal community.

Often there are a series of such spaces, each identified with all the others. For example, the Temple in Jerusalem (the center of the world where east, west, north, and south met), the Holy City of Jerusalem, and the country of Palestine all functioned as interlocking microcosms of the universe. At the same time, both Mount Zion, near Jerusalem, and Mount Sinai, in the wilderness, were also sacred spaces of the Hebrew faith. To enter any one of these was to enter all, yet each was symbolically *the* center of the world!

A sacred space is also often perceived to be a microcosm of the history of the cosmos. This is where the paradigmatic act of creation occurred in primordial time, where creation continues to recur, where the meaning of the contemporary struggle between the powers of good and evil is most fully manifest, and where the end of creation will be fulfilled. To enter sacred space means to make contact with the natural processes that are most real and effective in the world, and the events of history most determinative of human progress toward conformity with the cosmic way of life. It is here that human beings come to see and understand what it means to exist at this time in history and to be faced with the choice between death and life.

Of course this is a simplified description. The historical record shows that sacred centers take a great variety of forms and involve complex relationships to their cultural settings. Perhaps the most important differences among sacred spaces have to do with the different worldviews they symbolize. For example, compare the worldviews expressed in the cave paintings of Lascaux, the monuments of Stonehenge, and the basilica of St. Peter's. The first represents an attitude of geopiety—worship is directed toward the potencies of the earth; the second represents an attitude of cosmic reverence—worship is directed toward the cycles of the heavenly bodies; the third represents an attitude of worldly transcendence—worship is directed toward the invisible Creator of heaven and earth.

Granted the universal function of sacred spaces in human culture, the question arises: what kind of sacred spaces are needed to reorient contemporary society to the natural world? What form of sacred space could serve as a model for an ecological worldview? My answer is biosphere reserves. They are the emergent sacred spaces of an environmentally sustainable way of life appropriate to the twenty-first century.

How is this so?

Renewing the Sacred Bonds
✳

The Cévennes park appeals to its visitors to "discover things for yourselves, with no preconceived ideas, and no undue haste." The usual park list of prohibitions tells them, don't pick mushrooms and wild fruits, don't shoot (hunting is reserved for permanent residents), don't light fires, don't litter. But the emphasis is on the positive, on a way of being unlike the ordinary: walk lightly and cautiously, listen, see, respect your environment.

Encouraging a transformation of attitude in those who enter a protected area is customary the world over. It is part of the pilgrimage experience. But in this respect, the biosphere reserve is not just an alternative to, or replacement for, a national park. Rather, it incorporates the national park into an enlarged understanding of sacred space. In fact, what Americans call a national park has become the "core zone" of the biosphere reserve—the inner sanctuary where people are asked to tread *most* softly. There is a difference, however, in how a visitor approaches a national park and a biosphere reserve. In the former, the transition is abrupt: from outside to the inside, the spot usually marked by an entrance gate. In the latter, the transition is gradual. As we drove north through the Corniche des Cévennes, we were never sure where we left profane space and entered sacred space, although it became clear that we were in a very special place! This gradual transition is deliberate. According to the park literature, the park is not an area "set against" human life, a place with opening and closing times and entry fees. It is rather a place where there is a "delicate balance between different factors promoting life, or which are that life: soil, water, climate, as well as vegetation and animal populations, and above all, man." The park does not wall itself off from the rest of the country, but serves as a "nucleus" of an "ever-widening action" promoting the capacity of people to live well with the land.

This relationship of the park to the land around it bears reflection. It helps define the unique image of the biosphere reserve and its status as a new kind of sacred space.

The key to the meaning of a biosphere reserve is its holistic focus. A biosphere reserve seeks to harmonize and reconcile the great dichotomies of modern existence: past and present, nature and humanity, science and values. The ecological worldview it embodies is based on a vision of the coevolution of man and nature. The reserve affirms the responsibility of humankind for the future of evolution on earth and the consequent need to take fully into account the quality of life as a whole. This new worldview is suggested in such phrases as "human ecology" (the science of ecology must be both a natural and a human science), "ecological aesthetics" (our individual and shared perceptions of the environment are integral parts of the ecosystem as a whole), and "environmental ethics" (ecologically grounded science and values can be mutually reinforcing).

But this is overly abstract. Let us return to the concrete experience of the Cévennes Biosphere Reserve and see how I was led to such generalizations.

The overwhelming impression that my wife and I had in the Cévennes was that of *participating in the creative evolution of life*. What factors contributed to this impression?

First, the experience of time. The omnipresence of rock—the most permanent feature of the earth's surface—gave us the feeling of time as something deep and profound. In the Cévennes it was apparent that the earth is old and that plants, animals, and human beings alike have evolved through adaptation to the geologic, climatic, and topographic realities of its surface. All of these changes took time, patient eons of time—as Girard Collin phrases it, a "slower time." We sensed this time as a sacred, evolving rhythm that perfectly balances continuity and change. The neolithic dolmens and menhirs added substance to this impression, as did the evidence of centuries of laborious husbanding of soil through the removal of rocks from fields, rocks that were then used for fences and in the construction of terraces. We stood in awe of stone houses that must have taken generations to complete. And we identified with the Protestant farmers who fled to these remote and rugged slopes several centuries ago, in quest of religious freedom.

Through lifelike exhibits laid out on either side of an ascending spiral ramp, the Écomusée at Pont de Montvert mirrored the coevolution of landscape, plants, animals, and man. The Écomusée served as the temple of a new ecological and evolutionary faith. Here the sacred story was told, and in the movie that climaxed the exhibits, pilgrims and permanent residents alike were invited to participate consciously in the ongoing cosmic task of transmitting the past, improved and purified, to the future.

Secondly, there was the experience of integration itself, what the park literature calls the "ancient concord between man's actions and the forces of nature." We encountered this integration in several aspects of the reserve. One was the sacred geometry of the park—like that of all biosphere reserves, a series of inner cores where natural evolution continues as undisturbed as possible, surrounded by buffer zones in which traditional human communities are encouraged to flourish, where experimentation in more adaptive ways of life is pursued, and where education and ecological research occur. This geometry, which we knew in the abstract, was an extremely harmonious one to experience as we traveled about the park. The landscape is ideal, because it richly fulfills the role of aesthetic quality: unity in contrast. Almost every vista contained a view of one of the enduring centers of natural evolution, where man is essentially a visitor, and also of a community or farm where people live in balance with the land. The landscape was a microcosm of the unity of wild and humane.

We found a second instance of this integration in the traditional cultures and economies of the causse-dwellers and Cévenol people themselves: in their movement across the land, as they went out to cultivate their fields or lead their flocks along the roads; in their towns in which houses fit against one another as so many interpenetrating organs in a great stone body; in the chestnut trees that covered the schist countryside and provided timber and fruit; in the rare strains of rye that had been selected over centuries to grow on the mountain slopes. One activity that powerfully models this kind of integration, but which we experienced only vicariously, is *transhumance.* Each spring for generations, mountain dwellers have allowed sheepherders to lead their flocks from valleys far below the park up to pastures on the mountainsides because the sheep supply nutrients to the soil that the mountain dwellers need to cultivate their crops.

The great symbol that comes to mind to describe this integrative experience is "art." The traditional civilizations of the Cévennes are a precious heritage because they are "artful" civilizations. They exemplify a sustainable and fulfilling relationship between *homo faber* and his environment. In the Cévennes a great truth was disclosed to us: the dichotomies of the modern world, between technology and community, science and values, past and present, are due to our loss of the middle term—the integrative function of art, the creative capacity of human beings to pursue a way of life that adapts to, while simultaneously modifying, the environment, a way of life that turns the unconscious reciprocities of organism and environment into deliberately and freely chosen bonds of concord.

This brings us to a most significant point. Science in the Cévennes park is conceived as one of the human arts to be used on behalf of the total creative experience of the community of life. The scientific program of research serves to enhance both human actualization and natural evolution. The great vulture was reintroduced with the help of science, the strains of mountain rye are being preserved with the help of science, the fertility of the mountain soil is being increased with the help of science, new and more adequate building materials are being introduced with the help of science. In each of these cases, science is a means to the coevolution of humanity and nature. And in each of these cases, the contribution of science to sustaining life is made possible by visible working relationships between scientists and local people. Knowledge is constantly being looped back into consequences people can see and understand and into projects in which they can participate and from which they can benefit. When the literature of the biosphere reserves speaks of the human ecosystem as the ultimate unit of scientific accountability, this, concretely, is what it is talking about.

The cosmic order the biosphere reserve represents is not that of an objective eternal reality unaffected by human aspiration and choice, but the dynamic order of creative coevolutionary advance.

Microcosm of the Biosphere

※

The Egyptian anserated cross—the Nem Ankh—is the symbol for the Man and the Biosphere program of UNESCO. It is a striking symbol for Project 8 of the program, Biosphere Reserves.

In Egyptian hieroglyphics, the ankh stands for "Eternal Life," or simply "living," and forms part of such words as "health" and "happiness." Historians of religion suggest that the shape of the symbol represents the circle of life spreading outwards from the Origin and animating all existence. The shape may also be perceived as a knot binding together the elements to form one whole, and this may account for the ankh's association with various forms of organic symbolism. From these images, we may surmise that the ankh is being used to designate biosphere reserves as those special or sacred places that preserve and enable the evolutionary processes of life.

The ankh is in addition one of the most ancient forms of the cross, an archetypal symbol with many variations, but always pointing to some kind of conjunction of opposing forces. In the case of the ankh, the nature of the two opposing forces is indicated by two alternative traditional readings of the symbol: on the one hand, as representing the sun, the sky, and the earth (by reference to the circle, the vertical, and the horizontal lines); on the other hand, as representing a protean human figure (by reference to the circle as the head, the horizontal line outstretched arms, and the vertical line an upright body). The two forces that are conjoined in the biosphere reserves are the destinies of humanity and nature.

A morphological similarity between the ankh and a key is also readily apparent. Indeed, Egyptian gods are sometimes shown holding the ankh by the top as though it were a key, the key of Eternal Life opening the gates of death onto immortality. The biosphere reserves are the sacred spaces that show *how* the creative arts of civilization can be used for the successful coevolution of humanity and nature.

Such speculations on the overall symbolism of the MAB program and the biosphere reserve network suggest that if we are to read the full text of this new category of protected areas, we must grasp the relationship of each individual reserve to the system as a whole. Biosphere reserves derive their name from the fact that they are of importance to the survival of the entire biosphere. But only in the most general way may we consider the experience of any particular biosphere reserve a perfect microcosm of the biosphere itself, for the biosphere is not a formal unity; it is an organic unity, or unity-in-variety. The only true and perfect microcosm of the biosphere is the entire network of biosphere reserves in its interrelated diversity. This is a novel emergent in the history of human perceptions of sacred space, one that deserves careful explication.

The biosphere includes all living organisms and their interactions with one another and with nonliving matter over the surface of the globe. To our knowledge, this is the ultimate ecosystem, for it includes the most diverse collectivity of organisms mutually cooperating with the most comprehensive environment. The biosphere is composed of a complex unity-in-variety of some fourteen regional ecosystems, technically biomes or biogeographical provinces, each made up of distinctive types of vegetation and animal life. Tropical forests, grasslands, deserts, and deciduous forests are examples of biomes. Each biome, in turn, is composed of a unity-in-variety of ecosystems in the more proper sense of the word, that is, local communities of organisms in mutual cooperation with their local environments.

The general structure of the biosphere is roughly like that of a federal government. It is composed of an immense variety of local communal units (ecosystems) organized into a variety of distinctive regional wholes (biomes), which in turn make up the whole. Thus, in order to have a microcosm of the whole, there must be a network of representative portions of every significant local unit (comparable to provincial or state assemblies).

This is precisely what the system of biosphere reserves is designed to be: a microcosm of the biosphere, composed of a cooperative network of protected areas, each of which includes representative examples of each of the ecosystems of a particular biome. It is no coincidence that two key words that recur throughout the biosphere reserve literature are "representative" and "cooperative." The biosphere reserve system (when complete) will represent in microcosm as perfect a model of the biosphere conceived as a cooperative organic whole as it is possible to achieve.

Note that this mode of interlocking representative ecosystems also embraces representative examples of adaptive human economies (traditional and experimental). Thus the biosphere reserve network becomes a nearly perfect model of a sustainable global culture.

Taking the long view, it is possible to see three great stages in mankind's relationship to the earth. In the first, human evolution was limited to local communities functioning within the constraints of local ecosystems. In the second, the stage we are currently moving through, human evolution is alienated from the rest of nature, and is indiscriminately exploiting local ecosystems throughout the biosphere. In the third stage, the stage the biosphere reserves are preparing us for, human evolution will achieve a sustainable relationship to each particular ecosystem in the context of a cooperative global relationship to the biosphere as a whole. In this stage, if it comes, human civilization will be a true partner in the evolution of the earth conceived as a living, growing unity.

Restoration and the Reentry of Nature

❋

WILLIAM R. JORDAN III

HILE ECOLOGICAL RESTORA-
tion has been going on for the better
part of a century in our country and
has made dramatic strides during re-
cent years, it has yet to achieve a position in the foreground
of environmental thinking. Instead, it has tended to be regarded as an emergency measure, at best an environmental
palliative, a kind of last resort when the work of preservation has failed. Few have taken restoration seriously
either as a way of dealing with environmental problems, or
as an act implying, as I believe it does, an especially
healthy relationship between human beings and the rest of
nature.

Yet there are now hundreds and even thousands of
Americans engaged in attempts to restore ecological systems that have been destroyed or degraded as a result of
human activities. Through my work at the University of
Wisconsin Arboretum, where pioneering research on ecological restoration has been carried out for more than fifty
years, I have become acquainted with many of these people
and have come to think of their work not as marginal to the
aims and interests of environmentalism, but as crucial to
them.

Professionally, intellectually, and sociologically they are a diverse group, representing a dozen or so different disciplines and interests, and linked only by the conviction that human effort can lead to the improvement of the environment as well as to its degradation. Some are foresters. Many were trained as game managers or range scientists. Others are landscape architects, naturalists, or managers of parks or other natural areas. Some are responsible for the management of highway and railroad rights-of-way and utility corridors. A number are dedicated amateurs—gardeners more or less "going wild," as though following up the conclusions Thoreau reached in his reflections on agriculture in *Walden*. But although they may be very active in restoration efforts, few if any refer to themselves as "restorationists." Nor have they created a society.* The "literature" of their field is scattered through the journals of a dozen or more disciplines. And there is as yet no common language, no rhetoric of restoration comparable to that developed in support of environmental preservation during the sixties and seventies, or of conservation a generation before that.

It is easy to understand this lack of group identity when one looks at the way restorationists go about their work. The spirit is one of discovery and entrepreneurship: most have become involved on their own, coming up with restoration as their personal response to particular problems. John Berger is an example. While not an active restorationist himself, John is the author of the first popular book devoted entirely to restoration. As an environmental writer in the seventies, he found himself growing dissat-

*The Society for Ecological Restoration was founded in 1987, shortly after this essay appeared in *Orion*.

isfied with the defensive posture of much environmental reporting. "I began to think about what could be done to repair and reverse environmental damage rather than simply to accept it," he told me recently, "and that's how I got interested in restoration." For Berger, then, restoration was a personal discovery, an idea that grew out of the need he felt for a positive, active approach to balance the more negative aspects of environmentalism. Hundreds of people, he soon learned, were active in restoration projects all over the country, but no one had thought to write a book about them. So his book, *Restoring the Earth*, became a step toward identifying restoration as a distinctive undertaking.

Like Berger, many of the people he writes about "discovered" restoration more or less for themselves. He tells the story, for example, of Fred Ulishney, a Pennsylvania coal miner who became more interested in fixing up landscape that had been mined than in mining. And Bob Betz, a Northeastern Illinois University biochemist who fell in love with prairies and now supervises the restoration of six hundred acres of prairie at Fermilab near Chicago. Concern about the destruction of tropical forests in Mexico made Joyce Powers want to learn about ecosystem restoration closer to home and led to the creation of the Prairie Ridge Nursery near Madison.

One of my favorite restorationists, Ohioan George Palmiter, is not in John's book. I first read about him in a garden magazine. Since then I have paid him a visit and driven with him around his hometown of Montpelier, looking at creeks and streams and some of the things, both good and bad, that people do to them. A stream restorationist now, Palmiter started out as a switchman on the Norfolk and

Western Railroad who loved to hunt ducks. He spent a great deal of time paddling his canoe up and down the sluggish streams that meander across the low-country landscape of northwestern Ohio. When fallen trees killed by Dutch elm disease began clogging the waterways in the sixties, Palmiter organized a club to clear them. He began a practical study of streams and the way they respond to manipulation, and before long he had become an expert on the complex interaction of current, soil, and vegetation that shapes a waterway. He now works on streams full time, and methods he has devised are providing an ecologically sensitive alternative to the violence of traditional stream channelization techniques.

I can easily think of many others: Ron Bowen of Prairie Restorations near Minneapolis; Evelyn Howell, in the landscape architecture department at the University of Wisconsin; John Cairns, an ecologist at Virginia Polytechnic Institute; or Lee Purkerson, who supervised restoration of thirty-six hundred acres of redwood forest at Redwood National Park in California. Another restorationist is Lady Bird Johnson, who created the National Wildflower Research Center, an Austin-based organization whose work includes the development of methods for the restoration of native vegetation.

To me, this variety is both delightful and encouraging. Consider that not all of these people are even the sort who would have identified themselves as environmentalists. Yet coming from almost every conceivable direction and representing a remarkable range of interests, disciplines, and points of view, they have begun to converge around the idea, the mission, the commitment represented by the task of healing the land.

As the person responsible for publications and public relations at the University of Wisconsin Arboretum in Madison since 1977, I have been in an especially good position to think about restoration and its implications. The UW Arboretum is an unusual place. Like most arboreta, it has its collection of trees and shrubs, carefully labeled and growing in a semiformal setting. The greater part of the arboretum is devoted, however, to a collection of plant and animal *communities*, representing those native to Wisconsin and the upper Midwest. Some are more or less natural— i.e., growing where and as they have grown for centuries. But others have been created here on land that had been disturbed by farming, logging, and development—in other words, they are restored communities, partly natural and partly artificial. As far as we know, it is the oldest and most extensive collection of restored ecological communities anywhere.

So what? one might ask. This prairie or that forest is restored. What difference does it make? People do ask that question, in fact, and answering it has been a large part of my job for a number of years. There are, I think, some very good answers. In the course of finding them, I have come to consider ecological restoration an enterprise of immense significance. I certainly do not imagine that it represents the solution to all our environmental problems, but there is good reason to believe that in the long run restoration will play a major, perhaps even crucial, role in the preservation of biological diversity and of environmental quality generally. Just as important, restoration provides a model for a healthy relationship between our species and the environment—a kind of rite of reentry into nature, a step to-

ward that recovery of a harmonious balance with the rest
of the natural world that has been a recurring theme of environmental thinking since Thoreau.

To begin with, what exactly is ecological restoration?
This is another question that visitors here at the arboretum
often ask when they learn that many of our "natural" communities are actually restored. I usually reply by pointing
to Curtis Prairie, which stretches for about half a mile just
outside my office window, and which is in many ways the
centerpiece of the arboretum's collection of restored communities. Mine has been called the best office window view
in Madison, and it may well be. But fifty years ago, the
view here would have been not prairie but derelict farm
fields, mostly pasture. Prairie had covered much of this
land when European settlement began here a century and
a half ago, but by 1932, when the university began ac-
quiring land for an arboretum, all that was left was a small,
wet patch.

Distinctive in the arboretum development plan was the
emphasis on native ecological communities and the commitment not only to preserve those that still existed, but
to restore those that did not. Prairie restoration began
within two years of the first land acquisition. The pasture
sod was dug under. Plants and seeds collected from relict
prairies west of Madison were brought in. By 1941 more
than forty species had been planted. During the years
since, additional species have been introduced and fire has
been used to discourage invasion by trees and aggressive
exotic species. Surveys show that in some areas the vegetation now resembles closely that of the existing natural
prairies that served as models for the project. Today,

though the prairie is far too small for buffalo, it does provide habitat for a number of prairie animals such as the prairie vole, prairie garter snake, savannah sparrow, and sedge wren. In short, a kind of ecological time reversal has been accomplished, not simply by letting the land recover (which it probably never would have done), but by actively restoring it—gardening it—back into something resembling, though not necessarily matching exactly, its original condition. In this way, an ecosystem that might otherwise have been lost forever has been preserved. Tallgrass prairies, which once covered millions of acres in the Midwest, have been reduced to scattered remnants. The sixty-acre Curtis Prairie, though "artificial," is one of the largest tallgrass prairies in Wisconsin—a measure of its contribution to the biotic diversity of the area.

Curtis Prairie, then, is a good example of ecological restoration. It is a form of gardening—wildflower gardening, one might say, on a grand scale. What I am calling ecological restoration is distinguished from revegetation, land reclamation, or gardening, however, by its commitment to the re-creation of an entire community of plants and animals modeled strictly on one that occurs naturally. Usually the "model" community is one native to the site itself, but in some instances it may be another community that is judged ecologically appropriate to the site. In either case the motives for restoring a community are essentially the same as those for preserving it, and include the value of biotic diversity and other environmental, historical, and even economic considerations.

I might add that while Curtis Prairie illustrates the process of ecological restoration in the strictest sense of putting back together a community that had been eradicated, it also demonstrates how one might treat communities that have been only slightly degraded—by tree cutting, for example, road building, pollution, or invasion by exotic species. Treating such milder forms of ecological disturbance is more likely to be referred to as management than restoration, but the distinction between the two is basically a matter of degree. Both involve a measure of healing.

In thinking about restoration and its implications for the environment and for our relationship to nature, I have found it useful to compare restoration with three other, more traditional disciplines: agriculture, medicine, and ecology. Restoration borrows from all three for its methods, goals, ideas, and values. And as they converge in restoration, each of these more traditional activities is transformed and its scope enlarged.

The techniques and methods of restoration are those of agriculture—the cultivation of the land—in all its branches. Most conspicuous of these branches, especially in smaller, more intimate restoration efforts, is horticulture. Natural communities are generally made up of complex mixtures of species so that, with a few exceptions such as certain types of tidal marshes, re-creating a community is more like making a garden than managing a field of corn or soybeans. Small-scale restoration tends to look like horticulture and to employ familiar horticultural techniques for handling plants, propagating and introducing them, and also for controlling weeds, pests, and conditions through the use of fertilizer, irrigation, mulch, and so forth.

As the scale of the operation increases, restoration be-

gins to look less like horticulture and more like agronomy—real field agriculture. Combines are used to harvest
seeds, mechanical drills to sow them. Plows and various
kinds of earth-handling machinery are employed. One
even finds borrowings from animal husbandry—in the efforts of range managers to devise fences for confining bison
that have been returned to the prairies, for example.

The comparison to agriculture leads to an initial insight
into the significance of restoration as a way of dealing with
the natural world. Like agriculture, restoration brings the
practitioner into a relationship with nature that is active,
direct, intimate, and participatory. It gives the person real
business in nature and in this way reduces the danger of a
self-conscious distancing of self from environment that is
a hazard of many forms of nature *study*.

While restoration can be seen as a form of agriculture,
it represents agriculture radically transformed by ecology—or, more accurately, by the ecological consciousness.
In fact, restoration is agriculture in reverse. That is why it
looks and feels so different. Traditional forms of agriculture deal with nature analytically: they disassemble a complex ecosystem like a prairie and reduce it to a simplified,
more easily managed form, such as a field of corn or wheat.
Restoration goes just the other way. Inspired by the ecological consciousness and its sense of the primacy of the
whole, the restorationist deals with nature not analytically
but synthetically, working to reassemble the native ecosystem in its full complexity, the natural community in its
full variety.

This difference in approach requires a different attitude,
a different psychology on the part of the restorationist.
Where the farmer imposes his own will on the landscape,

the restorationist manipulates nature in imitation of models provided by nature itself. A certain freedom of choice of conventional agriculture becomes, in restoration, a deliberate subservience to nature. Implied is a self-abnegation, even a passivity, a deference that perhaps one has to be a gardener to appreciate fully. In my own experience, much of the pleasure of gardening derives from the opportunities it offers to order the landscape, to decide what will go where. This kind of activity is almost universally regarded as one of the most innocent forms of environmental manipulation, and I agree with Willa Cather's archbishop when he suggests that one is never closer to paradise than in one's garden. But the restorationist, as though following some counsel of perfection, forgoes even this modest pleasure for something humbler and more self-effacing.

Restoration diverges most radically from other forms of agriculture in its objectives. Unlike agriculture, restoration is not a mode of production, but like medicine, a healing art. So great is the difference between restoration and more traditional forms of medicine, however, that it is easy to miss the underlying similarity. Restoration is healing, not of individual organisms, but of the larger ecological whole of which they are a part. It is medicine transformed by the ecological consciousness—its scope enlarged beyond a preoccupation with single members of a single species. Restoration can be thought of as a kind of biocentric medicine. How much psychological distance, for instance, separates the work of healing people from the work of healing the land? I am not sure, but I cherish hints that the distance may not be so great as would at first seem. One of our volunteers at the arboretum is a retired nurse, and I have heard her, in referring to the homely clutter of clippers and sprayers used to remove unwanted plants from our restored communities, speak of "the instruments." A slip of the tongue, maybe, but then, maybe not. Perhaps in her mind she has already linked the work on the ruined hillside with her own lifetime of work in hospitals.

If restoration represents both agriculture and medicine transformed by the ecological consciousness, it also offers much to the science of ecology itself. As we have already noted, restoration has a strong connection with ecology; it is often considered a form of applied ecology. And in restoration, ecology finds new scope and opportunities. Restoration renews ecology's sense of mission as one of the healing arts—a meaning that is often declared but less often practiced. Moreover, restoration may prove in the end to be one of the most useful tools ecologists have for understanding the relationships between organisms and their environment—a possibility that ecologists and natural area managers have long been aware of, but which they have only recently begun to explore systematically. English ecologist Anthony Bradshaw, for example, has written of restoration as the "acid test" of ecological understanding, arguing in his "The Reconstruction of Ecosystems" that the critical proof of what ecologists know "is not whether we can take ecosystems to bits on pieces of paper, however scientifically, but whether we can put them together in practice and make them work." Viewed in this light, restoration becomes the ultimate challenge of ecology and one of its best prospects for reaching intellectual maturity as an experimental, predictive science.

In combining elements of agriculture, medicine, and ecology in this way, the act of restoration expresses an extremely attractive kind of relationship with nature, one in which the active and passive qualities in human nature are well balanced. Restoration entails an involvement with nature that is active and even aggressive—it draws on a full range of human abilities, including that of scientific enterprise; and yet it is fundamentally respectful of nature and wholly and deliberately benign toward it. To me such an activity seems more than marginal. To me it looks like a way for human beings to reestablish meaningful contact with nature.

To understand how this might be so, let's look at some of the implications of restoration, both for the environment and for our relationship to it. Consider first of all the ecological communities, including aquatic and marine communities, that have been disturbed and even destroyed by human activities. Many of these communities would take centuries to recover on their own and others are unlikely to recover at all. These damaged communities already cover a sizable fraction of the earth. Unless one is prepared to write them off until such time as they recover naturally, it is necessary to give thought to the problem of restoring them. If one is unwilling to take seriously the possibility of restoration, these areas—much agricultural land, for example, or open spaces in our cities—must be regarded as just so much land subtracted from the planet's reservoir of biological diversity and richness.

Second, consider that human influence is now extremely widespread. Up to now we have discussed restoration only in connection with the more dramatic forms of disturbance. Disturbance is relative, however. Human beings influence ecological communities in ways so subtle that we are barely aware of them.

We have a classic example here in the Midwest. When the settlers plowed the prairies in our region, they also reduced the frequency with which fires burned over the landscape. The absence of fire had a profound effect on those bits of prairie that had escaped the plow. For one thing, oaks that had been present in the sod as large-rooted sprouts began to grow. Within a generation many of the remaining prairies were well on the way to becoming oak forests, which is what they are today.

Thus, plowing the prairie in one place also destroyed other prairies indirectly by converting them into different kinds of communities. Such sequences of events are not exceptional; they are the rule. There is a dynamic tension within any landscape. Introduce any sort of change and you will likely alter the tensions and so the pattern of communities within that landscape. On the prairies of our area, the oak sprouts were there; only frequent fires prevented them from turning the landscape into a forest. Remove the fires caused by lightning or set by Indians and you have to replace them, or the prairie will quietly vanish, not in a roar of machinery but into the shadows of a forest. Replacing fire under these circumstances is an act of restoration. Restoration, then, is not an emergency measure, but the terms on which human beings coexist with the native landscape.

Finally, it is important to recognize that change is inevitable and will influence even those communities we are actively seeking to preserve. I refer not to human disturbances, which one might hope to prevent, but to events such as floods, tornadoes, volcanic eruptions, and the like, which are largely beyond human control. These are bound to occur and to have a profound effect on plant and animal communities we have succeeded in preserving and protecting from more immediate threats. Climatic change is one example. Such change has occurred in the past, of course, and plants and animals have managed to survive, often by shifting to new, more suitable areas. But what would climatic change mean today? Take, for example, a patch of preserved prairie in a cemetery near Chicago. Many of the surviving bits of prairie are in old cemeteries or along railroad rights-of-way. These tracts represent the last remnants of the vast prairies of the Midwest. They are reservoirs of biological diversity—astonishingly, new species of insects are still being found in them today. What will be the fate of such a prairie remnant if the climate begins to change? Suppose the average annual temperature goes up by a degree or so. Some of the species in the relict prairie would have to shift northward in order to survive. This kind of migration happened at the end of the last ice age. Today it is impossible, however, because the prairie is no longer a continuum but has been broken up into small tracts, each one surrounded by highways and cornfields. Moreover, as a result of increasing concentrations of carbon dioxide in the atmosphere, climatic change in the future is expected to be relatively rapid. Our relict prairie not only has to escape across those cornfields, it has to do so rapidly. It cannot, and so will begin to change in composition, losing native species and leaving ecological gaps that will be taken over by weedy exotics. Eventually, the prairie itself will be erased.

Robert Peters of the Conservation Foundation has looked into this kind of scenario in some detail. It suggests to him, among other things, that long-term survival of many communities is going to be determined by our ability to pick them up and move them—in other words, to restore them on new sites when conditions on their original site become unfavorable.

To a considerable extent, then, and whether we wish to admit it or not, the world really is a garden, and invites and even requires our constant participation and habitation. And the quality of the environment in the long run is going to depend not so much on the amount of land we are able to set aside and protect from disturbance as on our ability to achieve an equilibrium between the forces of degradation on the one hand and of regeneration on the other. So, far from being antagonistic to the interests of preservation as has sometimes been supposed, restoration may well be an integral part of a sound strategy for preserving the natural environment.

But what about restoration as regards our personal relationship with nature? For the real issue is not nature as environment, something "out there," but nature as habitat for innumerable species, including our own. That we tend to think of it otherwise, that we have somehow stepped outside the green, aboriginal world of our upbringing as a species, is the great dilemma of civilization. What does restoration offer us here?

In his 1970 book, *The Invisible Pyramid*, Loren Eiseley wrote that man had emerged from the original "first world" of nature and created a second, cultural world. He goes on to argue that man must make, by way of his cultural world, an actual, conscious reentry into the sunflower forest he had thought merely to exploit or abandon. He must do this in order to survive. If he succeeds he will, perhaps, have created a third world which combines elements of the original two and which should bring closer the responsibilities and nobleness of character envisioned by the axial thinkers who may be acclaimed as the creators, if not of man, then of his soul.

The question is, how to do this? How exactly do we reenter the green world of Eiseley's sunflower forest without denying history, without abandoning, as he puts it, "the knowledge gained on the pathway to the moon"?

By restoring it, of course. Restoration is one way to get back into the forest unself-consciously, with *our* full nature intact. It offers the ideal balance between action and contemplation, between manipulating the landscape and letting it be. It leads beyond appreciation of nature to actual participation. Restoration has the elements of a kind of ritual, even a sacrament, of reentry into nature.

It shares this quality, perhaps, with other such aboriginal activities as hunting, fishing, or gathering wild foods. But restoration goes beyond these because it not only reenacts the past but links the past with the future. Indeed, it recapitulates all the great stages in the development of our species' relationship with nature.

I have pointed out that restoration can be regarded as a form of agriculture. It really begins, though, before agriculture, in the seed-gathering, in which the restorationist reenacts the intimate, unself-conscious immersion in nature characteristic of hunting and gathering peoples. This connection became evident to me one bright fall day recently, as I was watching a group of volunteers harvesting seed on Curtis Prairie. There were perhaps a dozen of them, about as many as one might have found in a party gathering fruits and seeds on this plain a thousand years ago, and it occurred to me that in this act, these people—students, volunteers, and so forth—had in some sense leaped the psychological ground separating them from their ancestors of Eiseley's first world. I have done it myself, this gathering of wild things for use, and I knew just how it felt. I knew that it meant approaching nature not self-consciously with a field guide, but eagerly and even a little greedily. I knew that it gave each person a reason to be there that was in a way economic, and therefore ecological. It gave each one real business to transact on the prairie. Suddenly I saw in this seed-gathering the first stage in modern man's reentry into nature—the reenactment of ecosystem man, the symbolic recovery of the land not as environment, but as habitat. Only after the gathering does the restorationist proceed through the stages of cultural history—to agriculture and beyond it to natural history and finally to ecology and all it implies about questioning the ways of plants and animals: how they come together into communities, how they function in ecosystems. No other process I can think of carries us all this way so simply and naturally. Nothing else allows us to recover some of the sense, some of the feel, even a bit of the actual substance, of that original world.

Ecological restoration is in the odd condition of being a practice but still not quite an articulated idea. Yet, as a response to a problem it is full of promise. These thoughts turn in my mind as I walk in the arboretum's Wingra Woods on a day late in fall. A magnificent forest, this too is part of the garden. The plan was to create here on this hillside overlooking Lake Wingra a sample of the great hemlock-hardwood forest that once covered thousands of square miles in the northern part of the state. By the 1930s that forest had been destroyed, and the resulting slash fires, soil erosion, and economic devastation contributed to the great economic and ecological disasters of that decade. Here, however, someone decided to try again. Sugar maples and hemlocks were planted in the light shade under a stand of old oaks. Today their crowns are beginning to join those of the taller, older trees overhead. In summer this is now a shady spot under the maples, and the understory is thinning in places, becoming more like proper maple forest understory. On a bright fall day the place glows in sunlight filtered through a golden crown of maples.

The woods is not natural. It is not artificial. It simply defies these distinctions; it is both.

"This," I think, remembering the line from *A Winter's Tale* quoted by Frederick Turner in his essay "Cultivating the American Garden," "is an art / Which does mend Nature, change it rather; but / The art itself is nature."

Nowhere is this art more evident to me than here on this hillside, walking under the trees of this planted forest.

I T HAS BECOME COMMONPLACE to observe that Americans know little of the geography of their country, that they are innocent of it as a landscape of rivers, mountains, and towns. They do not know, supposedly, the location of the Delaware Water Gap, the Olympic Mountains, or the Piedmont Plateau; and, the indictment continues, they have little conception of the way the individual components of this landscape are imperiled, from a human perspective, by modern farming practices or industrial pollution.

I do not know how true this is, but it is easy to believe that it is truer than most of us would wish. A recent Gallup Organization and National Geographic Society survey found Americans woefully ignorant of world geography. Three out of four couldn't locate the Persian Gulf. The implication was that we knew no more about our own homeland, and that this ignorance undermined the integrity of our political processes and the efficiency of our business enterprises.

As Americans, we profess a sincere and fierce love for the American landscape, for our rolling prairies, free-flowing rivers, and "purple mountains' majesty"; but it is hard to imagine, actually, where this particular landscape is. It is not just that a nostalgic landscape has passed away—Mark Twain's Mississippi is now dammed from Illinois to Louisiana and the prairies have all been sold and fenced. It is that it's always been a romantic's landscape. In the attenuated form in which it is presented on television today, in magazine articles and in calendar photographs, the essential wildness of the American landscape is reduced to attractive scenery. We look out on a familiar, memorized landscape that portends adventure and promises enrichment. There are no distracting people in it and few artifacts of human life. The animals are all beautiful, diligent, one might even say well behaved. Nature's unruliness, the power of rivers and skies to intimidate, and any evidence of disastrous human land management practices are all but invisible. It is, in short, a magnificent garden, a colonial vision of paradise imposed on a real place that is, at best, only selectively known.

The real American landscape is a face of almost incomprehensible depth and complexity. If one were to sit for a few days, for example, among the ponderosa pine forests and black lava fields of the Cascade Mountains in western Oregon, inhaling the pines' sweet balm on an evening breeze from some point on the barren rock, and then were to step off to the Olympic Peninsula in Washington, to those rain forests with sphagnum moss floors soft as fleece underfoot and Douglas firs too big around for five people to hug, and then head south to walk the ephemeral creeks and sunblistered playas of the Mojave Desert in southern California, one would be reeling under the sensations. The contrast is not only one of plants and soils, a different array, say, of brilliantly colored beetles. The shock to the senses comes from a different shape to the silence, a difference in the very quality of light, in the weight of the air. And this relatively short journey down the West Coast would still leave the traveler with all that lay to the east to explore— the anomalous sand hills of Nebraska, the heat and frog voices of Okefenokee Swamp, the fetch of Chesapeake Bay, the hardwood copses and black bears of the Ozark Mountains.

No one of these places, of course, can be entirely fathomed, biologically or aesthetically. They are mysteries upon which we impose names. Enchantments. We tick the names off glibly but lovingly. We mean no disrespect. Our genuine desire, though we may be skeptical about the time it would take and uncertain of its practical value to us, is to actually know these places. As deeply ingrained in the American psyche as the desire to conquer and control the land is the desire to sojourn in it, to sail up and down Pamlico Sound, to paddle a canoe through Minnesota's boundary waters, to walk on the desert of the Great Salt Lake, to camp in the stony hardwood valleys of Vermont.

To do this well, to really come to an understanding of a specific American geography, requires not only time but a kind of local expertise, an intimacy with place few of us ever develop. There is no way around the former requirement: if you want to know you must take the time. It is not in books. A specific geographical understanding, however, can be sought out and borrowed. It resides with men and women more or less sworn to a place, who abide there, who have a feel for the soil and history, for the turn of leaves and night sounds. Often they are glad to take the outlander in tow.

These local geniuses of American landscape, in my experience, are people in whom geography thrives. They are the antithesis of geographical ignorance. Rarely known outside their own communities, they often seem, at the first encounter, unremarkable and anonymous. They may not be able to recall the name of a particular wildflower— or they may have given it a name known only to them. They might have forgotten the precise circumstances of a local historical event. Or they can't say for certain when the last of the Canada geese passed through in the fall, or can't differentiate between two kinds of trout in the same creek. Like all of us, they have fallen prey to the fallacies of memory and are burdened with ignorance; but they are nearly flawless in the respect they bear these places they love. Their knowledge is intimate rather than encyclopedic, human but not necessarily scholarly. It rings with the concrete details of experience.

America, I believe, teems with such people. The paradox here, between a faulty grasp of geographical knowledge for which Americans are indicted and the intimate, apparently contradictory familiarity of a group of largely anonymous people, is not solely a matter of confused scale. (The local landscape is easier to know than a national landscape—and many local geographers, of course, are relatively ignorant of a national geography.) And it is not simply ironic. The paradox is dark. To be succinct: the politics and advertising that seek a national audience must project a national geography; to be broadly useful that geography must, inevitably, be generalized and it is often romantic. It is therefore frequently misleading and imprecise. The same holds true with the entertainment industry, but here the problem might be clearer. The same films, magazines, and television features that honor an imaginary American landscape also tout the worth of the anonymous men and women who interpret it. Their affinity for the land is lauded, their local allegiance admired. But the rigor of their local geographies, taken as a whole, contradicts a patriotic, national vision of unspoiled, untroubled land. These men and women are ultimately forgotten, along with the details of the landscapes they speak for, in the face of more pressing national matters. It is the chilling nature of modern society to find an ignorance of geography, local or national, as excusable as an ignorance of hand tools; and to find the commitment of people to their home places only momentarily entertaining. And finally naive.

If one were to pass time among Basawara people in the Kalahari Desert, or with Kreen-Akrora in the Amazon Basin, or with Pitjantjatjara Aborigines in Australia, the most salient impression they might leave is of an absolutely stunning knowledge of their local geography—geology, hydrology, biology, and weather. In short, the extensive particulars of their intercourse with it.

In forty thousand years of human history, it has only been in the last few hundred years or so that a people could afford to ignore their local geographies as completely as we do and still survive. Technological innovations from refrigerated trucks to artificial fertilizers, from sophisticated cost accounting to mass air transportation, have utterly changed concepts of season, distance, soil productivity, and the real cost of drawing sustenance from the land. It is now possible for a resident of Boston to bite into a fresh strawberry in the dead of winter; for someone in San Francisco to travel to Atlanta in a few hours with no worry of how formidable might be crossings of the Great Basin

Desert or the Mississippi River; for an absentee farmer to gain a tax advantage from a farm that leaches poisons into its water table and on which crops are left to rot. The Pitjantjatjara might shake their heads in bewilderment and bemusement, not because they are primitive or ignorant people, not because they have no sense of irony or are incapable of marveling, but because they have not (many would say not yet) realized a world in which such manipulation of the land—surmounting the imperatives of distance it imposes, for example, or turning the large-scale destruction of forests and arable land into wealth—is desirable or plausible.

In the years I have traveled through America, in cars and on horseback, on foot and by raft, I have repeatedly been brought to a sudden state of awe by some gracile or savage movement of animal, some odd wrapping of a tree's foliage by the wind, an unimpeded run of dew-laden prairie stretching to a horizon flat as a coin where a pin-dot sun pales the dawn sky pink. I know these things are beyond intellection, that they are the vivid edges of a world that includes but also transcends the human world. In memory, when I dwell on these things, I know that in a truly national literature there should be odes to the Triassic reds of the Colorado Plateau, to the sharp and ghostly light of the Florida Keys, to the aeolian soils of southern Minnesota and the Palouse in Washington, though the modern mind abjures the literary potential of such subjects. (If the sand and floodwater farmers of Arizona and New Mexico were to take the black loams of Louisiana in their hands they would be flabbergasted, and that is the beginning of literature.) I know there should be eloquent evocations of the cobbled beaches of Maine, the plutonic walls of the Sierra

Nevada, the orange canyons of the Kaibab Plateau. I have no doubt, in fact, that there are. They are as numerous and diverse as the eyes and fingers that ponder the country—it is that only a handful of them are known. The great majority are to be found in drawers and boxes, in the letters and private journals of millions of workaday people who have regarded their encounters with the land as an engagement bordering on the spiritual, as being fundamentally linked to their state of health.

One cannot acknowledge the extent and the history of this kind of testimony without being forced to the realization that something strange, if not dangerous, is afoot. Year by year, the number of people with firsthand experience in the land dwindles. Rural populations continue to shift to the cities. The family farm is in a state of demise, and government and industry continue to apply pressure on the native peoples of North America to sever their ties with the land. In the wake of this loss of personal and local knowledge, the knowledge from which a real geography is derived, the knowledge on which a country must ultimately stand, has come something hard to define but I think sinister and unsettling—the packaging and marketing of land as a form of entertainment. An incipient industry, capitalizing on the nostalgia Americans feel for the imagined virgin landscapes of their fathers, and on a desire for adventure, now offers people a convenient though sometimes incomplete or even spurious geography as an inducement to purchase a unique experience. But the line between authentic experience and a superficial exposure to the elements of experience is blurred. And the real landscape, in all its complexity, is distorted even further in the public imagination. No longer innately mysterious and dignified, a ground from which experience grows, it becomes a curiously generic backdrop on which experience is imposed.

In theme parks the profound, subtle, and protracted experience of running a river is reduced to a loud, quick, safe equivalence, a pleasant distraction. People only able to venture into the countryside on annual vacations are, increasingly, schooled in the belief that wild land will, and should, provide thrills and exceptional scenery on a timely basis. If it does not, something is wrong, either with the land itself or possibly with the company outfitting the trip.

People in America, then, face a convoluted situation. The land itself, vast and differentiated, defies the notion of a national geography. If applied at all it must be applied lightly, and it must grow out of the concrete detail of local geographies. Yet Americans are daily presented with, and have become accustomed to talking about, a homogenized national geography, one that seems to operate independently of the land, a collection of objects rather than a continuous bolt of fabric. It appears in advertisements, as a background in movies, and in patriotic calendars. The suggestion is that there *can* be a national geography because the constituent parts are interchangeable and can be treated as commodities. In day-to-day affairs, in other words, one place serves as well as another to convey one's point. On reflection, this is an appalling condescension and a terrible imprecision, the very antithesis of knowledge. The idea that either the Green River in Utah or the Salmon River in Idaho will do, or that the valleys of Kentucky and West Virginia are virtually interchangeable, is not just misleading. For people still dependent on the soil for their sustenance, or for people whose memories tie them to those places, it betrays a numbing casualness, a utilitarian, expedient, and commercial frame of mind. It heralds a society in which it is no longer necessary for human beings to know where they live, except as those places are described and fixed by numbers. The truly difficult and lifelong task of discovering where one lives is finally disdained.

If a society forgets or no longer cares where it lives, then anyone with the political power and the will to do so can manipulate the landscape to conform to certain social ideals or nostalgic visions. People may hardly notice that anything has happened, or assume that whatever happens—a mountain stripped of timber and eroding into its creeks—is for the common good. The more superficial a society's knowledge of the real dimensions of the land it occupies becomes, the more vulnerable the land is to exploitation, to manipulation for short-term gain. The land, virtually powerless before political and commercial entities, finds itself finally with no defenders. It finds itself bereft of intimates with indispensable, concrete knowledge. (Oddly, or perhaps not oddly, while American society continues to value local knowledge as a quaint part of its heritage, it continues to cut such people off from any real political power. This is as true for small farmers and illiterate cowboys as it is for American Indians, native Hawaiians, and Eskimos.)

The intense pressure of imagery in America, and the manipulation of images necessary to a society with specific goals, means the land will inevitably be treated like a commodity; and voices that tend to contradict the proffered image will, one way or another, be silenced or discredited by those in power. This is not new to America; the pro-mulgation in America of a false or imposed geography has been the case from the beginning. All local geographies, as they were defined by hundreds of separate, independent native traditions, were denied in the beginning in favor of an imported and unifying vision of America's natural history. The country, the landscape itself, was eventually defined according to dictates of Progress like Manifest Destiny, and laws like the Homestead Act which reflected a poor understanding of the physical lay of the land.

When I was growing up in southern California, I formed the rudiments of a local geography—eucalyptus trees, February rains, Santa Ana winds. I lost much of it when my family moved to New York City, a move typical of the modern, peripatetic style of American life, responding to the exigencies of divorce and employment. As a boy I felt a hunger to know the American landscape that was extreme; when I was finally able to travel on my own, I did so. Eventually I visited most of the United States, living for brief periods of time in Arizona, Indiana, Alabama, Georgia, Wyoming, New Jersey, and Montana before settling twenty years ago in western Oregon.

The astonishing level of my ignorance confronted me everywhere I went. I knew early on that the country could not be held together in a few phrases, that its geography was magnificent and incomprehensible, that a man or woman could devote a lifetime to its elucidation and still feel in the end that he had but sailed many thousands of miles over the surface of the ocean. So I came into the habit of traversing landscapes I wanted to know with local tutors and reading what had previously been written about, and in, those places. I came to value exceedingly novels and essays and works of nonfiction that connected human enterprise to real and specific places, and I grew to be mildly distrustful of work that occurred in no particular place, work so cerebral and detached as to be refutable only in an argument of ideas.

These sojourns in various corners of the country infused me, somewhat to my surprise on thinking about it, with a great sense of hope. Whatever despair I had come to feel at a waning sense of the real land and the emergence of false geographies—elements of the land being manipulated, for example, to create erroneous but useful patterns in advertising—was dispelled by the depth of a single person's local knowledge, by the serenity that seemed to come with that intelligence. Any harm that might be done by people who cared nothing for the land, to whom it was not innately worthy but only something ultimately for sale, I thought, would one day have to meet this kind of integrity, people with the same dignity and transcendence as the land they occupied. So when I traveled, when I rolled my sleeping bag out on the shores of the Beaufort Sea or in the high pastures of the Absaroka Range in Wyoming, or at the bottom of the Grand Canyon, I absorbed those particular testaments to life, the indigenous color and songbird song, the smell of sun-bleached rock, damp earth, and wild honey, with some crude appreciation of the singular magnificence of each of those places. And the reassurance I felt expanded in the knowledge that there were, and would likely always be, people speaking out whenever they felt the dignity of the earth imperiled in these places.

The promulgation of false geographies, which threaten the fundamental notion of what it means to live somewhere, is a current with a stable and perhaps growing countercurrent. People living in New York City are familiar with the stone basements, the cratonic geology, of that island and have a feeling for birds migrating through in the fall, their sequence and number. They do not find the city alien but human, its attenuated natural history merely different from that of rural Georgia or Kansas. I find the countermeasure, too, among Eskimos who cannot read but who might engage you for days on the subtleties of sea-ice topography. And among men and women who, though they have followed in the footsteps of their parents, have come to the conclusion that they cannot farm or fish or log in the way their ancestors did; the finite boundaries to this sort of wealth have appeared in their lifetime. Or among young men and women who have taken several decades of book-learned agronomy, zoology, silviculture, and horticulture, ecology, ethnobotany, and fluvial geomorphology and turned it into a new kind of local knowledge, who have taken up residence in a place and sought, both because of and in spite of their education, to develop a deep intimacy with it. Or they have gone to work, idealistically, for the National Park Service or the fish and wildlife services or for a private institution like The Nature Conservancy. They are people to whom the land is more than politics or economics. These are people for whom the land is alive. It feeds them, directly, and that is how and why they learn its geography.

In the end, then, if one begins among the blue crabs of Chesapeake Bay and wanders for several years, down through the Smoky Mountains and back to the bluegrass hills, along the drainages of the Ohio and into the hill country of Missouri, where in summer a chorus of cicadas might drown out human conversation, then up the Missouri itself, reading on the way the entries of Meriwether Lewis and William Clark and musing on the demise of the plains grizzly and the sturgeon, crosses west into the drainage of the Platte and spends the evenings with Gene Weltfish's *The Lost Universe*, her book about the Pawnee who once thrived there, then drops south to Palo Duro Canyon and the irrigated farms of the Llano Estacado in Texas, turns west across the Sangre de Cristo, southernmost of the Rocky Mountain ranges, and moves north and west up onto the slickrock mesas of Utah, those browns and oranges, the ocherous hues reverberating in the deep canyons, then goes north, swinging west to the insular ranges that sit like battleships in the pelagic space of Nevada, camps at the steaming edge of sulphur springs in the Black Rock Desert, where alkaline pans are glazed with a ferocious light, a heat to melt iron, then crosses the northern Sierra Nevada, waist-deep in summer snow in the passes, to descend to the valley of the Sacramento, and rises through groves of elephantine redwoods in the Coast Range, to arrive at Cape Mendocino, before Balboa's Pacific, cormorants and gulls, gray whales headed north for Unimak Pass in the Aleutians, the winds crashing down on you, facing the ocean over the blue ocean that gives the scene its true vastness, making this crossing, having been so often astonished at the line and the color of the land, the ingenious lives of its plants and animals, the varieties of its darknesses, the intensity of the stars overhead, you would be ashamed to discover, then, in yourself, any capacity to focus on ravages in the land that left you unsettled. You would have seen so much, breathtaking, startling, and

outsize, that you might not be able for a long time to break
the spell, the sense, especially finishing your journey in the
West, that the land had not been as rearranged or quite as
compromised as you had first imagined.

After you had slept some nights on the beach, however,
with that finite line of the ocean before you and the land
stretching out behind you, the wind first battering then
cradling you, you would be compelled by memory, obli-
gated by your own involvement, to speak of what left you
troubled. To find the rivers dammed and shrunken, the
soil washed away, the land fenced, a tracery of pipes and
wires and roads laid down everywhere, blocking and chan-
neling the movement of water and animals, cutting the
eye off repeatedly and confining it—you had expected
this. It troubles you no more than your despair over the
ruthlessness, the insensitivity, the impetuousness of modern life. What underlies this obvious change, however, is a
less noticeable pattern of disruption: acidic lakes, skies
empty of birds, fouled beaches, the poisonous slags of industry, the sun burning like a molten coin in ruined air.

It is a tenet of certain ideologies that man is responsible
for all that is ugly, that everything nature creates is beautiful. Nature's darkness goes partly unreported, of course,
and human brilliance is often perversely ignored. What is
true is that man has a power, literally beyond his comprehension, to destroy. The lethality of some of what he man-
ufactures, the incompetence with which he stores it or
seeks to dispose of it, the cavalier way in which he employs
in his daily living substances that threaten his health, the
leniency of the courts in these matters (as though products
as well as people enjoyed the protection of the Fifth
Amendment), and the treatment of open land, rivers, and

the atmosphere as if, in some medieval way, they could still be regarded as disposal sinks of infinite capacity, would make you wonder, standing face to in the wind at Cape Mendocino, if we weren't bent on an errand of madness.

The geographies of North America, the myriad small landscapes that make up the national fabric, are threatened—by ignorance of what makes them unique, by utilitarian attitudes, by failure to include them in the moral universe, and by brutal disregard. A testament of minor voices can clear away an ignorance of any place, can inform us of its special qualities; but no voice, by merely telling a story, can cause the poisonous wastes that saturate some parts of the land to decompose, to evaporate. This responsibility falls ultimately to the national community, a vague and fragile entity to be sure, but one that, in America, can be ferocious in exerting its will.

Geography, the formal way in which we grapple with this areal mystery, is finally knowledge that calls up something in the land we recognize and respond to. It gives us a sense of place and a sense of community. Both are indispensable to a state of well-being, an individual's and a country's.

One afternoon on the Siuslaw River in the Coast Range of Oregon, in January, I hooked a steelhead, a sea-run trout, that told me, through the muscles of my hands and arms and shoulders, something of the nature of the thing I was calling "the Siuslaw River." Years ago I had stood under a pecan tree in Upson County, Georgia, idly eating the nuts, when slowly it occurred to me that these nuts would taste different from pecans growing somewhere up in South Carolina. I didn't need a sharp sense of taste to know this, only to pay attention at a level no one had ever told me was necessary. One November dawn, long before the sun rose, I began a vigil at the Dumont Dunes in the Mojave Desert in California, which I kept until a few minutes after the sun broke the horizon. During that time I named to myself the colors by which the sky changed and by which the sand itself flowed like a rising tide through grays and silvers and blues into yellows, pinks, washed duns, and fallow beiges.

It is through the power of observation, the gifts of eye and ear, of tongue and nose and finger, that a place first rises up in our mind; afterwards it is memory that carries the place, that allows it to grow in depth and complexity. For as long as our records go back, we have held these two things dear, landscape and memory. Each infuses us with a different kind of life. The one feeds us, figuratively and literally. The other protects us from lies and tyranny. To keep landscapes intact and the memory of them, our history in them, alive, seems as imperative a task in modern time as finding the extent to which individual expression can be accommodated, before it threatens to destroy the fabric of society.

If I were to now visit another country, I would ask my local companion, before I saw any museum or library, any factory or fabled town, to walk me in the country of his or her youth, to tell me the names of things and how, traditionally, they have been fitted together in a community. I would ask for the stories, the voice of memory over the land. I would ask to taste the wild nuts and fruits, to see their fishing lures, their bouquets, their fences. I would ask about the history of storms there, the age of the trees, the winter color of the hills. Only then would I ask to see the museums. I would want first the sense of a real place, to know that I was not inhabiting an idea. I would want to know the lay of the land first, the real geography, and take some measure of the love of it in my companion before I stood before the paintings or read works of scholarship. I would want to have something real and remembered against which I might hope to measure their truth.

PART THREE

✴

Other Walls,
Other Wildness

The Science of the Mebêngôkre

✳

DARRELL ADDISON POSEY

HEN I ARRIVED IN THE VIL-
lage of Gorotire in August of 1977,
the Kayapó were still best known for
their savageness and their distinctive
stretched lips. The last group of these Amazonian Indians
had been "pacified" less than ten years before. The lip disk,
sign of a valiant warrior, was in decline, but older men still
wore their "big lips" with pride.

One night shortly after my arrival, I was invited to sit
with the "big lips" in the Men's House for the elders' coun-
cil. The Brazilian government was finally demarcating the
Kayapó lands to protect Indian territory from land specu-
lators, and the leaders of the Kayapó villages had assembled to discuss how to defend their domain against en-
croaching plantations. The chiefs were meeting together
for the first time in peace and cooperation.

As a newcomer to Kayapó society, I was awed by the formal oratory of the elders. How could such large lip disks
be manipulated so artistically and with such authority? I
marveled even more at the ease and naturalness with which
two great warriors drank their coffee and ate their manioc
bread over their built-in plates.

Big lips, formal oratory, strange language, along with colorful dances and ceremonies, together formed an exotic filter between myself and the people I had come to study. It took six months of living with them before I could see through this filter and begin to realize that the Kayapó are people, too, with all the frailties and attributes that characterize the human creature: Kayapós fight and quarrel; they complain; they can be petty and selfish and can even lie. They love their families, cry for their dead, sacrifice for their children, work hard to provide for their households, and delight in joking and conversing.

The Kayapó year begins in the low-water season with agricultural activities that continue until the maturation of the corn, followed by the harvest period. The fall of wild fruits attracts animals, precipitating the hunting season, which coincides with the time of high water. Then there is a short period of heightened leisure and family activities, which ends when the water level in the river lowers again. Fishing intensifies, and a new year begins.

The different times of the year are celebrated with seasonal ceremonies, which are of great importance to the social identity of the group as well as to daily life. These ritual ceremonies are closely tied to the agricultural, hunting, and fishing cycles of the Amazonian environment. The people observe specific rituals before and after each trip to hunt or collect plants. Festivals celebrate the maize and manioc seasons as well as the seasons for hunting land turtles, tapirs, anteaters, and other game animals. Each ceremony requires certain foods and other natural objects, which means an organized trek to find the needed materials.

The bestowing of "beautiful names" on the youngest generations is perhaps the most important social event in the Kayapó society. Some of my most enjoyable times with the Kayapó are during their treks to get game and fish to feed the dancers for the naming ceremonies. We spend long days camped along the sandy river beaches, watching the strings of yellow and white butterflies as they hover over the waters, or on the river in a dugout, listening to the tucunare fish as they flop among the rocks near the cataracts, or watching the cranes fly, always just in front of the boat as we edge along quietly in hopes of surprising a tapir or deer drinking along the riverbank.

People who do not know the tropics always say to me, "But you must miss the seasons." Little do they know that among the Indians the seasons of the Amazon are not four, but dozens and dozens.

As an anthropologist trained in entomology, I went to live among the Kayapó to study their knowledge of and beliefs concerning the natural environment. The Kayapó, self-dominated Mebêngôkre, "people from the water's source," inhabit a vast area spreading across the states of Pará and Mato Grosso in Brazil. The great Mebêngôkre nation, formed by various subgroups, has a total population of above 3,500. Gorotire is the largest village, with more than 720 people.

One of the most significant questions facing Amazonian countries today is how large populations can be supported in and around the Amazon basin without destruction of the natural resource base. The biological knowledge held by Amerindians has customarily been considered irrelevant, because aboriginal populations were thought to have been sparse and scattered. Recent investigations, however, suggest that the size of these populations has been grossly underestimated. Archaeological and geographical data confirm historical accounts of the existence of large population centers in Amazonia.

Although the present number of the Mebêngôkre is relatively small, the evidence suggests that they and other Amerindians have profoundly influenced the Amazonian environment. Landscapes long regarded as "natural" have in fact been extensively managed by the Mebêngôkre for millennia. In their management of the tropical forest, they have developed a social and agricultural system that is vastly better adapted to the fragile ecosystem than anything the "civilizados" have attained even today in the same environment. As numerical estimates of Amerindian populations at the time of European discovery continue to increase, indigenous systems of ecological knowledge like those of the Mebêngôkre are becoming more and more relevant to modern development planning.

The knowledge of the Mebêngôkre Indians is an integrated system of beliefs and practices. In addition to the information shared generally, there is specialized knowledge held by a few. Each village has its specialists in soils, plants, animals, crops, medicines, and rituals. But each Mebêngôkre believes that he or she has the ability to survive alone in the forest indefinitely. This belief offers great personal security and permeates the fabric of everyday life.

A complete Mebêngôkre view of nature is difficult to convey because of its underlying cultural complexity. It is possible, however, to identify categories of indigenous knowledge that indicate new research directions, even shortcuts, for Western science, as well as alternatives to the destruction of Amazonia.

ETHNOECOLOGY

The Mebêngôkre identify specific plants and animals as occurring within particular ecological zones. They have a well-developed knowledge of animal behavior and know which plants are associated with particular animals. Plant types in turn are associated with soil types. Each ecological zone represents a system of interactions among plants, animals, soil, and the Mebêngôkre themselves.

The Mebêngôkre recognize ecosystems that lie on a continuum between the poles of forest and savanna. They have names, for example, for as many as nine different types of savanna—savanna with few trees, savannah with many forest patches, savanna with scrub, and so on. But the Mebêngôkre concentrate less on the differences between zones than on the similarities that cut across them. Marginal or open spots within the forest, for example, can have microenvironmental conditions similar to those in the savanna. The Mebêngôkre take advantage of these similarities to exchange and spread useful species between zones, through transplanting seeds, cuttings, tubers, and saplings. Thus there is much interchange between what we tend to see as distinctly different ecological systems.

Mebêngôkre agriculture focuses upon the zones intermediate between forest and savanna types because it is in these that maximal biological diversity occurs. Villages too are often sited in these transition zones. The Mebêngôkre not only recognize the richness of "ecotones," but actually create them. They exploit secondary forest areas and create special concentrations of plants in forest fields, rock outcroppings, trailsides, and elsewhere.

The creation of forest islands, or *apêtê*, demonstrates to what extent the Mebêngôkre can alter and manage ecosystems to increase biological diversity. *Apêtê* begin as small mounds of vegetation, about one to two meters round, created by transporting organic matter obtained from termite nests and ant nests to open areas in the field. Slight depressions are usually sought out because they are more likely to retain moisture. Seeds or seedlings are planted in these piles of organic material. The *apêtê* are usually formed in August and September, during the first rains of the wet season, and then nurtured by the Indians as they pass along the savanna trails.

As *apêtê* grow, they begin to look like upturned hats, with higher vegetation in the center and lower herbs growing in the shaded borders. In older *apêtê* the Indians usually cut down the highest trees in the middle to create a doughnut-hole center that lets the light in. Thus a full-grown *apêtê* has an architecture that creates zones varying in shade, light, and humidity. These islands become important sources of medicinal and edible plants, as well as places of rest. Palms, which have a variety of uses, are often grown in *apêtê*, as are shade trees. Even vines that produce drinkable water are transplanted here.

Apêtê look so "natural," however, that until recently scientists did not recognize that they were in fact human artifacts. According to investigators, of a total of 120 species inventoried in ten *apêtê*, about 75 percent could have been planted.

Such ecological engineering requires detailed knowledge of soil fertility, microclimatic variations, and species' niches, as well as the interrelationships among species that are introduced into these human-made communities. The eating habits of deer and tapir are well known to the Indians, and their favorite foods are propagated in forest islands. In this sense, forest islands must be viewed as both agroforestry plots and hunting reserves.

The Mebêngôkre are aware that some species develop more vigorously when planted together. They frequently speak of plants that are "good friends" or "good neighbors." One of the first of these "neighbor complexes" I was able to discover was the *tyryti-ombiqua*, or "banana neighbors." Among the plants that thrive near bananas are some of the *mekraketdjà* ("child-want-not") plants, which are very important in regulating fertility among the Mebêngôkre.

The Mebêngôkre characterize such synergistic plant groups in terms of "plant energy." These groups can include dozens of species and require complex patterns of cultivation. Thus a Mebêngôkre garden is created by carefully combining different "plant energies" just as an artist blends colors to produce a work of art. Indian fields thrive on diversity within the plots. Mebêngôkre fields look like a real mess to Westerners used to nice "clean" fields with orderly, symmetrical rows. The diversity is quite ordered to the Indian eye, however, with careful matchings between plant varieties and microenvironmental conditions. Apparently random fields turn out to have five more or less concentric zones, each with preferred varieties of cultivars and different cultivation strategies.

ETHNOPEDOLOGY

A survey of Mebêngôkre soil taxonomy shows sophisticated horizontal and vertical distinctions based on texture, color, drainage qualities, friability, and stratification. The Indians frequently identify certain indicator plant species that allow them to predict the plants and animals associated with specific soil types, each of which is managed differently according to individual characteristics. Sweet potatoes, for instance, like the hotter soils and thrive in the center of fields, where shade from the margins rarely penetrates. The plants must be well aerated, however, or soil compaction will smother the root system. Much handwork is necessary to turn over the soils, take out larger tubers, and replant smaller ones.

The Mebêngôkre use various types of ground cover such as vegetation, logs, leaves, straw, and bark to affect moisture, shade, and temperature of local soils. Holes are sometimes filled with organic matter, refuse, and ash to produce highly concentrated pockets of rich soil. Old banana leaves, stalks, rice straw, and other organic matter are piled and sometimes burned in selected parts of fields to create additional local variations.

The Mebêngôkre have dozens of types of plant ash, each said to have certain qualities preferred by specific cultivars. The ash is usually prepared from the vines, shucks, stalks, and leaves of plants that have been cut or uprooted during harvesting or weeding. Sometimes piles of organic matter are made, with the different varieties carefully separated and allowed to dry in the sun until they will give a complete burn. The ashes are then distributed to the appropriate part of the field.

ETHNOZOOLOGY

Like other tribes, the Mebêngôkre conscientiously study animal anatomy and are also astute observers of many aspects of animal behavior. The Mebêngôkre encourage their children to learn the behavior patterns and feeding habits of different animal species, which are considered to have their own "personalities." Part of this knowledge is gained through the rearing of pets. In a survey done with Kent Redford, we found over sixty species of birds, reptiles, snakes, amphibians, mammals—even spiders—being raised in the village.

The Mebêngôkre use a precise knowledge of insect behavior to control agricultural pests. For example, they deliberately place nests of "smelly ants"—*mrum kudja* (of the genus *Azteca*) in gardens and on fruit trees that are infested with leaf-cutting ants (*Atta spp.*). The pheromones of the "smelly ants" repel the leaf-cutters. These protective ants are also prized for their medicinal properties. The highly aromatic scents of the crushed insects are inhaled to open up the sinuses.

The Indians cultivate several plants containing extrafloral nectars, often on the leaves or stems, which attract predatory ants to serve as bodyguards for the plant. Banana trees are planted to form a living wall around their fields, because predatory wasps nest preferentially under the leaves.

Stingless bees (Meliponidae) are one of the most valued insect resources. During the dry season, groups of men often go off for days to find honey, which they frequently drink at the collection site. Beeswax is brought back to the village to be burnt in ceremonies and used in many artifacts.

One of my most knowledgeable and patient teachers, the shaman Kwyra-ka, was a great expert on stingless bees. When I went with him and his son Ira upriver to hunt, we spent most of our time searching for honey. His son had learned to draw at the missionary school and loved to sketch the bees' nests. I was originally trained in entomology and realized what a gold mine of information these two Indians possessed about the behavior of species our scientists still considered little known.

ETHNOMEDICINE AND ETHNOPHARMACOLOGY

Almost every Mebêngôkre household has its complement of common medicinal plants, many of which are domesticates or semidomesticates. Shamans specialize in the treatment of particular diseases. Diarrhea and dysentery remain the major killers in the humid tropics. The Mebêngôkre classify over fifty types of diarrhea/dysentery, each of which is treated with specific medicines. Folk categories can be more elaborate and detailed than their Western counterparts. Ethnopharmacologists and physicians frequently forget that disease categories, like all intellectually perceived phenomena, are culturally classified and not universal.

ETHNOBOTANY

Mebêngôkre plant classification is based on each plant's pharmacological properties—that is, for which disease it can serve as a cure. The shaman Beptopoop was the first Mebêngôkre to show me how rare medicinal plants could be brought from distant areas and transplanted to places near one's home or in special medicinal rock gardens. He specialized in curing the bites and stings of snakes, lizards, and scorpions, and knew the minutest details of these animals' behavior. I got a feeling for the sophistication of Mebêngôkre plant knowledge when he showed me how to graft a species prized for treating scorpion sting onto more common stock that grew near his favorite forest trail.

Indian plant categories cut across morphologically based botanical groupings. Nevertheless, these taxonomies often exhibit a high degree of correlation with Western botanical classification.

In addition to discovering medicinal plants, ethnobotany can establish new uses for known species and document the uses of unknown ones. "Kupa" (*Cissis gongylodes*), for instance, is an edible domesticate known only to the Mebêngôkre and some of their relatives. An estimated 250 plants have been collected that are used for their fruits alone.

ETHNOAGRICULTURE AND AGROFORESTRY

Indigenous agriculture begins with a forest opening into which useful species are introduced and ends with a mature forest of concentrated resources, including game animals. The cycle is repeated when the old-field forests develop canopies too high and dense for efficient production and are cleared again.

Agricultural plots are designed to be productive throughout this reforestation cycle. Contrary to persistent beliefs about indigenous slash-and-burn agriculture, fields are not abandoned within a few years of initial clearing and planting. On the contrary, old fields offer an important concentration of diverse resources long after primary cultivars have disappeared.

Mebêngôkre "new fields," for example, peak in production of principal domesticated crops in two or three years but continue to bear produce for many years: sweet potatoes for four to five years, yams and taro for five to six years, papaya for five or more years. The Mebêngôkre consistently revisit old fields seeking these lingering riches.

Fields take on new life as plants in the natural reforestation sequence begin to appear. These plants soon constitute a type of forest for which the Mebêngôkre have a special name that means mature old fields. Such fields provide a wide range of useful products and are especially valuable for their concentrations of medicinal plants.

Old fields also draw wildlife to their abundant low leafy plants. The wide spacing of old fields and the deliberate attraction of game animals extend the human influence over the forest by providing, in effect, large "game farms" near human population centers.

The Mebêngôkre do not make a clear distinction between field and forest, nor between wild and domesticated species. Gathered plants are transplanted, concentrated in spots near trails and campsites, to produce "forest fields." The sides of trails themselves are planting zones. It is not uncommon to find trails composed of four-meter-wide strips of cleared forest.

The processes of domestication, frequently assumed to be historical, are still occurring in indigenous groups like the Mebêngôkre. With the team members of the Kayapó

Project, we have collected literally hundreds of plant varieties that have been systematically selected by the Mebêngôkre and planted in human-modified ecological systems. It is fair to conclude that similar activities have gone on and continue to go on throughout the Amazon among native peoples. Thus plant species are probably being led toward domestication as you read this article.

NEW DIRECTIONS

It is always easy to interest people in the exotic side of Indian life—big lips, strange customs—as I tried to do in the beginning of this article. But behind this exotic filter are lessons that our own society desperately needs. Mebêngôkre ecological adaptations and agricultural strategies offer new models for resource management of the Amazon. Past efforts to develop the Amazon have been such clear failures that the necessity for new directions is obvious.

Changes must begin by treating Indians and caboclos not as obstacles in development to be overcome or planned for, but rather as active participants in the process, whose ideas are integrated into new, more socially and ecologically rational strategies of change. If indigenous experience were taken seriously by modern science and incorporated into research and development programs, the Indians would be recognized as a diligent, intelligent, and practical people who have adapted successfully for thousands of years in the Amazon, and they would participate, with the respect and esteem they deserve, in the construction of a modern Brazil.

One important question remains unanswered, and this

is one of the most difficult. How do we compensate native peoples for their knowledge? How do we legally recognize the intellectual property rights of native peoples? Unless we find the answer, we will be a part of just another colonial invasion to mine and exploit the last knowers of the secrets of the Neotropics.

Wildness and Walls

✳

JOHN ELDER

I TRAVELED SLOWLY TOWARD Japan, through a landscape of literature, observing the beauty of each new season as it flowed into the life of the people. Lady Murasaki slid open the door, disclosing gardens of Heian courtiers. Her shining company played their flutes under the moon, in time to the swaying of the bamboo; they dyed the bamboo of those flutes to match the green of the pines and dressed in the "wild aster combination" as fields around the palace gave way to magenta and green. Later, in the time of the shoguns, Bashō walked north toward the bay of Matsushima, "the pine islands." Looking over that world of wind-sculpted rock, of trees bent out over the thousand coves, he composed a haiku in which the Japanese name gusted into the rush of water, of wind:

> *Matsushima ya*
> *aa matsushima ya*
> *matsushima ya*

The more I read, the more I wanted to follow Japan's testimonies of natural freshness back to the landscape of their origin, to experience a sensitivity to the earth transcending the dichotomies of the American wilderness movement. The American system of national parks, culminating in the Wilderness Act of 1964, had made a unique contribution to the stewardship of nature in the twentieth century. But it had also contributed in certain ways to the polarization of "nature" and "culture." At any rate, that phase of our environmental evolution seemed to have come to an end with the passage of the Alaska Lands Bill in 1980. I wondered whether the Japanese perception of a natural harmony that included humanity might now help Americans become more attuned to nature within urban and suburban settings.

In May, when I laid the books down and boarded a plane for Narita Airport, a visit to Matsushima was the first item on my Japanese itinerary. I took the bullet train from Tokyo to Sendai, then transferred to a local carrying commuters and tourists out to the bay. Since Bashō wrote, Matsushima has become celebrated as one of Japan's three most beautiful landscapes. My route from the station to the harbor was marked by souvenir stands and by plastic statues of the poet, featuring the large nose that is his trademark. But wherever I stood to look across the water—from the ridge of an island attached to the mainland by a long footbridge, from the teahouse constructed on shore by the daimyo Date Masamune, from the Zuigenji Temple on the high ground further inland—the view focused on the enormous smokestacks of a power plant. Not only were they far taller than any other natural or human form along the coast, but the tops were encircled by commanding red and white stripes. As the tour boats, their prows shaped like the heads of peacocks and dragons, cruised out through the islands, it seemed that they were bearing straight for these overwhelming verticals.

Despite all the careless "development" I have witnessed in America, I was startled that the Japanese would allow construction at the focal point of one of their most revered natural and cultural sites. In the following weeks, however, as I traveled around the country with my Japan Rail Pass, I saw major building projects just about everywhere I went. Even when taking a ferry to Hiroshima through the Inland Sea, I was rarely out of sight of a derrick on the shore, or out of sound of earth-moving machinery. The nineteenth-century prints depicting this coastal landscape hovered in my mind; I looked through them, as through tinted transparencies, at the emerging gray face of a new Japan.

Arriving in Hiroshima, I was taken out to dinner by several friends of an American colleague. As was true everywhere I went on this trip, my Japanese hosts were wonderfully gracious. We sat on tatami mats around a long, low table in the restaurant's upper dining room, with relay after relay of Kirin beer loosening our tongues. One man, a professor at the university, shared my interests in Japanese and American literature. As the conversation with him bobbed and turned, there came a moment when I could ask the question growing in my mind. Could the love of nature so distinctive and central to Japanese culture survive the current boom of construction, industrialization, and natural exploitation?

With no hesitation, Professor Aihara answered yes. Take a stroll down any alley in Hiroshima, he advised me. Beside the doorways and in the windows I would see lovingly tended bonsai trees, set out to take the morning air. Or for that matter, he said, look down at the platter on our table. Tiny raw octopus were bedded on seaweed, looking just as they had when they were netted that morning. Chrysanthemum heads were arrayed around raw prawns and lightly grilled whole fish. Such meals celebrated the forms of nature. They were daily experiences of communion, reinforced by facts such as that many Japanese family names derive from natural objects, that the graceful strokes of traditional calligraphy grow out of the twining lines of grass, the drooping curves of willows. Nature was not just the background of Japan's culture: it was its heart.

I knew that Professor Aihara's examples were true to the Japanese tradition. Bashō's poems offer moments, not landscapes in the conventional Western sense. In my favorite of his haiku a single raven on a bare branch hones the edge between seasons—*aki no kure*, "the fall of autumn." The Ryoanji garden of Kyoto offers another kind of distillation. It is a rectangle of fine, light gravel, surrounded by low earthen walls on three sides and opening into an airy hall on the fourth. Fifteen rocks of varying size and shape are arrayed the length of the rectangle, sometimes rising out of thick beds of moss. Though mature trees tower above the walls, the pattern of rocks and gravel, in its mysterious balance, becomes the onlooker's whole world. Some people have discovered in this arrangement a mother tiger leading her cubs across a stony riverbed. Others have found an ocean in the ripples of raked gravel, with islands, or continents, rising up from the mossy surf. As one sits down on the hall's long wooden steps and opens up to the presence of Ryoanji, though, this dry garden gradually conveys the resistant, refreshing integrity of wildness itself.

The architect Yoshinobu Ashihara has pointed out that the Ryoanji garden, while separated from the surrounding landscape by its walls, is not meant to be viewed by a person standing inside it. Its balance and significance are available only from the temple building, looking out at it. The importance of this removed perspective follows from the special status of the floor as a "sanctified" space in a Japanese building. "It is from this elevated position inside that the landscape outside is intended to be viewed," he writes. In my limited experience of Japanese culture, two details confirm Ashihara's statement. One is the verb that describes entering a house, a tea cottage, a temple: *hairu*, to go up. The other is the fact that one always leaves one's shoes at the door, and leaving them, turns from the dusty mundane world.

I recognize another version of Ryoanji's ironic enclosure and separation within the walls of my experience. I have a passion for *go*, the national game of Japan. It is a territorial game, played with round stones on a grid of 361 intersections, formed by 19 lines running vertically on the board, 19 horizontally. The players, one of whom uses stones of black slate while the other uses white clamshell stones, alternately place a single piece on the board, with the eventual goal of surrounding as much territory as possible. Since the corners of a board offer the areas that are easiest to control, a game's opening frequently involves contests to see who can achieve dominance in them. But a strong player will sometimes choose in the opening to establish positions outside the corners. Giving up secure territory for the sake of what is called "outside influence," such a player begins in effect to wall in the *center*. I have always enjoyed hearing the inner part of the board described as the outside. Like looking at a Klein bottle or a Moebius strip, this way of speaking bends my mind around. The paradoxical language also feels very natural, though. Moving inward from the edge leaves a certain security behind. Aesthetically and psychologically, it is a venture *out*, into a landscape of potential.

But I'm not sure Professor Aihara's "yes" was right. I spent a morning at Ryoanji, sitting on that wooden veranda beside the garden. Every half-hour or so a bus would pull up and a school group would bustle around the temple grounds. Again and again, a boisterous knot of blue-uniformed teenagers would walk out onto the platform and begin to count the rocks loudly. It's hard to take in all of the garden from any one vantage point. The kids would usually stop with a laugh when they got to eleven and race off to the next building in the compound. They seemed to be having a great time and were certainly not noisier than American youngsters on a similar outing. Nor were they less attentive to the morning's miracle than, say, the occupants of most tour buses pulling up to the South Rim of the Grand Canyon. The point may simply be that in Japan, as in America, Edward Abbey's "industrial tourism" exerts its deadening effect.

The speed of our transportation and of our mass media makes it harder for citizens of the modern world to find the meditative openness for which Ryoanji was designed. It's clear, too, that many Japanese teenagers would rather eat a *hambaaga* from the golden arches of *Makudonarudo* than partake of the traditional table's cool, fresh offerings from sea and garden. For that matter, they will probably spend less time than their parents did learning to write in naturalistic calligraphy. Pocket computers can remind them of characters they would otherwise have to learn through practice with a brush. The Japanese tradition of sensitivity to nature is today beset, just as American culture is, by heedless consumerism.

Japanese sensitivity to human connections with nature will endure. Regardless of the changing outward face of the island, people will remember to begin their letters with a reference to the season, and will notice when the plum tree comes into flower, when the branches are white. When the cherry blossoms are white they will still gather as families beneath them, too, raising glasses of sake to the return of spring. Though these traditions help to alleviate the dreariness of technological life, they are finally no antidote to the environmental damage suffered by either Japan or America. I traveled to Japan looking for an alternative to the nature-culture split troubling American culture. What I experienced was a society that, no matter how different its traditional perspective, faces the same essential problems.

In Ashihara's book *The Aesthetic Townscape*, he compares the refreshing balance of the garden at Ryoanji to the garish advertising displays that dominate downtown buildings in Tokyo and Osaka. "How is it," he asks, "that Japanese, so attentive to the design of exquisitely beautiful interior spaces, end up with such unsightly building exteriors? The only explanations I can find are in the priority given interior over exterior space that arises from the attitude toward garden scenery viewed from within. . . ." Looking at his photographs of street scenes in Tokyo's Shibuya quarter, I can see what he means. The arrows, flashing neon signs, and towers erected atop the buildings to hold even more ads act to shatter any sense of architectural integrity. But glancing at these pictures, before I focus on the *kanji* within the advertisements, I see nothing foreign to the disorder of Times Square or Los Angeles. This unsightly familiarity strengthens a growing impression that, while the Japanese genius for nature has been expressed microcosmically and our American contribution has been in the development of national parks and wilderness areas, our cultures are in another way fundamentally similar. We both suffer from a tendency to celebrate the preciousness of nature hermetically.

Just as the developers of Ryoanji enclosed it with a wall, our wilderness areas are bounded by a congressional mandate, decreeing that within them shall be no lumbering or permanent building and that motorized vehicles shall be prohibited. The Wilderness Act of 1964 erected a high wall, to protect and define a series of precious landscapes. I rejoice in this achievement. But the negative implication of such a distinction is that, outside the wall, nature can be exploited without restraint. Cities are "beyond the pale," outside the sheltering bounds of wilderness. New York, like Tokyo, shows the result of such a distinction.

Perhaps our two very different, though similarly *extreme* experiences of space have led Japanese and Americans to this shared predicament. Japan has been a densely populated country for centuries, with a large part of its terrain too mountainous to support much settlement. The southern plain has thus been dominated by an urban corridor since the seventeenth century, when it included the world's two largest cities. Small wonder that the Japanese genius so early developed an inward appreciation for nature, or that emblematic celebrations of the seasons should remain essential even as Japanese strive to sustain economic growth on their crowded islands. America, well into the present century, felt empty to the settlers from Europe. In the rush to make some visible impact on the land, we achieved a record of natural despoliation distressing even to ourselves. By the outbreak of the Civil War, vast herds of buffalo had been slaughtered, and much of New England had been deforested. Our wilderness areas were a belated decision to draw the line, remanding a few last patches of unspoiled nature into protective custody.

I celebrate the protective and enhancing enclosures that have brought us the gardens of Japan and the wilderness legislation of America. But their hermetic limitations become clearer as we confront the global nature of environmental devastation in our time. Neither the garden at Ryoanji nor Alaska's Gates of the Arctic Wilderness Area can be walled off from the larger degradation of life on earth. Natural integrity can never be exclusive. As I write this essay, hundreds of square miles of Prince William Sound are covered with oil slick, and blackened seals, otters, fish, and birds are washing ashore. The millions of acres of wilderness set aside in the interior of that state can never correct or compensate for such a disaster in the area traded off to industrial and commercial development. Nor can the bonsai of Hiroshima replace or make up for the disappearing rain forests of Brazil. Carefulness identifies the mountains with the sea and acknowledges the larger balance planted in the woods of opposing hemispheres. Love of nature must be comprehensive.

The environmental disasters suffered, and perpetrated, by Japan and America do not mean that our national visions of nature were false, nor that the hermetic celebrations of garden and wilderness were a mistake. They show instead that these insights must now go further. In a game of *go*, the enclosing energies of black and white propel the game beyond closed territories into a swirl of interfolding patterns—a beautiful, balanced complexity beyond either player's intention or control. In his essay "The Land Ethic," from *A Sand County Almanac*, Aldo Leopold describes cultural evolution as an extension of ethical relations to broader and broader circles of life, and finally to the land itself. For Leopold, such a mature ethical vision will grow out of "love, respect, and admiration for land, and a high regard for its value; I mean value in the philosophical sense." Love for the land has been nurtured in the garden, heightened in the wilderness. Now, perhaps, we can find the ways to express and enact it more expansively, more consistently.

Literature, in conveying the Japanese tradition of response to nature, did not mislead me. Poets of nature are not policymakers but prophets, telling us what we need to do if we are to remember where we are. In America, too, we have had such prophets. Thoreau, one of the first writers to point America toward the East, can serve as a bridge between America and Japan with his statement that "in wildness is the preservation of the world." John Muir, much as he admired Thoreau, felt that Concord was no place for such an assertion. What could that region of towns and farms, puckerbrush and second-growth woods have to do with wildness? When Muir formulated his own version of Thoreau's credo, he said, "In God's wilderness is the preservation of the world." For him, the sacred expression of wildness demanded the vastness and the dramatic contrasts provided by the western wilderness. What Thoreau may have understood more clearly, however, was that wildness is finally a quality of experience as much as an outward fact. A suburban creek, or the electrically dimmed sky above a city, can be wild to one who brings openness of eye and spirit. A pattern of rocks and gravel can refresh and inspire city dwellers just as a passage through the high peaks can. Wildness is an essential quality about which the wilderness, like the garden, can remind us. Thoreau tells us, wherever we may find ourselves, to "live in infinite expectation of the dawn." Bashō, too, strengthens our ability to identify with nature's freshness with his simple, integral pictures of life within the flowering world:

> *Asagao ni*
> *ware wa meshi ku*
> *otoko kana*
>
> *I am one*
> *who eats his breakfast*
> *gazing at the morning-glories.*
> (translated by R. H. Blyth)

Recalling our own naturalist legacies, and learning about each other's, perhaps Japanese and Americans can learn how to value nature on both sides of the wall. No part of the earth is less precious, natural, or "wild" because it lies outside congressionally drawn and protected bounds. In the same way, the Ryoanji sea depends upon the beauty of the Inland Sea: they ratify one another. The placement of each stone in the gravel reflects the larger, nonhierarchical balance of nature.

We look at bonsai to remember the pine islands of a bay that has been cultivated by the wind. We hike into the wilderness not just to climb the mountains, but to see grasses shining with dew. Looking outward, looking inward, we regain our bearings as human beings in community, sustained by and celebrating the physical earth.

Sleeping with Lions

THE WILD AND THE HOLY

✳

SUSAN POWER BRATTON

N A RECENT MOVIE ABOUT the American West, Kevin Costner plays an army officer who wishes to experience the fast-disappearing frontier. Stationed at a remote prairie post, he befriends a wolf and a community of Lakota Sioux. The officer's idyllic stay on the plains is terminated by the conquering cavalry, who use his wolf friend for target practice. The scene's message is simple: invading Euro-Americans did not value wildness and destroyed much that was beautiful in their abrupt cultural occupation of lands that had belonged to better caretakers. The message by now is a familiar one, given authority by the environmental historians of the last twenty years who have traced the degradation of nature in the New World back to the roots of Western culture.

It would be a mistake, however, to assume that Western culture has no traditions of living with or befriending the wild. For evidence of such traditions we have only to examine the stories of the early Christian monks. While this might seem at first a barren area of study, there are three well-developed, related literatures that describe numerous peaceful interactions between people and wildlife.

Take for example a story about Kevin, the great Irish saint who lived into the early seventh century C.E. Early Celtic Christians believed they would be resurrected where they had been buried; thus they established churches and cemeteries in aesthetically pleasing localities, suitable for eternal residence. Kevin had gone to live in an isolated wood in the "Glen of the Two Lakes," Glendalough, when an angel came and guided him to the site for a new monastery and his place of resurrection at the east end of the lesser lake. Too Irish to leave well enough alone, Kevin objected that the valley was hemmed in by mountains and that his monks would not feel comfortable there. The angel promised that if Kevin would bring fifty monks to the site, as each one died, he would be replaced by another until the Day of Judgment. Kevin objected again. Fifty was too few. The angel then offered to make the number many thousands and to raise a great monastic city on the spot. This, of course, would require leveling the surrounding mountains into fertile meadow lands. Kevin, however, rejected the offer in favor of leaving the mountains as God had created them. Walking back across the lake, Kevin told the angel he had no desire to displace God's creatures, and that the animals of the peaks and glens were his gentle housemates, who would be saddened by the angel's proposal. The angel apparently accepted Kevin's decision, for the glen was left as the saint had found it.

As quaint as this story may seem, it has a pleasing moral: that human pursuit of the holy (or of the highest and most worthy of human endeavors) should not destroy the rest of God's created order. Kevin would not expand his congregation if it meant tearing down the mountains and turning beautiful Glendalough into a monastic megalopolis. The original Celtic audience for the "adventures of Kevin" would have concluded that the irascible hermit believed God could produce a settlement for the faithful without doing violence to his favorite corner of the cosmos.

To the typical modern reader, the story appears to be an anomaly. It diverges from the more familiar portrayal of Western religion as pursuing personal salvation while treading on the community of creation. Roderick Nash, in his widely cited volume *Wilderness and the American Mind*, suggests that historic Judaism and Christianity associated wildness with the accursed and the demonic. In his view, the early Christian ascetics who withdrew into the wilderness had little appreciation for the surrounding environment or its native species. Nash proposes Francis of Assisi, with his love for birds and wolves, as the one major exception to this negative pattern.

Nash's conclusions concerning monastics, however, do not account for Kevin's behavior. Kevin could not have been a follower or admirer of Saint Francis, since he stood and prayed waist-deep in the waters of Glendalough a good five hundred years before the humble Italian wandered through the farm fields of Assisi.

To understand Kevin's response to the angel, and perceptions of wildlife in early Christian tradition, we can turn to three literatures spanning nearly a thousand years of monastic history: the writings of the desert fathers, the poetic efforts of Celtic monasticism, and the Franciscan biographies. Although neglected by environmental historians, each of these literatures contains many accounts of interactions between saints—exemplary Christians—and animals. These stories, intended to teach virtue and proper Christian behavior, strongly reflect the highest social and ethical ideals of their respective eras.

The Desert Fathers

❋

The beginning of the Christian monastic movement is usually attributed to Antony, who died in 355. Wishing to avoid the sinful influences of Hellenism, Antony withdrew to a solitary cell on a mountain in the "Inner Desert" of Egypt. Antony's lifestyle, which was widely imitated, was based on subsistence gardening. Athanasius, his biographer, relates that when Antony cleared a little garden, desert animals coming to the nearby spring for water trampled the beds. Antony caught one of the unknowing offenders and asked the animal why he was harming Antony when Antony was doing nothing to harm him. The solitary saint then commanded the animal not to come into the garden again, and in apparent obedience to his orders, the local wildlife ceased trespassing on the cultivated area. In another version of the story, Jerome reports that the animals, wild asses in this instance, returned after the rebuke from Antony, but only drank water and never again molested the vegetable patch. The animals' obedience to Antony's word was a sign of the man's holiness.

Antony himself was appreciative of nature and his theology of creation was simple and profound. Once when a philosopher asked how he got along in the desert without the comfort of books, Antony answered, "My book, philosopher, is the nature of created things, and as often as I have a mind to read the words of God, it is at my hand."

Athanasius's *Life of Antony*, written shortly after the saint's death, initiated a literature that recorded the lives and sayings of the early Christian ascetics and included many stories about desert wildlife. In these stories, the monks often live in special relationships with animals. Another work of the same period, *The History of the Monks of Egypt*, for example, describes the life of a hermit named Theon, who was always accompanied by a troop of wild creatures when he went into the desert. Theon would provide the gazelles, wild goats, and wild asses with water, and their tracks were everywhere around his cell. The texts concerning Theon portray him not as master, but more as friend to his fellow creatures. The description of his relationship to the animals, in fact, completes a list of his noble attributes, which included wisdom in discourse and powers of healing.

A dramatic example of wild beasts responding to a Christian holy man is found in *The Life of St. Paul the First Hermit* by Jerome. In this work of the late fourth century, Antony heard there was a man who had been in the desert longer than he had and was much holier. Antony wandered the desert seeking the hermit, until he saw a she wolf "panting in a frenzy of thirst" enter a cave at the bottom of a mountain. Antony guessed that the hermit was providing the wolf with water and went into the cave, where he found Paul. After Paul received Antony, a crow "softly flying down" deposited an entire loaf of bread in front of them.

Paul had already been near death when Antony arrived. As Antony was on his way home, he had a vision that directed him to return to the cave, where he found an erect corpse with hands outstretched in prayer. Antony wanted to bury the body but had no tool for digging. Before he could otherwise resolve this dilemma, two lions came running up to the dead saint, and, roaring and wagging their tails, lamented the passing of their friend. They then walked a little way off and began digging a grave in the sand. When they had finished, they came to Antony with bowed heads, and licked his hands and feet. He realized they wanted him to bless them, and did so. Again the theme of the story is relationship, not raw power over nature.

Some of the monastic histories do include instances of power being employed to subdue nature, but it is always in response to need. A monk named Benus, for example, drove away a hippopotamus that was disturbing the countryside and presumably damaging crops, and did the same to a troublesome crocodile. Rarely is violence done to an animal.

Large carnivores, and particularly lions, appear often in the histories about the desert fathers. Antony's adventures were the first of many stories in which the lion is portrayed as a friend of the monks. One virtuous old man welcomed lions into his cell and was "so full of grace" that he fed them from his lap. Another hermit, living alone in a cave, slept with a lion who kept him warm. Sometimes the animals defended the hermits. One story tells of a dedicated monk who was living away from his monastic community when desert marauders began terrorizing the neighborhood. Fearing for his safety, the fathers called him back, but he did not want to leave his solitude. He entrusted himself to God, who sent a great lion for his protection.

Although he was uncomfortable at first with the animal lying beside him, the lion stayed with him and warded off the raiders.

The stories convey the thought that the lion could express the foundational virtues of faith, hope, and love, and that animals were capable of joining the monks in service to God. The Abbot Gerasimus found a lion with an infected paw, removed the reed causing the injury, and cleaned the wound. The lion refused to leave him, so the abbot gave him charge of the donkey that drew water for the monastery. When a camel driver stole the donkey, the lion returned downcast to Gerasimus. The abbot assumed the lion had eaten the donkey and commanded him to haul water in the donkey's place. The lion was finally vindicated when the camel driver returned, saw the lion, and fled, leaving his animals behind. The lion picked up the donkey's halter rope in his mouth and led him, with three camels, back to the monastery. Such was the lion's devotion that at the abbot's death, he lay down, roaring, on the old man's grave and eventually died there.

In looking for the cultural roots of these stories of the desert fathers, we find that older Jewish and Christian traditions provided some of the themes. The texts about the lions, for example, reflect the Old Testament idea that the true prophet will not be injured by wild animals. Other stories recall the prophecies in Isaiah, including Isaiah 11, "The wolf lives with the lamb . . ."; and 43, "The wild beasts will honor me. . . ."

In addition to biblical stories, Greek fables and the lives of Greek philosophers may have influenced the monks. A number of philosophers of the Pythagorean school were said to have had special relationships with animals. Pythagoras supposedly called down an eagle from the sky and befriended a bear. The desert fathers may not have read Pythagoras, but the values expressed by these works were presumably widespread in Hellenistic culture.

Philosophy aside, some of the stories may be based on real events. In more recent times there have been verified cases of animals befriended by hermits or others who have lived in wild areas for a long time. If left unmolested, animals lose their fear of humans and when given food or water, may learn to trust individuals or safe locations. There could have been monks like Theon who provided water and soon had animals gathering around their cells. Although some of the stories, such as Antony and the lions burying Paul the Hermit, depend on the miraculous, many do not. When Sabas, for example, was establishing a monastery, he needed a source of water. One night as he prayed, he heard a wild ass's hoof striking the ground in the valley below. Following the sound to the bottom of a cliff, he found the aquifer. The story may have been based in fact since wild horses and asses have been known to excavate for water.

While it is impossible to determine the factual basis of these stories, we can be more certain about the monks' attitudes toward nature. The stories were written by monks about other monks, and their primary purpose was to teach values. Although some of these tales portray the desert monks as having special power over wild animals, they seldom use it to harm animals, and most stories portray monks and animals as living in a relationship of reciprocity. The monks can communicate with the animals and enjoy their friendship. The hermits thus regain the position of Adam and Eve before the Fall and the expulsion from the Garden of Eden. Their peaceful coexistence with wild nature is a sign of holiness and of the blessings of God.

Celtic Literature

✳

The *Life of Antony* reached Gaul a mere twenty years after it was written, and it took another fifty years for monastic values to infiltrate the kingdoms of Ireland, on the outer reaches of the Western world. The infusion of Christianity into one of the purest remnants of Celtic culture that began in the fifth century C.E. resulted in a great outpouring of art. Throughout the sixth century and into the seventh, Celtic Christianity produced illuminated manuscripts, biographies of saints, and religious poetry characterized by repeated use of natural imagery and motifs.

Like that of the desert fathers, the Celtic monastic literature suggests a fondness for animals. Surprisingly for a people with a pastoralist heritage, the Celtic monks show little animosity toward predators. Maedoc of Ferns, for example, fed starving wolves more than once, using both wethers from his foster mother's flock and a calf belonging to his monastery. The stories directly cite pity or compassion as the motive.

Often the monks protect wild animals from human hunters. Kevin once had a wild boar rush to him for protection from hunting dogs, whose feet he bound to the ground through his spiritual power. Godric found a stag that was being pursued by hounds. The exhausted animal seemed to beg for the saint's assistance with its plaintive cries. Godric let the stag enter his hermitage. When the hunters arrived, he diverted their questions. The hunters, recognizing the saint as holy, asked his pardon and departed. The stag remained with Godric until the evening, when the saint released it. The stag for many years afterwards would return to Godric and lie at his feet to show its gratitude.

As with the desert fathers, animals frequently offer assistance to Celtic monks. Again, the animals' response identifies the saint as a holy person. A life of St. Cuthbert, of Lindisfarne in Britain, tells how, while visiting a monastery, the saint kept his nightly prayer vigil. After soaking in the sea up to his armpits, he withdrew to the shore to pray. Two sea otters came at once and rolled up on his feet, rubbing them with their soft pelts and warming them with their breath. In appreciation of their ministry to him, Cuthbert blessed the animals and they happily returned to their home in the waves.

Animals volunteer for other services to the monks. Kevin accidently dropped his psalter into a lake and an otter returned it to him, dry and readable. A stag came daily to Ciaran and lay down so that the monk could use his antlers as a reading stand. During a long voyage, Brendan had no sanctuary for church services. At Easter a great whale appeared, and Brendan celebrated mass on the willing leviathan's back.

The Celts had a special love for birds. From the diminutive wren to the tall, graceful crane, the saints showed compassion for these delicate creatures. One Lent Kevin was kneeling in prayer in a solitary hut, his hands outstretched toward heaven, when a blackbird settled on his unmoving palm, constructed a nest, and laid an egg in it. The saint was so moved by the bird's trust that he patiently held the nest in his cupped hand until the young ones were hatched. Kevin was also said to pray with flocks of birds circling around his head.

Numerous other stories in the Celtic monastic literature encourage protection of animals. When a cleric saw a bird lamenting Molua's death, an angel spoke to him and said: "Molua MacOcha has died, and therefore all living creatures bewail him, for never has he killed any animal, little or big; so not more do men bewail him than the other animals, and the little bird thou beholdest."

Another story tells of an otter that "in his great kindness" would bring some monks a salmon every day. One of the brothers decided the otter would look better as a glove. Sensing danger, the otter no longer came with the fish. The covetous monk realized his guilt and repented.

There are few places in the Celtic literature where a saint does harm to an animal. In one of the few reported exceptions, Columba killed a wild boar by praying that it would die. Many Celtic monks kept a vegetarian diet and therefore would have had little need to kill animals.

In the stories that have come down to us, the Celtic monks show a greater tendency than the desert fathers to display power over nature. Such stories were intended to prove the spiritual power and influence of the saint. Abban, for example, ordered wolves to tend his sheep. Mochuda commanded two deer to pull a poor man's plow. And Kevin commanded a doe to provide milk for a foster child. When a wolf came and killed the doe's fawn, Kevin ordered the wolf to take the place of the fawn so the doe would continue to give milk.

The Celtic literature differs from that of the desert monks in other ways. First, the Celtic monks mention a much greater diversity of animals in their literature than do the desert monks, who primarily interact with large mammals, like lions and wild asses, and a few reptiles. In addition to stories about birds, there are Celtic stories about fish, mice, and flies.

Second, the Celts wrote a great many poems celebrating nature or using it to teach spiritual values. This literature is full of color and sound, describing the song of the blackbird, the belling of stags, the calls of noisy seabirds, the plumage of birds, the bright fruits of the rowan, and the flashing sides of the salmon. The desert monks did not produce an equivalent genre of literature.

Third, and perhaps most important, the Celtic literature shows a much greater concern for protecting animals from humans than does that of the Levant. The desert fathers saved animals, but the sources of danger were usually natural ones, such as a thorn in a lion's paw. In turn, the animals frequently protected desert monks from human foes. This theme probably reflects the unstable social and military environment of the ancient Middle East, where the Persians and desert raiders were far more likely than the lions to exterminate the monks. In contrast, Celtic monasticism arose at a time when agriculture and overhunting were taking a toll on wolves and other wildlife in the British Isles. Even if they didn't understand the intensity of the threat or the potential degree of landscape change, it seems that the Irish monks had a concern for the well-being of individual creatures and recognized their need for protection from humans.

Saint Francis

※

The monastic sources best known to most environmentalists are the medieval biographies of Francis of Assisi and Francis's own writings. It should now be clear that to consider Francis's attitude toward nature to be an anomaly is to misunderstand his place in history. Far from being the first or only nature-loving monastic, Francis was the ultimate expression of traditions that had been growing and interweaving for centuries.

As Edward Armstrong has pointed out in his book *Saint Francis, Nature Mystic*, most of the animal stories in the Franciscan biographies have precursors in the lives of the Celtic saints, many of which would have been available in Italian monastic libraries. What then did Francis add to Christian love and respect for nature? An interest in the variety of nature, often attributed to Francis, was actually a contribution of the Celts. Francis, however, thoroughly incorporated his fellow creatures into his Christology and made care for nature part of the Christian mission.

He also extended Celtic enjoyment of diversity into an appreciation of the diminutive. Although the conversion of the wolf of Gubbio is perhaps the best-known Franciscan animal tale, Francis didn't spend much time with large vertebrates. He lived in an urbanizing Europe, where most of the bigger wild mammals had already been driven from the countryside into refuges in the mountains. While the desert fathers fraternized with lions and gazelles, Francis cared for swallows and doves. He fed the bees a little wine during the winter and picked up worms that might be trampled underfoot. To a greater extent than the Celtic monks, Francis sought opportunities to serve the small and humble of the natural world.

If Kevin became one of the first Western preservationists when he refused the angel's offer to level Glendalough, we might consider Francis both a preservationist and an early conservationist. On the one hand, Francis could ask a boy to free caged doves offered for sale. On the other, he could instruct his monks to coppice a woody stem so it would continue to grow and produce branches, or to leave the borders around a garden untilled so there would be space for a few wildflowers.

In Kevin Costner's film, the Indians observe the army officer playing with his lupine companion and name the white man "Dances with Wolves." If the Lakota Sioux had met some of the Christian saints, they might well have given them names such as "Walks with Gazelles," "Stands with Otters," "Speaks with Swallows," and "Sleeps with Lions." Great lovers of the earth and all its creatures, the Sioux might have understood the stories about the saints better than most of us who are cultural heirs to this literature.

We do a disservice to the saints (and to the Sioux) if we treat them as mere curiosities or as cultural relics useful only for nourishing wilderness romanticism. The saints, like the Sioux, have something very important to say to us. They tell us that our relationship with nature is a reflection of the state of our own souls. When we put aside our self-interest and look to the good of the entire cosmos, we will live at peace with all Creation. Then we, too, will sleep with lions.

The Ecology of Magic

✳

DAVID ABRAM

ATE ONE EVENING I STEPPED out of my little hut in the rice paddies of eastern Bali and found myself falling through space. Overhead the black sky was rippling with stars, densely clustered in some regions, almost blocking out the darkness between them, and loosely scattered in other areas, pulsing and beckoning to each other. Behind them streamed the great river of light with its several tributaries. But the Milky Way churned beneath me as well, for my hut was set in the middle of a large patchwork of rice paddies, separated from each other by narrow two-foot-high dikes, and these paddies were all filled with water. By day, the surface of the pools reflected perfectly the blue sky, or the monsoon clouds, a reflection broken only by the thin, bright green tips of new rice. By night, the stars glimmered from the surface of the paddies, and the river of light whirled through the darkness underfoot; there seemed to be no ground in front of my feet, only the abyss of star-studded space falling away forever.

I was no longer simply beneath the night sky, but also above it—the immediate impression was of weightlessness. I might perhaps have been able to reorient myself, to regain some sense of ground and gravity, were it not for a

fact that confounded my senses entirely: between the galaxies below and the constellations above drifted countless
fireflies, their lights flickering like the stars, some drifting
up to join the clusters of stars overhead, others, like graceful meteors, slipping down from above to join the constellations underfoot, and all these paths of light upward and
downward were mirrored in the still surface of the paddies.
I felt myself at times falling through space, at other moments floating and drifting. I could not dispel the profound vertigo and giddiness; the paths of the fireflies and
their reflection in the water's surface held me in a sustained
trance. Even after I crawled back to my hut and shut the
door on this whirling world, the little room in which I lay
seemed itself to be floating free of the earth.

Fireflies! It was in Indonesia that I was first introduced
to the world of insects, and there that I first learned of the
great influence that such diminutive entities could have
upon the human senses. I had traveled to Indonesia on a research grant to study magic—more precisely, to study the
relation between magic and medicine, first among the traditional sorcerers, or *dukuns*, of the Indonesian archipelago, and later among the *dzankris*, the traditional shamans
of Nepal.

The grant had one unique aspect: I was to journey into
rural Asia not outwardly as an anthropologist or academic
researcher, but as an itinerant magician, in hopes of gain-
ing a more direct access to the local sorcerers. I had been a
professional sleight-of-hand magician for five years back in
the United States, helping put myself through college by
performing in clubs and restaurants throughout New England. I had also taken a year off from my studies to travel
as a street magician through Europe, and toward the end

of that journey had spent some months in London, where I explored the use of sleight-of-hand magic in a therapeutic setting, as a way to open communication with distressed individuals largely unapproachable by clinical healers. As a result of this work I became interested in the relation, largely forgotten in the West, between folk medicine and magic.

It was this interest that eventually led to the grant, and to my sojourn in rural Asia. There my sleight-of-hand skills proved invaluable as a means of stirring the curiosity of the local shamans. Magicians, whether modern entertainers or indigenous, tribal sorcerers, have in common the fact that they work with the malleable texture of perception. When the local sorcerers gleaned that I had at least some rudimentary skill in altering the common field of perception, I was invited into their homes, asked to share secrets with them, and eventually encouraged—even urged—to participate in various rituals and ceremonies.

But my interest gradually shifted from a concern with the application of magical techniques in medicine and ritual curing toward a deeper pondering of the relation between traditional magic and the natural world. This broader concern seemed to hold the key to the earlier one. For *none* of the several island sorcerers that I came to know in Indonesia, nor any of the *dzankris* with whom I lived in Nepal, considered their work as ritual healers to be their major role or function within their communities. Most of them, to be sure, *were* the primary healers or "doctors" for the villages in their vicinity, and they were often spoken of as such by the inhabitants. But the villagers *also* sometimes spoke of them, in low voices and in very private conversations, as witches (or "leyaks" in Bali)—as dark magicians who at night might well be practicing their healing spells backwards, or, by turning to the left instead of to the right, might be afflicting people with the very diseases that they would later work to cure. I myself never saw any of those magicians or shamans with whom I became acquainted engage in magic for harmful purposes, nor any convincing evidence that they had ever done so. (Few of the shamans that I came to know even accepted money in return for their services, although they did accept gifts in the way of food, blankets, and the like.) Yet I was struck by the fact that none of them ever did or said anything to counter such disturbing rumors and speculations. Slowly I came to recognize that it was through the agency of such rumors, and the ambiguous fears these rumors engendered, that the sorcerers were able to maintain a basic level of privacy. By allowing the inevitable suspicions and fears to circulate unhindered in the region (and sometimes even by encouraging and contributing to such rumors), the sorcerers ensured that only those who were in real and profound need of their skills would dare approach them for help. This privacy, in turn, left the magicians free to attend to their primary craft and function.

A clue to this role may be found in the circumstance that shamans rarely live at the heart of their village; rather, their dwellings are commonly at the spatial periphery of the community or, most often, out beyond the edges of the village, amid the rice fields, or in a forest, or a wild cluster of boulders. We can easily attribute this location to the just-mentioned need for privacy, yet for the magician in a traditional culture it also serves another purpose, providing a spatial expression of his or her symbolic position with regard to the community. For the magician's intelligence is not encompassed within the society—its place is at the edge, mediating between the human community and the larger community of beings upon which the village depends for its nourishment and sustenance. This larger community includes, along with the humans, the multiple nonhuman entities that inhabit and constitute the local landscape, from the myriad plants and diverse animals—birds, mammals, fish, reptiles, insects—of the region, to the particular winds and weather patterns that inform the local geography, as well as the various landforms—rivers, forests, mountains, caves—that lend their specific character to the surrounding earth.

The traditional shaman, as I came to discern in the course of my twelve months in Asia, is in many ways the "ecologist" of a tribal society. He or she acts as intermediary between the human community and the larger ecological field, regulating the flow of nourishment, not just from the landscape to the human inhabitants, but from the human community back to the local earth. By his or her constant rituals, trances, ecstasies, and "journeys," the shaman ensures that the relation between human society and the larger society of beings is balanced and reciprocal, and that the village never takes more from the living land than it returns—not just materially, but with prayers, propitiations, and praise. The scale of a harvest or the size of a hunt is ever negotiated between the tribal community and the natural world that it inhabits. To some extent every adult in the community is engaged in this process of listening and attuning to the other presences that surround and influence daily life. But the shaman or sorcerer is the exemplary voyager in the intermediate realm between the human and the more-than-human worlds, the primary strategist and negotiator in any dealings with the Others.

It is only as a result of his or her ongoing engagement with the animate powers that dwell beyond the human community that the traditional magician is able to alleviate many illnesses that arise *within* that community. Disease, in most such cultures, is conceptualized as a disequilibrium within the sick person, or as the intrusion of a demonic or malevolent presence into his or her body. There are, at times, destructive influences within the village or tribe that may disrupt the health and emotional well-being of susceptible individuals. Yet such influences are commonly traceable to an imbalance between the human community and the larger field of forces in which it is embedded. Any healer who is not attending to the relations between the human community and the larger field will likely dispel an illness from one person only to have it arise, perhaps in a new guise, somewhere else in the community. Hence the traditional magician or medicine-person functions primarily as an intermediary between human and nonhuman worlds, and only secondarily as a healer. Without a continually adjusted awareness of the relative balance or imbalance between the local culture and its nonhuman environs, along with the skills necessary to modulate that relation, any "healer" is worthless, indeed, not a healer at all. The medicine-person's primary allegiance, then, is not to the human community, but to the earthly web of relations in which that community is entwined, and it is from this that his or her power to alleviate human illness derives.

The primacy of the magician's relation to other species

and to the earth is not always evident to Western researchers. Countless anthropologists have managed to overlook
the ecological dimension of the shaman's craft, while writing at length of the shaman's rapport with "supernatural"
entities. We must attribute much of this oversight to the
modern assumption that nonhuman nature is largely determinate and mechanical, and that that which is regarded
as mysterious, powerful, and beyond human ken must
therefore be of some other, nonphysical realm outside nature—"supernatural." The oversight becomes still more
comprehensible when we recognize that many of the earliest ethnologists were Christian missionaries, for the
church has long assumed that only human beings have
souls, and that the (other) animals, to say nothing of trees
and rivers, were "created" for no other reason than to serve
humankind. It is not surprising that most of these early
ethnologists, steeped in the dogma of institutionalized
Christianity, assumed a belief in supernatural, other-
worldly powers among those tribal persons whom they observed awestruck and entranced by nonhuman (but nevertheless natural) forces. What is remarkable is the extent to
which contemporary attitudes preserve their anthropocentric bias. We no longer dismiss the shaman's "spirit-
helpers" as the superstitious claptrap of heathen primi-
tives, yet we still refer to these enigmatic presences,
respectfully now, as "supernaturals"—for we are unable to
shed the sense, so endemic to our civilization, that nature
is a rather prosaic and predictable realm, unsuited to such
mysteries. Nevertheless, that which is regarded with the
greatest awe and wonder by indigenous, oral cultures is, I
suggest, none other than what we view as *nature* itself. The
deeply mysterious powers and beings with whom the sha-

man enters into a rapport are ultimately the same entities—the very same plants, animals, forests, and winds—
that to literate, "civilized" Europeans are just so much
scenery, the pleasant backdrop to our more pressing human concerns.

To be sure, the shaman's ecological function, his or her
role as intermediary between human society and the land,
is not always obvious at first, even to a sensitive observer.
We see the shaman being called upon to cure an ailing
tribesperson of sleeplessness, or to locate some missing
goods; we witness the shaman entering into a trance and
sending his or her awareness into other dimensions in
search of insight and aid. Yet we should not be so ready to
interpret these dimensions as "supernatural," nor as realms
entirely "internal" to the personal psyche of the practitioner. For it is likely that the "inner world" of our Western
psychological experience, like the supernatural heaven of
Christian belief, originated in the loss of our ancestral reciprocity with the living landscape. When the animate
presences with whom we have evolved over several million
years are suddenly construed as having less significance
than ourselves, when the fecund earth that gave birth to us
is interpreted as a soulless or determinate object devoid of
sensations and feelings, then the numinous mysteries with
which we have always been in touch must migrate, either
into a supersensory heaven beyond the natural world, or
else into the human skull itself—the only allowable refuge, in this world, for what is ineffable and unfathomable.

But in genuinely oral, tribal cultures, the sensuous
world itself remains the dwelling place of the gods, the
mysterious powers that can either sustain or extinguish
human life. It is not by sending awareness out *beyond* the

natural world that the shaman makes contact with the purveyors of life and health, nor by journeying into the personal psyche; rather it is by propelling awareness *laterally*,
outward into the depths of a landscape at once sensuous
and psychological, the living dream that we share with the
soaring hawk, the spider, and the stone silently sprouting
lichens on its coarse surface.

The sorcerer's intimate relation to nonhuman nature becomes most evident when we attend to the easily overlooked background of his or her practice, not just to the
more visible tasks of curing and ritual aid to which the sorcerer is called by individual clients, or to the larger ceremonies at which he or she presides and dances, but to the
content of the prayers made in preparation for such ceremonies and the countless ritual gestures enacted when
alone, the daily propitiations and praise that flow from the
sorcerer toward the land and its many voices.

The most sophisticated definition of "magic" that circulates today through the American counterculture is "the
ability or power to alter one's consciousness at will." No
mention is made of any reason for altering one's state of
consciousness. In tribal cultures, however, that which we
call "magic" takes all of its meaning from the fact that humans in an oral context experience their own intelligence
as simply one form of awareness among many others. The
traditional magician cultivates an ability to shift out of his
or her common state of consciousness precisely in order to
enter into rapport with the other organic forms of sensitivity and awareness that animate the local landscape. Only
by temporarily shedding the accepted perceptual logic of
his or her culture can the sorcerer hope to enter into rela-

tion with other species on their own terms. It is this, we might say, that defines a shaman: the ability to readily slip out of the perceptual boundaries that demarcate his or her particular culture—boundaries reinforced by social customs, taboos, and most importantly, the common speech or language—in order to make contact with and learn from the other powers in the land. The shaman's magic is precisely this heightened receptivity to the meaningful solicitations—songs, cries, gestures—of the larger, more-than-human field.

Magic, then, in its perhaps more primordial sense, is the experience of living in a world made up of multiple intelligences, the intuition that every natural form one perceives—from the swallows swooping overhead to the fly on a blade of grass and indeed the blade of grass itself—is an experiencing form, an entity with its own predilections and sensations, albeit sensations that are very different from our own.

The magician's relation to nonhuman nature was not at all my intended focus when I embarked on my research into the medical uses of magic in Indonesia, and it was only gradually that I became aware of this more subtle dimension of the native magician's craft. The first shift in my preconceptions came when I was staying for some days in the home of a young "balian," or magic practitioner, in the interior of Bali. I had been provided with a simple bed in a separate, one-room building in the balian's family compound (most homes in Bali are comprised of several separate small buildings set in a single enclosed plot of land). Early each morning the balian's wife came by to bring me a small plate of delicious fruit, which I ate by myself, sitting on the ground outside, leaning against my hut and watching the sun slowly climb through the rustling palm leaves.

I noticed, when she delivered the plate of fruit, that my hostess was also balancing a tray containing many little green bowls—small, boat-shaped platters, each of them woven neatly from a freshly cut section of palm frond. The platters were two or three inches long, and within each was a small mound of white rice. After handing me my breakfast, the woman and the tray disappeared from view behind the other buildings, and when she came by some minutes later to pick up my empty plate, the tray was empty as well.

On the second morning, when I saw the array of tiny rice-platters, I asked my hostess what they were for. Patiently, she explained to me that they were offerings for the household spirits. When I inquired about the Balinese term that she used for "spirit," she repeated the explanation now in Indonesian, that these were gifts for the spirits of the family compound, and I saw that I had understood her correctly. She handed me a bowl of sliced papaya and mango and slipped around the corner of the building. I pondered for a minute, then set down the bowl, stepped to the side of my hut, and peered through the trees. I caught sight of her crouched low beside the corner of one of the buildings, carefully setting what I presumed was one of the offerings on the ground. Then she stood up with the tray, walked to the other corner, and set down another offering. I returned to my bowl of fruit and finished my breakfast.

That afternoon, when the rest of the household was busy, I walked back behind the building where I had seen her put the two offerings. There were the green platters resting neatly at the two rear corners of the hut. But the little mounds of rice were gone.

The next morning I finished the sliced fruit, waited for my hostess to come by and take the empty bowl, then quietly headed back behind the buildings. Two fresh palm-leaf offerings sat at the same spots where the others had been the day before. These were filled with rice. Yet as I gazed at one of the offerings I noticed, with a start, that one of the kernels of rice was moving. Only when I knelt down to look more closely did I see a tiny line of black ants winding through the dirt to the palm leaf. Peering still closer, I saw that two ants had already climbed onto the offering and were struggling with the uppermost kernel of rice; as I watched, one of them dragged the kernel down and off the leaf, then set off with it back along the advancing line of ants. The second ant took another kernel and climbed down the mound of rice, dragging and pushing, and fell over the edge of the leaf, and then a third climbed onto the offering. The column of ants seemed to emerge from a thick clump of grass around a nearby palm tree. I walked over to the other offering and discovered another column of ants dragging away the rice kernels. This line emerged from the top of a little mound of dirt about fifteen feet away from the buildings. There was an offering on the ground by a corner of my building as well, and a nearly identical line of ants.

I walked back to my room chuckling to myself. The balian and his wife had gone to so much trouble to placate the household spirits with gifts, only to have them stolen by little six-legged thieves. What a waste! But then a strange thought dawned within me. What if the ants themselves were the "household spirits" to whom the offerings were being made?

The idea became less strange as I pondered the matter. The family compound, like most on this tropical island, had been constructed in the vicinity of several ant colonies. Since a great deal of cooking took place in the compound (which housed, in addition to the balian and his wife and children, various members of their extended family), and also the preparation of elaborate offerings of foodstuffs for various rituals and festivals, the grounds and buildings were vulnerable to infestations by the ant population. Such invasions could range from rare nuisances to a periodic or even constant siege. It became apparent that the daily palm-frond offerings served to preclude such an attack by the natural forces that surrounded (and underlay) the family's land. The daily gifts of rice kept the ant colonies occupied—and presumably, satisfied. Placed in regular, repeated locations at the corners of various structures around the compound, the offerings seemed to establish certain boundaries between the human and ant communities; by honoring this boundary with gifts, the humans apparently hoped to persuade the insects to respect the boundary and not enter the buildings.

Yet I remained puzzled by my hostess's assertion that these were gifts "for the spirits." To be sure there has always been some confusion between our Western notion of "spirit" (often defined in contrast to matter or "flesh") and the mysterious presences to which tribal and indigenous cultures pay so much attention. I have already alluded to the misunderstandings arising from the circumstance that many of the earliest Western students of these other customs were Christian missionaries all too ready to see ghosts and immaterial specters where the tribespeople were simply offering their respect to the local winds. While the notion of "spirit" has come to have, for us in the West, a primarily anthropomorphic or human association, my encounter with the ants was the first of many experiences suggesting to me that the "spirits" of an indigenous culture are primarily those modes of intelligence or awareness that do *not* possess a human form.

As humans we are well acquainted with the needs and capacities of the human body—we *live* our own bodies and so know from within the possibilities of our form. We cannot know, with the same familiarity and intimacy, the lived experience of a grass snake or a snapping turtle; we cannot readily experience the precise sensations of a hummingbird sipping nectar from a flower, or a rubber tree soaking up sunlight. Our experience may be a variant of these other modes of sensitivity, yet we cannot, as humans, experience entirely the living sensations of another form. We do not know with full clarity their desires or motivations—we cannot know, or can never be *sure* that we know, what they know. That the deer *does* experience sensations, that it carries knowledge of how to orient in the land, of where to find food and how to protect its young, that it knows well how to survive in the forest without the tools upon which we depend, is readily evident to our human senses. That the apple tree has the ability to create apples, or the yarrow plant the power to reduce a child's fever, is also evident. To humankind, these Others are purveyors of secrets, carriers of intelligence that we ourselves often need: it is these Others who can inform us of unseasonable changes in the weather, or warn us of imminent eruptions and earthquakes—who show us where we may find good berries to eat when we are lost, or the best route to follow back home. By watching them build their shelters and nests we glean clues regarding how to strengthen our own dwellings, and their deaths teach us of our own. We receive from them countless gifts of food, fuel, shelter, and clothing. Yet still they remain Other to us, inhabiting their own cultures and enacting their own rituals, never wholly fathomable. Finally, it is not only those entities acknowledged by Western civilization as "alive," not only the other animals or the plants that speak, as spirits, to the senses of an oral culture, but also the meandering river from which those animals drink, and the torrential monsoon rains, and the stone that fits neatly into the palm of the hand. The mountain, too, has its thoughts. The forest birds whirring and chattering as the sun slips below the horizon are vocal organs of the rain forest itself.

Bali, of course, is hardly an aboriginal culture—its temple architecture, irrigation systems, festivals, and crafts all bespeak the influence of various civilizations, most notably the Hindu complex of India. In Bali, nevertheless, these influences are thoroughly intertwined with the indigenous animism of the Indonesian archipelago; the Hindu gods and goddesses have been appropriated, as it were, by the more volcanic spirits of the local terrain.

Yet the underlying animistic cultures of Indonesia, like those of many islands in the South Pacific, are steeped as well in beliefs often referred to by anthropologists as "ancestor-worship," and some may argue that the ritual reverence paid to one's long-dead human ancestors, and the assumption of their influence in present life, easily invalidates the assertion that the various "powers" or "spirits" that move throughout the discourse of these peoples are ultimately tied to *nonhuman* (but nonetheless sentient or intelligent) forces in the surrounding landscape.

This objection trades on certain notions fundamental to Christian civilization, such as the assumption that the "spirits" of dead persons necessarily retain their human form, and that they reside in a domain beyond the physical world. However, most indigenous tribal peoples have no such ready recourse to an immaterial realm outside earthly nature. For almost all oral cultures, the enveloping and sensuous earth remains the dwelling place of both the living and the dead. The "body"—whether human or otherwise—is not yet a mechanical object in such cultures, but a magical entity, the mind's own sensuous aspect, and at death the body's decomposition into soil, worms, and dust can only signify the gradual reintegration of one's elders and ancestors into the living landscape, from which all, too, are born. Each indigenous culture elaborates this recognition of metamorphosis in its own fashion, taking its clues from the natural environment in which it is embedded.

Often the invisible atmosphere that animates the visible world, the subtle presence that circulates both within us and around all things, retains within itself the breath of the dead person until the time when that breath will enter and animate another visible body—a bird, or a deer, or a field of wild grain. Some cultures may burn or "cremate" the body in order more completely to return the person, as smoke, to the swirling air, while that which departs as flame is offered to the sun and stars, and that which lingers as ash is fed to the dense earth. Still other cultures, like some in the Himalayas, may dismember the body, leaving parts in precise locations where they will likely be found by condors, or where they will be consumed by leopards or wolves, thus hastening the reincarnation of that person into a particular animal realm within the landscape. Such examples illustrate simply that death, in tribal cultures, initiates a metamorphosis wherein the person's presence does not "vanish" from the sensible world (where would it go?) but rather remains as an animating force within the vastness of the landscape, whether subtly, in the wind, or more visibly, in animal form, or even as the eruptive, ever to be appeased, wrath of the volcano. "Ancestor-worship" in its myriad forms, then, is ultimately another mode of attentiveness to nonhuman nature; it signifies not so much an awe or reverence of *human* powers, but rather a reverence for those forms that awareness takes when it is *not* in human form, when the familiar human embodiment dies and decays to become part of the encompassing cosmos.

This cycling of the human back into the larger world ensures that the other forms of life that we encounter, whether ants, or willow trees, or clouds, are never absolutely alien to ourselves. Despite their obvious differences in shape and ability and style of being, they remain distantly familiar, even familial. It is, paradoxically, this perceived kinship and consanguinity that renders the difference or otherness so eerily potent.

Several months after my arrival in Bali, I left the village where I was staying to visit one of the pre-Hindu sites on the island. I arrived on my bicycle early in the afternoon, after the bus carrying tourists from the coast had departed. A flight of steps took me down into a lush, emerald valley lined by cliffs and awash with the sound of the river and the sighing speech of the wind through high, unharvested grasses. I crossed a small bridge and stood in front of a great moss-covered complex of passageways, rooms, and courtyards carved by hand out of the black volcanic rock.

I noticed, at a distant bend in the canyon downstream, a further series of caves carved into the cliffs. These appeared more isolated and remote, unapproached by any footpath I could discern, and so I set out in their direction. After getting somewhat lost in the head-high grass and fording the river three times, I at last found myself beneath the caves. A short scramble up the rock wall brought me to the mouth of one of them, and I entered on my hands and knees.

It was a wide opening, maybe four feet high, and the interior receded only about five or six feet into the cliff. The floor and walls were covered with mosses, painting the cave with green patterns and softening the harshness of the rock; the place, despite its small size, or perhaps because of it, had an air of great friendliness. I climbed to two other caves, each about the same size, but felt drawn back to the first one, to sit cross-legged on the cushioning moss and gaze out across the canyon. It was quiet inside, a kind of intimate sanctuary. I began to explore the rich resonance of the enclosure, first just humming, then intoning a chant taught to me by a balian some days before. I was delighted by the overtones that the cave added to my voice and sat there singing for a long while. I did not notice the change in the wind outside, or the cloud-shadows darkening the valley until the rains broke, suddenly and with great force. The first storm of the monsoon!

I had experienced only slight rains on the island before then and was startled by the torrential downpour now sending stones tumbling along the cliffs, building puddles and then ponds in the landscape below, swelling the river. There could be no question of returning home—I would be unable to make my way back through the flood to the valley's entrance. And so, thankful for the shelter, I recrossed my legs to wait out the storm. Before long the rivulets falling along the cliff outside gathered themselves into streams, and two small waterfalls cascaded across the cave's mouth. Soon I was looking into a solid curtain of water—thin in some places, where the canyon's image flickered unsteadily, and thickly rushing in others. My senses were all but overcome by the wild beauty of the cascade and by the ferocious roar of sound, my body trembling inwardly at the weird sense of being sealed into my hiding place.

And then, in the midst of this tumult, I noticed a small, delicate activity just in front of me. Only an inch or two to my side of the torrent, a spider was climbing a thin thread stretched across the mouth of the cave. As I watched, it anchored another thread to the top of the opening, then slipped back along the first thread and joined the two at a point about midway between the roof and floor. I lost sight of the spider then. For a while it seemed to have vanished, thread and all, until my focus rediscovered it. Two more filaments now radiated from the center to the floor, and then another; soon the spider began to swing between these as on a circular trellis, trailing an ever-lengthening thread which it affixed to each radiating rung as it moved from one to the other, spiraling outward. Now and then it broke off its spiral dance and climbed to the roof or the floor to tug on the radii there, assuring the tautness of the threads, then crawled back to where it had left off. The spider seemed wholly undaunted by the tumult of waters spilling past. Whenever the web disappeared from my view, I waited to catch sight of the spinning arachnid, and then let its dancing form gradually draw the lineaments of the web back into visibility, tying my focus into each new knot of silk as it moved, weaving my gaze into the deepening pattern.

Abruptly, my vision snagged on a strange incongruity: another thread slanted across the web, neither radiating nor spiraling from the central juncture, violating the symmetry. As I followed it with my eyes, pondering its purpose in the overall pattern, I discovered that it was on a different plane from the rest of the web, for the web slipped out of focus when this new line became more clear. I soon saw that it led to its own center, about twelve inches to the right of the first, another nexus of forces from which several threads stretched to the floor and the ceiling. And then I saw that there was a different spider spinning this web, testing its tautness by dancing around it like the first, now setting the silken cross-weaves around the nodal point and winding outward. The two spiders spun independently of each other, but to my eyes they wove a single intersecting pattern. This widening of my gaze soon disclosed yet another spider spiraling in the cave's mouth, and suddenly I realized that there were *many* overlapping webs coming into being, radiating out at different rhythms from myriad centers poised—some higher, some lower, some minutely closer to my eyes and some farther away—between the stone above and below.

I sat mesmerized before this complexifying expanse of living patterns upon patterns—my gaze drawn like a breath into one converging group of lines, then breathed out into open space, then drawn down into another con-

vergence. The curtain of water had become utterly silent.
I tried at one point to hear it, but could not. My senses
were entranced. I had the distinct impression that I was
watching the universe being born, galaxy upon galaxy.

Night filled up the cave with darkness. The rain had not
stopped. Yet strangely, I felt neither cold nor hungry, only
remarkably peaceful and at home. Stretching out upon the
moist, mossy floor near the back of the cave, I slept.

When I awoke the sun was staring into the canyon, the
grasses below rippling with blue and green. I could see no
trace of the webs, nor their weavers. Thinking that they
were invisible to my eyes without the curtain of water behind them, I felt carefully with my hands around and
through the mouth of the cave. But the webs were gone. I
climbed down to the river and washed, then hiked across
and out of the canyon to where my bicycle was drying in
the sun and headed back to my own valley.

I have never, since that time, been able to encounter a
spider without feeling a great strangeness and awe. To be
sure, insects and spiders are not the only powers, or even
central presences, within the Indonesian universe. But
they were *my* introduction to the spirits, to the magic afoot
in the landscape. It was from them that I first learned of
the intelligence that lurks in nonhuman nature, the ability
of an alien form of sentience to echo one's own—to instill
in one a reverberation that temporarily shatters habitual
ways of seeing and feeling, leaving one open to a world all
alive, awake, and aware. It was from such small beings that
my senses first learned of the countless worlds within
worlds that spin in the depths of this world that we commonly inhabit, and it was from them that I learned my
body could, with practice, enter sensorially into these di-

mensions. The precise, minuscule craft of the spiders had so honed and focused my awareness that the very webwork of the universe, of which my own flesh was a part, seemed to be being spun by their arcane art. I have already spoken of the ants, and of the fireflies, whose sensory likeness to the lights in the night sky had taught me of the impermanence of galaxies and the fickleness of gravity. The long and cyclical trance that we call malaria was also brought to me by insects, in this case mosquitoes, and I lived for three weeks in a feverish state of shivers, sweat, and visions.

I had rarely paid much attention to the natural world before, but my exposure to traditional magicians and seers was rendering me increasingly susceptible to the solicitations of nonhuman things. I began to see and to hear in a manner I never had before. When a magician spoke of a power or "presence" lingering in the corner of his house, I learned to notice the ray of sunlight that was pouring through a chink in the wall, illuminating a column of drifting dust, and to realize that that column of light was indeed a power, influencing the air currents by its warmth, even influencing the mood of the room. Although I had not consciously seen it before, it had already been structuring my experience. My ears began to attend in a new way to the songs of birds—no longer just a melodic background to human speech, but meaningful speech in its own right, responding to and commenting on events in the surrounding world. I became a student of subtle differences: the way a breeze may flutter a single leaf on a tree, leaving the others silent and unmoved (had not that leaf, then, been brushed by a magic?); or the way the intensity of the sun's heat expresses itself in the precise rhythm of the crickets. Walking along the dirt paths, I learned to slow my pace in order to feel the difference between one hill and the next, or to taste the presence of a particular field at a certain time of day when, as I had been told by a local *dukun*, the place had a special power and proffered unique gifts. It was a power communicated to my senses by the way the shadows of the trees fell at that hour, and by smells that only then lingered in the tops of the grasses without being wafted away by the wind, and other elements I could only isolate after many days of stopping and listening.

Gradually, other animals began to intercept me in my wanderings, as if some quality in my posture or the rhythm of my breathing had disarmed their wariness; I would find myself face to face with monkeys, and with large lizards that did not slither away when I spoke, but leaned forward in apparent curiosity. In rural Java I often noticed monkeys accompanying me in the branches overhead, and ravens walked toward me on the road, croaking. While at Pangandaran, a peninsula jutting out from the south coast of Java ("a place of many spirits," I was told by nearby fishermen), I stepped out from a clutch of trees and discovered I was looking into the face of one of the rare and beautiful bison that are found only on that island. Our eyes locked. When it snorted, I snorted back; when it shifted its shoulders, I shifted my stance; when I tossed my head, it tossed its own in reply. I found myself caught in a nonverbal conversation with this Other, a gestural duet with which my reflective awareness had very little to do. It was as if my body were suddenly being motivated by a wisdom older than my thinking mind, as though it were held and moved by a logos—deeper than words—spoken by the Other's body, the trees, the air, and the stony ground on which we stood.

I returned to North America excited by the new sensibilities that had stirred in me—my newfound awareness of a more-than-human world, of the great potency of the land, and particularly of the keen intelligence of other animals, large and small, whose lives and cultures interpenetrate our own. I startled neighbors by chattering with squirrels, who quickly climbed down the trunks of their trees and across the lawns to banter with me, and by gazing for hours on end at a heron fishing in a nearby estuary, or at gulls dropping clams on the rocks along the beach.

Yet, very gradually, I began to lose my sense of the animals' own awareness. The gulls' technique for breaking open the clams began to appear as a largely automatic behavior, and I could not easily feel the attention that they must bring to each new shell. Perhaps each shell was entirely the same as the last, and no spontaneous attention was necessary. . . .

I found myself now observing the heron from outside its world, noting with interest its careful, high-stepping walk and the sudden dart of its beak into the water, but no longer feeling its tensed yet poised alertness with my own muscles. And, strangely, the suburban squirrels no longer responded to my chittering calls. Although I wished to, I could not focus my awareness on engaging in their world as I had so easily done a few weeks earlier, for my attention was quickly deflected by internal verbal deliberations of one sort or another, by a conversation I now seemed to carry on entirely within myself. The squirrels had no part in this conversation.

It became increasingly apparent, from books and articles and discussions with various people, that other animals were not as awake and aware as I had assumed, that they lacked any genuine language and hence the possibility of real thought, and that even their seemingly spontaneous responses to the world around them were largely "programmed" behaviors, "coded" in the genetic material now being mapped by biologists. Indeed, the more I spoke *about* other animals, the less possible it became to speak *to* them. I slowly came to discern that there was no common ground between the unlimited human intellect and the limited sentience of other animals, no medium through which we and they might communicate and reciprocate one another.

As the sentient landscape gradually receded behind my more exclusively human concerns, threatening to become little more than an illusion or fantasy, I began to feel, particularly in my chest and abdomen, as though I were being cut off from vital sources of nourishment. I was indeed reacclimating to my own culture, becoming more attuned to its styles of discourse and interaction, yet my bodily senses seemed to be losing their edge, becoming less awake to certain patterns and changes. The thrumming of crickets, like the songs of the local blackbirds, readily faded from my awareness, and it was only by a great effort of will that I could bring them back into my perceptual field. The flights of sparrows and of dragonflies no longer carried my attention very long, if I noticed them at all. My skin quit registering the changes in the breeze, and smells seemed to have vanished from the world almost entirely. My nose woke up only once or twice a day, perhaps while cooking, or when taking out the garbage.

In Nepal, the air had been filled with smells—whether in the cities, where burning incense combined with the aromas of roasting meats and honeyed pastries and fruits for trade in the open market, and the stench of organic refuse rotting in the ravines, and sometimes of corpses being cremated by the river; or in the high mountains, where the wind carried the whiffs of countless wildflowers, and of the newly turned earth outside the villages, where the fragrant dung of the yaks was drying in round patties on the outer walls of the houses, to be used when dry as fuel for the household fires, and where smoke from those many home fires always mingled in the outside air. And sounds as well: the chants of aspiring monks and Buddhist adepts blended with the ringing of prayer bells on near and distant slopes, accompanied by the raucous croaks of ravens, and the sigh of the wind pouring over the passes, and the flapping of prayer flags, and the distant hush of the river cascading through the far-below gorge. There the air was a thick and richly textured presence, filled with invisible but nonetheless tactile, olfactory, and audible influences. In America, however, the air seemed thin and void of substance or influence. Here it was not a sensuous medium—the felt matrix of our breath and the breath of the other animals and plants and soils—but merely an absence, and indeed was commonly spoken of as empty space. I found myself lingering near wood-fires and even garbage dumps—much to the dismay of my friends—for only such an intensity of smells served to remind my body of its immersion in an enveloping medium, and with this experience came a host of body-memories from my sojourn among the shamans and village people of rural Asia.

Today, in the "developed world," many persons in search of spiritual meaning or self-understanding are enrolling for workshops in "shamanic" methods of personal discovery and revelation. Meanwhile some psychotherapists have begun to specialize in "shamanic healing techniques." "Shamanism" has thus come to denote an alternative form of therapy; the emphasis among these practitioners of popular shamanism is on personal insight and curing. These are noble aims, to be sure. But they are secondary to, and derivative from, the primary role of the indigenous shaman, a role that cannot be fulfilled without long and sustained exposure to wild nature, its patterns and vicissitudes. Mimicking the indigenous shaman's curative methods without his intimate knowledge of the wider natural community cannot, if I am correct, do anything more than trade certain symptoms for others, or shift the locus of dis-ease from place to place within the human community. For the source of illness lies in the relation *between* the human culture and the natural landscape in which it is embedded. Western industrial society, of course, with its massive scale and hugely centralized economy, can hardly be seen in relation to any particular landscape or ecosystem; the more-than-human ecology with which it is directly engaged is the biosphere itself. Sadly, our society's relation to the living biosphere can in no way be considered a reciprocal or balanced one. With thousands of acres of nonregenerating forest disappearing every hour and hundreds of species becoming extinct each month as a result of our excesses, we can hardly be surprised by the amount of epidemic illness in our culture, from increasingly severe immune dysfunctions and cancers, to widespread psychological distress, depressions, and ever more frequent suicides, to the growing number of murders committed for no apparent reason by otherwise coherent individuals.

From an animistic perspective, the clearest source of all this distress, both physical and psychological, lies in the aforementioned violence needlessly perpetrated by our civilization upon the ecology of the planet; only by alleviating the latter will we be able to heal the former. This may sound at first like a simple statement of faith, yet it makes eminent and obvious sense as soon as we recognize our thorough dependence upon the countless other organisms with whom we have evolved. Caught up in a mass of abstractions, our attention hypnotized by a host of human-made technologies that only reflect us back upon ourselves, it is all too easy for us to forget our carnal inherence in a more-than-human matrix of sensations and sensibilities.

Our bodies have formed themselves in delicate reciprocity with the manifold textures, sounds, and shapes of an animate earth—our eyes have evolved in subtle interaction with other eyes, as our ears are attuned by their very structure to the howling of wolves and the honking of geese. To shut ourselves off from these other voices, to continue by our lifestyles to condemn these other sensibilities to the oblivion of extinction, is to rob our own senses of their integrity, and to rob our minds of their coherence. We are human only in contact and conviviality with what is not human. Only in reciprocity with what is Other will we begin to heal ourselves.

PART FOUR

❋

A Child's Sense of Wildness

Days at Bear River
✳
TERRY TEMPEST WILLIAMS

I WAS RAISED TO BELIEVE IN A spirit world, that life exists before the earth and will continue to exist afterward, that each human being, bird, and bulrush, along with all other life forms, had a spirit life before it came to dwell physically on the earth. Each occupies an assigned sphere of influence, each has a place and a purpose.

It made sense to a child. And if the natural world was assigned spiritual values, then those days spent in wildness were sacred. We learned at an early age that God can be found wherever you are, especially outside. Family worship was not just relegated to Sunday in a chapel.

Our weekends were spent camped alongside a small stream in the Great Basin, in the Stansbury Mountains or Deep Creeks. My father would take the boys rabbit hunting while Mother and I sat on a log in an aspen grove and talked. She would tell me how when she was a girl she would paint red lips on the trunks of trees to practice kissing. Or how she would lie in her grandmother's lucerne patch and watch clouds.

"I have never known my full capacity for solitude," she would say.

"Solitude?" I asked.

"The gift of being alone. I can never get enough."

The men would return anxious for dinner. Mother would cook over a green Coleman stove as Dad told stories from his childhood—like the time his father took away his BB gun for a year because he shot off the heads of every red tulip in his mother's garden, row after row after row. He laughed. We laughed. And then it was time to bless the food.

After supper, we would spread out our sleeping bags in a circle, heads pointing to the center like a covey of quail, and watch the Great Basin sky fill with stars. Our attachment to the land was our attachment to each other.

The days I loved most were the days at Bear River. The bird refuge was a sanctuary for my grandmother and me. I call her "Mimi." We would walk along the road with binoculars around our necks and simply watch birds. Hundreds of birds. Birds so exotic to a desert child it forced the imagination to be still. The imagined was real at Bear River.

I recall one bird in particular. It wore a feathered robe of cinnamon, white, and black. Its body rested on long, thin legs. Blue legs. On the edge of the marsh, it gracefully lowered its head and began sweeping the water side to side with its delicate, upturned bill.

"*Plee-ek! Plee-ek!*"

Three more landed. My grandmother placed her hand gently on my shoulder and whispered, "Avocets." I was nine years old.

At ten, Mimi thought I was old enough to join the Audubon Society on a special outing to the wetlands surrounding Great Salt Lake. We boarded a Greyhound bus in downtown Salt Lake and drove north on U.S. Highway 91, paralleling the Wasatch Mountains on our right and Great Salt Lake on our left. Once relaxed and out of the city, we were handed an official checklist of birds at the Bear River Migratory Bird Refuge.

"All members are encouraged to take copious notes and keep scrupulous records of birds seen," proclaimed the gray-haired, ponytailed woman passing out cards.

"What do copious and scrupulous mean?" I asked my grandmother.

"It means pay attention," she said. I pulled out my notebook and drew pictures of the back of birdwatchers' heads.

Off the highway, the bus drove through the small town of Brigham City with its sycamore-lined streets. It's like most Utah settlements with its Mormon layout: a chapel for weekly worship, a tabernacle for communal events, and a temple nearby (in this case Logan) where sacred rites are performed. Lawns are well groomed and neighborhoods are immaculate. But the banner arched over Main Street makes this town unique. In neon lights it reads, BRIGHAM CITY: GATEWAY TO THE WORLD'S GREATEST GAME BIRD REFUGE. So welded to the local color of this community, I daresay no one sees it anymore, except newcomers and perhaps the birds that fly under it.

A small, elderly man with wire-rimmed glasses and a worn golf cap stood at the front of the bus and began speaking into the hand-held microphone: "Ladies and gentlemen, in approximately ten miles we will be entering the Bear River Migratory Bird Refuge, America's first waterfowl sanctuary, established by a special act of Congress on April 23, 1928."

I was confused. I thought the marsh had been created in

the spirit world first and on earth second. I never made the connection that God and Congress were in cahoots. Mimi said she would explain the situation later.

The man went on to say that the bird refuge was located at the delta of the Bear River, which poured into the Great Salt Lake. This I understood.

"People, this bus is a clock. Eyes forward, please. Straight ahead is twelve o'clock; to the rear is six. Three o'clock is on your right. Any bird identified from this point on will be noted accordingly."

The bus became a bird dog, a labrador on wheels, which decided where high noon would be simply by pointing in that direction. What time would it be if a bird decided to fly from nine o'clock to three o'clock? Did that make the bird half past nine or quarter to three? Even more worrisome to me was the possibility of a flock of birds flying between four and five o'clock. Would you say, Twenty birds after four? Four-thirty? Or simply move the hands of the clock forward to five? I decided not to bother my grandmother with these particulars and, instead, retreated to my unindexed field guide and turned to the color plates of ducks.

And then it happened: "Ibises at two o'clock!"

The brakes on the bus squeaked to a halt. The doors opened like bellows and we all filed out. And there they were, dozens of white-faced glossy ibises grazing in the field, just like the man said. Their feathers on first glance were chestnut, but with the slightest turn they flashed iridescences of pink, purple, and green.

Another flock landed nearby. And another. And another. They coasted in diagonal lines with their heads and necks extended, their long legs trailing behind them, seeming to fall forward on hinges the second before they touched ground. By now, we must have been watching close to a hundred ibises probing the farmlands adjacent to the marsh.

Our leader, who was now speaking through a megaphone, told us they were eating earthworms and insects.

"Good eyes," I thought, as I could only see their decurved bills like scythes disappearing behind the grasses. I watched the wind turn each feather as the birds turned the soil.

Mimi whispered to me how ibises are the companions of gods. "Ibis escorts Thoth, the Egyptian god of wisdom and magic, who is the guardian of the Moon Gates in heaven. And there are two colors of ibis—one black and one white. The dark bird is believed to be associated with death, the white bird a celebration of birth."

I looked out over the fields of black ibis.

"When an ibis tucks its head underwing to sleep, it resembles a heart. The ibis knows empathy," my grandmother said. "Remember that, alongside the fact it eats worms."

She also told me that if I could learn a new way to tell time, I could also learn a new way to measure distance.

"The stride of an ibis measures exactly one cubit, which was the measurement used in building the great temples of the Nile."

I sat down by the rear wheels of the bus and pondered the relationship between an ibis at Bear River and an ibis foraging on the banks of the Nile. In my young mind, it had something to do with the magic of birds, how they bridge cultures and continents with their wings, how they mediate between heaven and earth.

Back on the bus and moving, I wrote in my notebook, "one hundred white-faced glossy ibises—companions of the gods."

Mimi was pleased. "We could go home now," she said. "The ibis makes the day."

But there were more birds. Many, many more. Within the next few miles, ducks, geese, and shorebirds were sighted around "the clock." The bus drove past all of them. With my arms out the window, I tried to touch the wings of avocets and stilts. I knew these birds from our private trips to the refuge. They had become relatives.

As the black-necked stilts flew alongside the silver bus, their long legs trailed behind them like red streamers.

"*Ip-ip-ip! Ip-ip-ip!*"

Their bills were not flattened and upturned like avocets', but straight as darning needles.

The wind massaged my face. I closed my eyes and sat back in my seat.

Mimi and I got out of the bus and ate our lunch on the riverbank. Two western grebes, ruby-eyed and serpentine, fished, diving at good prospects. They surfaced with silver minnows struggling between sharp mandibles. Violet-green swallows skimmed the water for midges as a snowy egret stood on the edge of the spillway.

With a crab sandwich in one hand and binoculars in the other, Mimi explained why the bird refuge had in fact been created.

"Maybe the best way to understand it," she said, "is to realize the original wetlands were recreated. It was the deterioration of the marshes at Bear River Bay that led to the establishment of a sanctuary."

"How?" I asked.

"The marshes were declining for several reasons: the diversion of water from the Bear River for irrigation, the backing-up of brine from Great Salt Lake during high-water periods, excessive hunting, and a dramatic rise in botulism, a disease known then as 'western duck disease.'

"The creation of the Bear River Migratory Bird Refuge helped to preserve the freshwater character of the marsh. Dikes were built to hold the water from the Bear River to stabilize, manage, and control water levels within the marsh. This helped to control botulism and at the same time keep out the brine. Meanwhile, the birds flourished."

After lunch, I climbed the observation tower at the refuge headquarters. Any fear of heights I may have had moving up the endless flights of steel stairs was replaced by the bird's-eye view below me. The marsh appeared as a green and blue mosaic where birds remained in a fluid landscape.

In the afternoon, we drove the twenty-two-mile loop around the refuge. The roads capped dikes where deep channels of water were bordered by bulrush and teasel. We saw ruddy ducks (the man sitting behind us called them "blue bills"), shovelers, teals, and wigeons. We watched herons and egrets and rails. Red-winged blackbirds poised on cattails sang with long-billed marsh wrens as muskrats swam inside shadows created by clouds. Large families of Canada geese occupied the open water, while ravens flushed the edges for unprotected nests with eggs.

The marsh reflected health as concentric circles rippled outward from a mallard feeding "bottoms up."

By the end of the day, Mimi and I had marked sixty-seven species on our checklist, many of which I had never seen before. A short-eared owl hovered over the cattails. It was the last bird we saw as we left the refuge.

I fell asleep on my grandmother's lap. Her strong, square hands resting on my forehead shielded the sun from my eyes. I dreamed of water and cattails and all that is hidden.

When we returned home, my family was seated around the dinner table.

"What did you see?" Mother asked. My father and three brothers looked up.

"Birds . . ." I said as I closed my eyes and stretched my arms like wings.

"Hundreds of birds at the marsh.".

Tokens of Mystery

✳

SCOTT RUSSELL SANDERS

THERE IS A SAYING THAT YOU can take the boy out of the country but you cannot take the country out of the boy. My mother, who grew up in the steel-and-concrete hive of Chicago, frequently applied this remark with a roll of her eyes to my father, who grew up on a red dirt farm in Mississippi. It was true enough in his case, and it holds true for many another country boy and girl I have known, myself included. The legacy of a rural childhood entails more than a penchant for going barefoot, say, or an itch for digging in dirt, or a taste for black-eyed peas, or a habit of speaking with lazy tongue. It also entails a relationship with the land, its rhythms and creatures. The country lingered in my father and lingers in me as a recollected intimacy with particular wild places, a memory of encounters with muskrats and mules, tornadoes and hickory trees, crickets and flooded creeks, the whole adding up to an impression of nature as grander, more intricate, and wiser in its ways than we two-leggers.

It is quite possible to grow up in the country without learning to honor nature. Drive the back roads of America, and you will see many a butchered forest, eroded field, and poisoned creek, many a trash dump, many a tattered animal shot up for the sheer joy of killing, all the handiwork of country people. In fact, the history of rural America has been largely one of slash and plunder. Familiarity with a landscape may breed no more than contempt, if our eyes have been trained to see contemptuously, or it may breed devotion, if we have learned to see reverently. In the book of Job, the beleaguered man cries out that all creatures, himself included, rest in the hand of God:

> *But ask the beasts, and they will teach you;*
> *the birds of the air, and they will tell you;*
> *or the plants of the earth, and they will teach you;*
> *and the fish of the sea will declare to you.*

The key word here is *ask*. What the birds and beasts and countryside teach us depends on the questions we pose. A person wielding a fifty-ton digger in search of coal will learn quite different lessons from one who wields a pair of binoculars in search of warblers. Job assumed that anybody who listened to the creation would hear the whisper of the creator. But generally we hear what our ears have been prepared for, and if we do not go seeking divinity we are not likely to find it. In the long run and in a blunt manner, nature has its own say: species that poison or exhaust their habitat die out. But in the short run, nature does not declare how we should approach it; that lesson we learn from culture.

For me as a child, "culture" meant first of all my parents, and then a few neighbors, then books and teachers, and only much later, when I was largely set in my ways, photographs and paintings and films. Whether plucking a pheasant, sawing down a tree, walking through a woods, planting beans, gathering blackberries, watching the moon, my parents acted out of a joyous, wondering regard for nature. To my mother, the budding of pussy willows or the reddening of maples announced the eras of our lives with more authority than anything the calendar or newspaper had to say. To my father, the pawprints of a raccoon in the mud beside a creek, or the persistent flowing of the creek itself, were tokens of an inexhaustible mystery. I learned from my parents a thousand natural facts, but above all I learned how to stand on the earth, how to address the creation, and how to listen.

Because of their example, I was drawn to those of our neighbors who shared this regard for nature—the elderly Swedish couple who let me help with maple sugaring, the carpenter who brooded on the grain in wood, the biology teacher who lived in a wild meadow (sight of her musing among the waist-high flowers left a deeper impression on me than any lecture or textbook), the dairy farmers, horse trainers, muskrat trappers, hunters of fossils, feeders of birds. Their example in turn prepared me to read with gusto about Mark Twain's Mississippi River, Thoreau's Walden Pond, Black Elk's High Plains, Annie Dillard's Roanoke Valley, Wendell Berry's Kentucky, Barry Lopez's Arctic, and the many other intimate landscapes in our literature. I moved easily from literary visions of nature to visions inspired by science in the pages of Rachel Carson, Loren Eiseley, Lewis Thomas, and Stephen Jay Gould. Reading prepared me to relish the paintings of Thomas Cole and George Innes, the photographs of Ansel Adams, the films of Jacques Cousteau, the music and ceremonies of Native Americans.

Thus begun on a path of ardent inquiry about the cosmos, I hope to make new discoveries so long as I live.

Needless to say, I haven't always lived up to these models for how one should dwell in nature—I close myself inside human shells, I stop my ears and blinker my eyes, I squander the fruits of the earth—and yet, inscribed with those models in childhood, I always know when I have fallen away.

Meanwhile, just down the road from us lived a man and woman who whipped their horses, kicked their dogs, ruined their soil, and threw trash out the back door. Their children grew up doing likewise. Surrounded by the same landscape, the same beasts and weather as our family, these neighbors inhabited a radically different "nature" from the one we knew. Their conversation with the earth was carried on in a language foreign to the one I learned in my own household. You can grow up in the country and remain blissfully ignorant of nature, and you can behave as callously toward the earth as any city slicker. But still, love the land or hate it, attune yourself to its rhythms or mine it for dollars, the one thing you cannot do, having grown up in the country, is ignore it. You know in your bones that nature surrounds and sustains our tiny human play.

I am never more aware of being an overgrown backwoods boy than when I sojourn in a city. Transplanted this year from a small Indiana town, where deer still occasionally graze in backyards, to Boston, where the yards have been paved and the deer pose on billboards, I find myself wondering how children in cities experience nature. When these children grow up, and some of them become the potentates who decide how we should occupy the planet, what images of nature will govern their decisions? For me this is a question of private as well as public consequence, because my nine-year-old son and fourteen-year-old daughter are sharing Boston with me. Having them on hand means I can snoop on youth without going far afield. I have emerged from some months of this snooping with a gloomy opinion of cities as places for learning about nature, but with an increased respect for the imagination, resourcefulness, and curiosity of children.

Suppose you are a child taking a walk in downtown Boston. What ghosts of wildness do you see amid the skyscrapers, glassy shops, condominiums, and parking lots? Well, you see dogs on leashes, sickly trees and shrubs (not quite on leashes, but planted in boxes and surrounded by fences to protect them from human assault), an occasional strip of grass that is kept alive by infusions of chemicals, cut flowers for sale on street corners, pigeons roosting on windowsills, rats nosing in alleys. If you make your way to that fabled green space, the Public Garden, which is entirely hemmed in by a palisade of buildings, you will discover a concrete pond aswim with pinioned ducks (except after frost, when authorities drain the pool to avoid lawsuits), a row of elms bearing name tags, a cemetery, a baseball diamond, two subway stops, a six-lane boulevard, an expanse of trampled lawn planted with statues, and signs everywhere announcing what is forbidden. Since the avenues yield no glimpses of robust or unfettered nature, you might seek out water. But like most rivers that have the ill fortune to wind through cities, the Charles is a docile and filthy gutter, girded by walls, laced with bridges, hemmed in by highways, and slick with oil. The river's poisons collect in the harbor, which has become a gray desert encircled by shipyards, airport, docks, and high-rise apartments.

In this great outdoors of Boston, the only remnants of nature, aside from rats, that look as though they might survive without our ministrations are the sun and sky glimpsed overhead between glass towers. If you are bold enough to walk abroad at night, you will search for the stars in vain through the glare of streetlights. The breeze is laden with diesel fumes and the rumble of engines. By going indoors—into a shopper's nirvana such as Copley Place, for example, or a corporate stronghold such as the Prudential Building—you can escape even the sky and its weathers, withdraw from seasons and the vagaries of sunlight. In grocery stores, cows show up sliced and weighed into red hunks, chickens go featherless in styrofoam tubs, wheat disappears along with a dose of additives into gaudy packages, even apples and oranges wear a camouflage of dye. Day or night, indoors or out, nature in the city appears as a slavish power, rather puny and contemptible, supplying us with decoration, amusement, or food, always framed by our purposes, summoned or banished according to our whims.

Of course, like all reasonably affluent cities that take the burdens of enlightenment seriously, Boston provides its children with places to confront nature, as it were, in the flesh. Chief among these are the zoo, where morose animals pace in cages; the aquarium, where fish circle in tanks; the arboretum, where trees that never rub limbs in the wild grow side by side and bear identifying labels; and the science museum, where the universe comes packaged in mind-sized dollops, usually jazzed up with electronics.

Fitted with a pair of child's eyes, let us pay a visit to the New England Aquarium. Outside you watch three seals cruise in a small white pool shaped like a rhomboid. Two beats of the rear flippers carry them from end to end. You admire their grace, but soon realize that you have seen every move they are likely to make in such a cramped, sterile space. Inside the building, on the ground floor, you hang over the rail of a larger pool to observe a colony of jackass penguins, some of them zipping through the green shallows, some teetering across the fiberglass islands. Just when you are beginning to feel a sense of how these dapper birds might carry on in their own realm, a diver splashes into the pool. From plastic buckets he doles out fish to the assembled penguins, noting on a clipboard the dietary selection for each bird. Meanwhile, from the balcony overhead, a second diver lowers a thermometer on a wire above the head of each penguin in turn and records the temperatures on yet another clipboard. If you are like my son, you find the electronics and wet suits more impressive than these birds that must be fed like babies. If you are like my daughter, you are distracted by the other kids who shoulder you aside for a view of the proceedings.

From the ground floor you climb a spiral ramp, passing tank after tank in which sea creatures browse or snooze in tiny simulated habitats—inky murk for the ocean depths, crashing surf for the coastal shallows, weedy thickets, and algal pools. These exhibits go some way toward showing us nature on its own terms, as a web of life, a domain of non-human forces. And yet these miniature habitats with their listless swimmers are still merely pictures framed and labeled by the masters; they are images viewed, like those on television, through windows of glass.

From the top floor you gaze down into a huge cylindrical tank, which houses a four-story fiberglass replica of a coral reef and several hundred species of fish. The size of it, the painted reef, the mixture of species all give some feel for the larger patterns of the sea. And yet immediately a naturalist begins lecturing while a diver descends to feed the sharks. "You think they'll bite him?" the children ask, their minds bearing Hollywood images of underwater killers, nature measured on a scale of menace. By means of another ramp you spiral down along the circumference of this tank, stopping to press your nose through a wavery thickness of glass against the snout of a moray eel. That is communion of a sort. Downstairs, a film about the artificial reef celebrates the imitation more than the ocean's original, dwelling on the ingenuity of the builders, the strength of the walls, the weight of glass and steel, thereby confirming your sense that nature is fortunate indeed to have been packaged by such clever artisans.

A bell rings, calling you to the eleven o'clock water show. You rush to the auditorium, squeeze into a seat, then watch as a trainer puts a seal and three dolphins through their paces. The trainer is an earnest woman, who carries on about how intelligent these animals are, how cantankerous, how creative, but all you see are dolphins jumping through hoops and retrieving rubber toys, a seal balancing a ball on its nose and smacking its flippers at jokes; all you hear are the synchronized splashes, whistles, and grunts of programmed clowns.

Visit the zoo in Franklin Park—or any zoo, even the most spacious and ecologically minded—and you find nature parceled out into showy fragments, a nature demeaned and dominated by our constructions. Thickets of bamboo and simulated watering holes cannot disguise the elementary fact that a zoo is a prison. The animals are captives, hauled to this place for our edification or entertainment. No matter how ferocious they may look, they are wholly dependent on our care. A bear squatting on its haunches, a tiger lounging with half-lidded eyes, a bald eagle hunched on a limb are like refugees who tell us less about their homeland, their native way of being, than about our power. In the zoo they exist without purposes of their own, cut off from their true place on earth and from the cycles demanded by their flesh.

Visit the Museum of Science, a lively playhouse aimed at luring children into a reasoned study of the cosmos, and again you find nature whittled down to fragments. Most of the exhibits have to do, not with nature, but with our inventions—satellites, steam engines, airplanes, computers, telephones, lasers, robots, cars, Van de Graaff generators—a display of human power that merely echoes the lessons of the city. As though to compensate, a number of the creaturely exhibits are gigantic—a full-scale model of *Tyrannosaurus rex*, a grasshopper the size of a delivery van, an immense brain (ours, of course, thereby reminding us where the center of the cosmos lies). But no matter how large, the beasts themselves are manifestly artificial, further proofs of our ingenuity. "Wow," cry the children, "how did they make *this*?" The nearest you come to nature's own products is in the hall of dioramas, where stuffed animals, encased in glass, pose in habitat groups against painted backdrops. How long will you stand before these dusty, silent, rigid carcasses, while, from elsewhere in the museum, our own handiworks beckon with luminous colors, bright lights, synthetic voices, and flashy movements?

On a wall of the museum there is a quotation from Aristotle: "The search for the Truth is in one way hard and in another easy—for it is evident that no one of us can ever master it fully, nor miss it wholly. Each one of us adds a little to our knowledge of nature and from all the facts assembled arises a certain grandeur." Worthy sentiments; yet the facts assembled in the museum, like the bits of nature scattered through the city, point to no grandeur except our own. So long as we meet nature in fragments and in human containers, we cannot see it truly. Even when science is called in to explain what we are beholding, it comes to seem not so much a way of reading the cosmos as an instrument of power. Without wishing to deny the educational zeal of those who run the museum, the zoo, the aquarium, or the other city arenas for the display of nature, I want to emphasize how belittling, how dangerously one-sided are the impressions these arenas create. Sight of stuffed antelope, trees behind fences, gorillas behind bars, penguins in tanks, and flowers in pots will more likely inspire contempt than awe. Snared in our inventions, wearing our labels, the plants and animals stand mute. In such places, the loudest voice we hear is our own.

None of the foregoing is meant as a diatribe against Boston in particular—a place I delight in—nor against cities in general, but rather as a sober account of the peculiar, even pathological image of nature the city provides. Recognizing how distorted this image is, we should feel the necessity of making available to our children a wiser and healthier one. Although my view of cities as places for learning about nature is gloomy, my view of children as learners is hopeful. Against all odds, many an urban child acquires a sense of the dignity, integrity, and majestic self-sufficiency of nature. How does this come about? For the beginnings of an answer, let me describe a recent conversation with my son Jesse.

One day this past winter he and I set out for the library on foot. Whenever Jesse steps outdoors, all his senses come alert. Before we had even crossed the street, he squatted down to examine a slab of ice in the gutter. The slab had broken in two, and the pieces, gliding on their own meltwater, had slipped a hand's width apart. After a moment of scrutiny, tracing the ice with a finger, he observed, "These are like the continents drifting apart on molten rock."

This led us to discuss the geological theory of plate tectonics, about which we had seen a documentary on television. According to the theory, earthquakes are caused by the friction of adjoining plates as they rub against one another. We tried this out on the ice, shoving the two pieces together until their edges grated, and were rewarded by the feel of tremors passing up through our gloved hands. Continuing our walk to the library, we then recalled what a friend of the family, a seismologist, had told us concerning his study of earthquakes in the Soviet Union, and what that study revealed about the structure of the earth.

"I read in school," Jesse told me excitedly, "how Chinese scientists have discovered a kind of fish that can feel when earthquakes are coming, even before machines can."

In reply, I told how one time John James Audubon was riding near the Ohio River, when his usually obedient horse stopped dead in its tracks and spread its legs as though to keep from tumbling over. What in blazes? Audubon thought. Neither word nor whip could make the horse budge—and a good thing, too, for several minutes later the ground buckled and the trees rocked from the New Madrid earthquake.

"You know," Jesse mused, "lots of animals have keener senses than we do. Like the way coon dogs can smell, and the way birds can travel using landmarks and stars and the earth's magnetism."

He had learned of coon dogs from a grandfather's stories, of celestial navigation from a visit to a whaling museum, of migration from magazines and from our habit of watching, every spring and fall, for the unerring movements of ducks and geese overhead. We then talked about the night vision of owls and the daylight vision of ospreys, birds we had seen on our camping trips.

"If I could see like an eagle," said Jesse, "I'd be able to spot tiny things like field mice from way high up. But would I be able to see in color?"

Since that question stumped me, and since by then we had reached the library, we decided to look up the answer. None of the books gave a clear-cut answer, but one of them did say that birds of prey owe their acute vision to the dense packing of rods and cones in their retinas. From the dictionary we then learned that rods are sensitive to dim light, cones to bright light and colors. So we had our answer, and in our excitement gave one another a boisterous high-five hand slap that provoked a glower from the librarian.

In skimming the encyclopedia articles, Jesse had noticed that birds have a rapid heartbeat. How fast was his own? We timed his pulse: eighty beats per minute. How fast was mine? Fifty-five. How come his was faster? I told him it was partly because of our relative size—small bodies lose heat more quickly than large ones—and partly because children have a higher rate of metabolism than adults. What's metabolism? Jesse wanted to know. So we talked about how cells turn food into energy and tissue.

"Like we get energy from milk," said Jesse, "and the cow gets energy from grass, and the grass gets energy from the sun. I bet if you go back far enough, you can track every kind of food to the sun."

By now, our rucksacks filled with a new supply of books, we were moseying toward home. On the way, Jesse kept up his flurry of questions and speculations. Could humans live by eating grass? Why doesn't grass use up the soil and wear it out? How much grass would a big wild critter like a buffalo have to eat every day to stay alive? Smoke rising from a chimney then set him talking about wind patterns, acid rain, forests. If bad chemicals fall on the grass—lead, say, from diesel trucks—and cattle graze on it, and we eat the cattle in our hamburgers, the poison winds up in us, right? And so, within the space of an hour, driven forward by Jesse's curiosity, we moved from a broken slab of ice to the geology of earth, from earthquakes to eagles, from the anatomy of eyes to the biology of food chains. No telling where we might have gone next. Out front of our place one of Jesse's buddies led him off to play street hockey.

Such conversations do not happen every day, but they happen frequently enough to persuade me that Jesse, at age nine, is persistently, eagerly building a model of nature, one that will make sense of the full variety of his experience. As that experience enlarges, so he continually revises his model. In this one conversation he drew from books, magazines, school, radio and television (public radio and public television: to seek knowledge of nature on the commercial channels is like searching for a moose in a parking lot), drew from his memories of camping trips, gardening, hikes in the woods, seaside rambles, mealtime conversations, family stories, visits to museums, talks with adult friends (a geologist, a physician, a bird-watcher, a farmer), drew from all these sources in an attempt to see nature whole. He needed every scrap of this experience, and would have used anything else his nine years might have provided.

Jesse shares with all children this voracious hunger to make sense of things, but his *way* of making sense bears the stamp of his upbringing. Having lived most of his nine years in a house with a wildflower garden in the backyard, in a small town surrounded by forests and creeks, having known farmers and stone quarriers and biologists, and having spent many hours with his family tramping through the countryside, he knows without being told that nature is our ultimate home. What the city has to say about nature—in museums, zoos, parks—he understands in light of what he has already learned from the country. Watching California gray whales migrate along the Pacific coast prepared him to view without condescension the dolphins that jump through hoops; because he has watched pileated woodpeckers graze on dead trees and white-tailed deer cross a meadow like ripples of pure energy, he knows that beasts in cages are lords in exile.

In Thoreau's exultant phrase, "We need to witness our own limits transgressed, and some life pasturing freely where we never wander." This is all the more crucial for urban children, who live in a maze of human invention. If a child is to have an expansive and respectful vision of nature, there is no substitute for direct encounters with wildness. This means passing unprogrammed days and weeks in the mountains, the woods, the fields, beside rivers and oceans, territories where plants and beasts are the natives and we are the visitors. Ideally, children should witness "life pasturing freely" in the company of adults who are intimately aware of nature's pulse and pattern. As parents, we can assure our children of such company, not by turning them over to experts, but by cultivating this awareness in ourselves.

My own parents never *told* me how I should feel about nature; they communicated their own deep regard for that larger order by their manner of living. On hearing the call of geese, my father would drop whatever he was doing and rush outside. On visiting a new place, he would scoop up a handful of dirt to get the feel of it, the smell and taste of it. When I was small enough to ride in his arms, during thunderstorms he would bundle me in a blanket and carry me onto the porch and hold me against his chest while we listened to the rain sizzle down. My mother would tramp across a bog to admire a lady-slipper or a toad. When I first came across Dylan Thomas's fierce lines,

> *The force that through the green fuse drives the flower*
> *Drives my green age; that blasts the roots of trees*
> *Is my destroyer,*

it was a truth I had already learned from her. She was alive to designs everywhere—in the whorls of her palm and the spirals of a chambered nautilus, in the crystals of milky quartz, the carapace of a snapping turtle, the flukes of a mushroom, the whiskers of a mouse. Neither of my parents was a scientist, but they were both eager to learn everything science could tell them about the workings of the world.

Fashioning a vision of nature is one of the urgent enterprises of childhood. I believe that Jesse's curiosity, his desire to understand and feel at home on the earth, is typical of young children. The child inhabits a compact wilderness called the body, with which he or she reaches out to all other living things. Look at a child, and you see an organism perfectly equipped for investigating the world—wide-awake eyes, quick brain, avid mouth, irrepressible hands. Nothing is lost on children, so long as it brings news from previously unknown regions. Their questions not only probe the universe; they probe us. How much do we understand of the workings of the cosmos and of our place within it? Where we are ignorant, do we know how (or care) to search for answers? Daily companionship with a questioning child is a reminder of what intelligence is *for*—not, ultimately, for dominion, but for communion. Children are transcendentalists by instinct, reading in the humblest natural fact a sign of some greater pattern. Unlike a grown-up—who might often with more accuracy be called a grown-rigid—children will only settle for a cramped, belittling, domineering view of nature if that is all we offer them. So let us offer them tokens of the creation, that elegant wildness, that encompassing order which calls for our full powers of understanding and, when mind has stretched as far as it will go, for love.

A Child's Sense of Wildness

✳

GARY NABHAN

 SHOULD HAVE SENSED THE difference in perception during the weeks just prior to our wilderness encounter. The kids seemed somewhat bored by the photo previews of parks we might see and by the litany of place-names sung into their ears during our packing and preparation.

My children—Dustin Corvus, age seven, and Laura Rose, age five—were born, raised, and baptized in the cactus-stippled basins of the Sonoran Desert, where volcanic and granitic mountain ranges have rimmed their horizons. Little did they know what lay ahead of them in the geological jumble of northern Arizona and southern Utah: "more hills, holes, humps and hollows, reefs, folds, salt domes, swells and grabens, buttes, benches and mesas, synclines, monoclines and anticlines than you can ever hope to see and explore in one lifetime," as that childlike mortal Ed Abbey once described them. Little did I know what my children's minds would open for me: Lilliputian landscapes often overlooked by educated adults seeking the Big Picture.

We were off, headed north for the canyon country of the Colorado Plateau, my mind set on our destination, Dustin's dwelling on what was immediately around us. As we worked our way beyond Phoenix, he was preoccupied with the earthmovers cruising along outside his window. They were reshaping the land around a new, multistoried office complex of the Salt River Project, the dam-and-ditch bureaucracy that controls where water flows in our stretch of the Sonoran Desert. Dustin watched intently, then warbled a sad note about the state of the world as he saw it.

"Papa, I don't like what they're doing. Scraping up all the dirt like that. They're taking more and more of the earth away until pretty soon it will be so small that we'll all be bumping into one another."

He shook his head, then selected a Smokey the Bear propaganda piece from the pile of field guides and comic books he had brought along and perused it between conversations with his sister. An hour and a half later, as we rose in elevation from the desert to the ponderosa pine forest, his attention turned once more to the world outside his window.

"Papa, where are we?"

"Coming into Coconino National Forest," I answered. "We'll be in the forest until dark, I guess."

Another forty minutes passed.

"Are we coming into a city? I thought you said we would be in the forest until dark."

"Well, this is Flagstaff. It has grown up in the middle of Coconino National Forest. We'll be getting back into the pine trees pretty soon."

He glanced out at the sluggish traffic along muddy roads under construction, the enormous but empty parking lots around new shopping malls, and the raw logs piled high along the railroad tracks.

"Papa," he asked, tentatively, "when they cut the forest down to make a city, what do the forest rangers do then? Do they become policemen?"

Worried aphorisms stopped flowing from Dustin's tongue once the camping began. During the following eight days, Dustin and Laura Rose were busy looping lizards, then letting them go. They made perfumes out of mashed sagebrush leaves and juniper berries soaked in their breakfast bowls. They searched for water striders in mountain rivulets and netted butterflies above them. They scrambled up slopes to inspect petroglyphs and down washes to enter into keyhole canyons.

In contrast, the adults kept their eyes out for picturesque panoramas and scenic overlooks. We had in mind those classic photos of burnt orange and buff sandstones juxtaposed with mauve shales or cliffs covered with cobalt blue desert varnish. We would position ourselves to peer out over a precipice, hoping to see what the light was like as it interacted with ridgeline after ridgeline, reaching out toward the ultimate horizon. Whenever we arrived at a promontory, the children would pause a moment to hold my hands, then retreat to scour the ground for bones, pine cones, sparkly sandstones, feathers, or wildflowers.

Dustin's photos from the trip are crisp close-ups of sagebrush lizards, yuccas, rock art, and sister's funny faces. His obligatory overviews of scenery seem dull and blurry by contrast.

I have noticed the same phenomenon when I have taken the children to a zoo in the Sonoran Desert. Enraptured, they will watch native round-tailed ground squirrels picking up popcorn on the trail a few feet away, oblivious to the elephants and giraffes in the zoo's featured exhibits across the moat. Framed nature hardly captures their attention.

Only once last summer did the larger landscape elicit a response from my two playmates. After a half day of four-wheeling up an eroded jeep road in Navajo country, we turned a corner and suddenly gazed out over the preposterous landforms that make up Monument Valley. The adults were dumbstruck, left literally speechless by what we saw. Laura, the youngest among us, casually broke the silence.

"Papa, it's so pretty!" she sang. The next moment she hopped out of the vehicle, happy to have her seatbelt off and her feet on the ground again. She skipped away, to find a good place her dolls could use as a dressing room, to gather deadfall branches for the fire, and to search out nooks and crannies along the mesa top with her brother, the snake hunter.

Late in our canyon country journey, I could not resist asking Dustin what he thought the word *wilderness* meant.

"Wilderness . . ." Dustin sighed, "is full of plants and animals and rocks."

"Well," I replied in a tone that only a father would try, "so is the botanical garden where I work. So is the zoo. What's the difference with wilderness?"

"Wilderness is where there are no roads. It is not caged in," and then he added, "not surrounded by chicken wire."

Dustin offered an interesting constellation of traits. Wilderness is full of things, some living, some perhaps not, all palpable. It has few intrusions, few inroads from civilization. Yet it is not easily circumscribed, not conveniently fenced to keep its wildness within or away from us.

It is too early to tell how long such a sense of wilderness will stay with Dustin and Laura. But whenever I wonder and worry about whether their links to nature will remain strong, I think of some of my own earliest recollections, times alone when I sat as a toddler out in the great sand pile called the Indiana Dunes. I remember the feeling of the dry, sugarlike sand on the dunes' surface, of the wet, doughlike texture of the deeper sand when I dug in my hands. I sat for hours on end in that sand, playing, listening to birds and frogs and toads and squirrels fill the air with thick sound. I still see the bluejays chasing one another through the oaks, the trees themselves being buried by the moving front of the dune, the dazzle of the dragonflies, and red-winged blackbirds and wrens weaving through the cattails in the wetlands tucked between the dunes. The organisms and elements I sighted, squeezed, or smelled when I was young have become psychophysical touchstones that I have carried with me the rest of my life.

In Edith Cobb's essay "The Ecology of the Imagination in Childhood," she claims that there is a special period "between the striving of animal infancy and the storms of adolescence when the natural world is experienced in a highly evocative way. This experience provides the child with a sense of profound continuity with natural processes." Cobb suggests that within such experiences, "there may be evidence of the biological basis of intuition."

What happens, then, when children become isolated from wild settings that nurture this intuitive sense? When natural diversity and habitat heterogeneity are lacking, is an individual's psychological metamorphosis somehow arrested? Driving back through Phoenix near the end of our trip, and seeing again the barrios and tract house sub-divisions where contact with other life forms is virtually suspended, I sensed that urban society is driving into ex-tinction the wild creatures that would otherwise inhabit the minds of the young who live there. Within the next generation, as many as a fourth of the children in the United States will be born into inner city wastelands. What will be the fate of those who become adults unable to conjure up a single memory of nature from their childhood?

Near the end of our trip with Dustin and Laura, we met up with two women who did have an early immersion in wild nature. Julie and Caroline Wilson are daughters of Bates Wilson, for many years the superintendent of Arches National Monument and a pivotal figure in the cre-ation of Canyonlands National Park. The Wilson girls grew up outside Moab, Utah, in a wild playground of sed-imentary landforms. From the side door of their stone house in Arches, they were but one hop, skip, and a jump away from slickrock benches, bluffs, cliffs, slopes, and ti-najas which conformed to no human design.

The girls spent hours, together or alone, in this jungle gym of geomorphology, acting out dramas, staging dances, mounting expeditions, or watching clouds roll by. A little over a quarter century later, they escorted my chil-dren through their fantasyland, pointing out the Indian Cave, the Penguins, the Ballroom, the Princess's Bed-room, the Train, and the Deer Pond. The scale of these little niches, crawl spaces, shelters, and passages fit Dustin and Laura to a T.

"The smoothness of the rock is what attracts kids," Caroline said. "You can scoot up and down it without scraping yourself."

We spent a morning scrambling on the rocks behind their former home and listening to the sisters tell of events from years before as if they had happened yesterday. At one point Caroline crushed a few leaves of big sage in her hands. "That smell!" she cried. "It's the one I grew up with, one that means home to me!" Moments later, the bruised leaves of wild rosemary mint gave her much the same welcome.

Caroline still lives in wildlands, in Organ Pipe Cactus National Monument, where she is an interpretive specialist for the National Park Service. Her sister, Julie, spends much of the year near windswept dunes and barren malpais at Tuba City, Arizona. Their time in wild settings seems to have lent them a healthy perspective about humankind: a warmth for reunions with old friends, a willingness to share with other hikers or campers, a great courtesy to strangers. These traits, I sensed, were shaped during the years of campouts, jeep rides, and short hikes when their father would host visitors to the Canyonlands. Ultimately, their social graces are not unrelated to their feeling at home in the wild.

There was a moment on the tour of their childhood playground that stands out above others. It was when Caroline led us into the Ballroom, an almost flat bench of creamy white sandstone overlooking her former home, surrounded by nearly animate rockforms and a dozen floral fragrances. "This, Laura Rose," Caroline explained, "is where we danced!" She shut her eyes. Then, feeling the tilt of the rock beneath her feet, she spun around and danced up an image she had carried with her from childhood.

"I *remember* these rocks!" Caroline whispered, somewhat astonished by the sudden upwelling of tears in her eyes. "They are as familiar to me as the freckles on my arm. . . ."

I glanced down at Laura Rose, at my side. Her eyes grew wide. I closed mine, and hoped that I would be around one day when, as a young woman, Laura Rose will dance herself in place.

PART FIVE

✻

Metaphors of
Desire

Drawing on Experience

✳

ANN ZWINGER

HERE COMES A TIME WHEN, as an illustrator, I bite the bullet and draw the plants that I have put off doing, having been enchanted by brighter, more visually interesting plants. Bur sage (*Franseria dumosa*) is one of those I put off. It is not what one would call a knockout of a plant.

Bur sage, or burrobush, is often as ubiquitous as the ultra-ubiquitous creosote bush, with which it grows in the Mohave and Sonoran deserts. Acres of creosote bush checker across the sandy, gravelly flats of the desert, wide-spaced, counting into the distance like an exercise in perspective. In many places, bur sage grows between them— low, rounded shrubs, grayer than the olive-green creosote, not anything to catch the eye except that there are so many of them. They don't have showy flowers, they don't have thorns and spines, they don't have any distinctive characteristics. They're just there.

I've collected bur sage branches over time, out of a sense of duty, and they have remained in the ice chest because they keep well, and I draw everything else because I really don't want to draw them. When I finally throw them out I feel guilty and wasteful. At some point discipline usually triumphs, and I take out a sprig and begin to draw.

That's when the learning begins, on a nondescript plant with nondescript flowers, when I discover that it is both fascinating and beautiful.

Smaller branches take off from larger in a stalky, angular pattern, the angle of stem and branch consistent. The repeated angles build a nest of branches that are then wind-trimmed into a low, rounded shrub. From the branch ends rise racemes of flowers, male and female separate. The distinction can only be appreciated with a hand lens.

The stamens are packed into an involucre, yellow buttons held close by gray-green bracts. They hang like little lanterns among the female flowers, which in the beginning are also enclosed in bracts, with protruding, shaggy pistils. The female flowers, when fertilized, ripen into fruits that have hairs and glands with scattered spines. "Glandular-puberulent" is the botanical term. It describes the hairy fruits, but not how the glands glisten in the light. The fruits look tough and spiny, but in the early part of bloom they are soft, becoming small burs that catch in everything only when they are dry.

The leaves seem intricately made, confusingly complex, until you look at them through a hand lens and find the inherent order of lobe and vein, and note that the leaves are ashen in color because they are covered with fine, stiff, short hairs. All these characteristics spell "desert"—wind-pollinated plants in a hot, windy environment, where growing is so difficult that no energy is expended upon showy flowers, and leaves must be protected from the insolation of a brutal desert sun by a matting of fine hairs.

Last week, surrounded by bur sage in the lower Colorado Desert in Arizona, I found plants very different from the ones I had drawn. In late June the leaves were ashen, papery-dry, and crumbly when touched. They were much smaller than the ones I drew from the Mojave Desert, because their habitat was so much more difficult. The comparison is embedded in my mind and expands what I perceive of deserts: that there are dry and drier and sometimes driest. The memory that permits the comparison would not be in my mental file drawer had I not drawn the bur sage.

It really doesn't matter whether you can draw or not—just the time taken to examine in detail, to turn a flower or a shell over in your fingers, opens doors and windows. The time spent observing pays, and you can better observe with a hand lens than without one. A hand lens is a joy and a delight, an entrée to another world just below your normal vision. Alice in Wonderland never had it so good—no mysterious potions are needed, just a ten- or fifteen-power hand lens hung around your neck. There's a kind of magic in seeing stellate hairs on a mustard stem, in seeing the retrorsely barbed margin of a nettle spine—there all the time but never visible without enhancement.

But to take the next step—to draw these in the margin of your notebook, on the back of an envelope, in a sketch pad, or even in the sand—establishes a connection between hand and eye that reinforces the connection between eye and memory. Drawing fastens the plant in memory.

I speak of plants because they are what I enjoy drawing. I find small plants easier to translate to paper than a minute ant's antennae or a full-blown, horizon-to-horizon landscape. Landscapes are beautiful for what you leave out; the most magnificent landscapes I know are those Rembrandt did with a wash from a couple of brush strokes enlivened with a crisp pen. But that took years of practice and a large dose of genius, which are not the point here—I speak of the enjoyment of learning from precise observation.

With a plant, I start with a small detail and build up because it's easier to extend outward into the infinite space of the page than to be caught in the finite space of an outline. If you begin with the big outline and fill in, and if you have any of the proportion problems I do, you often draw yourself into a corner. I begin with the stigma and stamens, or perhaps a petal, or perhaps the part that's closest, and work outward, relating each part to what's been put down before rather than blocking in a general outer shape and working down to detail.

When I begin in the center, as it were, and move outward, I build up a reality in which each detail relates to the one before. I wonder if this is also a way of apprehending a world, of composing it from many observations, a detail here, a detail there, creating an infinitely expandable universe. I always thought I worked this way because I was myopic, but maybe it's deeper than that and has to do with judgments, perceived realities, and whether there are five or six stamens.

Small things, large enough to see easily, but small enough to hold in the hand or put on the table in front of you, small enough to translate more or less one-to-one, seem to me the easiest subjects for the neophyte illustrator. Why deal with complex proportions if you don't have to? Forget the tea rose and the peony. Forgo the darlings of the garden that have been bred into complex, complicated flowers with multiple petals and fancy shapes. Try instead an interesting leaf, noting how the veining webs, or the edges curl or notch. Or try a simple flower—a phlox or lily-of-the-valley or an open, five-petaled wild rose.

Pale-colored plants are easier to draw: dark or brilliant colors often obscure the shape and character of the flower. Seedheads, summer's skeletons, are often felicitous subjects. So are cow parsnip's umbrella ribs or pennycress's orbicular pods, shepherd's purse or lily pods, which likewise give a sense of seasons past and springs to come.

Plants are nice because they stay still. I draw insects but only deceased ones, collected, pinned, and dried. Trying to portray a moving bug is a ridiculous task ending only in frustration.

Quick sketches of larger moving animals are difficult but greatly rewarding. If you are a birdwatcher and have the patience, drawing is a good way to learn how birds move, orient and tilt their bodies, and to pick up a lot on animal behavior because the observation is focused. (I happen to find birds hard to draw but suspect it's because I don't practice.) An afternoon sketching at the zoo with pencil and pad will astound anyone who's never tried it before. Pick out the movement, never mind the details, and by the end of the afternoon the improvement, both in drawing and observation, is measurable.

Shells, beach debris, offer endless possibilities. Think of what you are doing as doodling, not immortalizing a shell for posterity. Play with different points of view and different scales. Find out how a snail builds its shell by the Fibonacci numbers, how the inside of an oyster shell reveals in color and pattern where the oyster was attached and how it lived.

Or go to your local natural history museum and draw stuffed animals, although a weasel in the bush is worth two in the display. I remember wanting to draw a pocket gopher, and the sole specimen easily available was in a natural history museum. Only the front part was visible, the rest of the specimen having presumably been blown to bits on capture. It was not a successful drawing, and I never used it.

Drawing is like practicing the piano: you have to do it on a fairly regular basis to keep your hand in.

I have no patience with the "Oh,-if-I-could-only-draw!" school. Drawing is a state of mind—how much you want to do it, how much time you're willing to practice. It is, after all, simply a neural connection between eye and mind and hand, and the more that connection is reinforced, the more satisfying the result is going to be. I knew an art teacher who required students in his class to draw their own hand, once a week. His theory was that the subject was always on the premises, had infinite possibilities of outline and pose, and was not very easy to draw. The difference between the first hand drawn and the last was remarkable, a real confidence builder.

I'm also impatient with those who say "It doesn't *look* like what I wanted it to look like!" So what? Don't demand of yourself what you're not able to do at the time. Enjoy the feel of pencil on paper without imposing goals you can't meet.

I don't know why this setting of impossible goals happens more with drawing than with other creative endeavors. People who accept that they can't sit down and write a symphony in a week expect to produce a skilled drawing the first time out. Potters spend hours learning how to center on the wheel; violinists practice scales all their lives. Drawing is in the same category: it takes time to develop the basic skills. And patience. When you hit a wrong note on the piano it fades off into the air before you play the correct one. If you make a wrong line, you can erase it. Or start over.

There are some wonderful books on drawing—Frederick Franck's *The Zen of Drawing* and, best of all, *Drawing on the Right Side of the Brain* by Betty Edwards. The exercises she suggests, along with her practical how-tos, open a whole new way of looking and seeing.

A drawing class can also be useful, but it's not necessary. What *is* necessary is to toss out some preconceived notions, and to accept and appreciate your fallibility and then forget it. Masterpieces of self-expression are not devoutly to be wished. Drawing is an experience of the facts and figures of a visual world that you can learn about in no other way.

Fancy tools aren't necessary either. Although I used to carry a full complement of pencils, I now carry a single automatic one with a .5 mm lead that I buy at the supermarket. I prefer a spiral sketch pad because the papers remain anchored better, and I like one with little "tooth," as smooth as will comfortably take pencil. And if there's space in your pack or purse, carry a can of workable spray fixative. It's dismaying in the extreme to see a labored-over drawing reduced to a smear, and know that it can't be restored.

Colored pencils are a delight to use, but there's a great deal to be said for learning with black pencil on white paper. The analogy of black-and-white and color photography comes to mind: color is lovely, but color obfuscates. I don't learn as much about a plant when I draw with color. The structure and the detail are clearer in black and white.

When I am drawing I am usually very content in the pleasures of focusing outward. I think of drawing not as an end in itself but as a learning process, of doing research with a hand lens and pencil instead of a book and note cards. I think of it as seeing what I did not see before, of discovering, of walking around in the stamens and the pistil, of pacing off the petals, of touching the plant and knowing who it is.

In touch, you are given knowledge in an immediate and practical way. You find out quickly that a cholla spine stings, that a blue spruce stabs, that a juniper prickles, that a mullein leaf is soft. There is also a communication established, an intimacy between mind and plant.

I remember a morning an April ago. I had been out in the desert for three days and had an ice chest full of plants. No matter how hard I worked in the evening, I couldn't catch up with all there was to draw, so I took that morning just to draw. And I'm not sure but what it isn't a good time for drawing—your mind is yet uncluttered, energy is high, the capacity for concentration undiluted. The light tends to be bright and cool and better for drawing than the artificial light needed at night.

Two days prior a kindly hostess had said, "Let me get you a glass to put the lily in so you don't have to hold it in your hand." I had replied without thinking, "No thank you—I need to see what's on the other side." I thought of that that morning as I drew the lily, which had been carefully cossetted in the ice chest since.

When I had acquired the lily, it had five buds. That morning only one remained closed, two were open, and two were spent. It was a delicate, difficult flower, spreading its sepals and petals into a six-pointed star, stretching out gold-powdered sepals that would attract no pollinator, extending a white, three-partite stigma beyond where it could catch its own pollen, a stigma that now, in the end, would catch none. But even as I had plucked the stalk (there was no time to draw it on site) I knew the bulb would endure, to produce another stalk of flowers next year, nourished by the ruffled leaves that spread across the dry, hard ground.

I propped the lily up in the folds of the bedspread, arranged it so that the two open flowers gave different aspects of the same reality, arranged it so it said not only *Hemerocallis* but *undulata* and Sonoran Desert at ten o'clock on an April morning. A light breeze came in the window at my right shoulder and the perfect light, bright but soft, illuminated the ruffled edges of the petals, revealing a trace of where they had overlapped in the bud.

The quintessential lily, based on a trinity of shapes: I drew three lines, enough to put a turned-back sepal on paper, layered pencil lines to limn the greenish stripe down the middle, checked the proportions, width against length, ruffle against sweep of edge. And picked it up. Unconsciously. Turned it over, looked it round, set it back, realized that knowing what was on the other side mattered a great deal. How do you know where you're going if you don't know where you've been?

The appearance of the lily on the page is the future, but I've already seen it in my mind's eye, turned it in my hand, seen all lilies in this lily, known dryness in my roots, spreading in my leaves, sunshine polishing my stalk. Because of this lily, which I never saw until a few days ago, I know all about waiting for enough warmth, all about cool dawns and wilting noons. Because of this lily I know about desert heat and winter sleep and what the desert demands.

This lily is fixed in my mind's memory, on the page and blowing in a desert spring. No matter what the season, this lily blooms as part of experience, part of understanding, a deep part of knowledge beyond words. Words, visual images, straight memory—none bring that lily to flower in the mind like the notation of its curve and the line of its flare, a memory of the eye and the hand inscribed in the simple act of pencil rotating softly on paper.

The Case of
the Pain of Whales

✳

JIM NOLLMAN

✳

The expert who steps forward
is no expert;
the reaction that shows
is no reaction.

✳

Since the cetacean revelations of 2024, osmotic tuning
has revolutionized the way our civilization experiences the
natural world. Whereas a century ago human beings relegated the stewardship of nature to their nation states, and
inevitably to the scientific establishment, now each individual is capable of feeling the network of Gaia as an inner
pulse. And whereas adherents to the twentieth-century biological paradigm sincerely believed that they were discovering or gathering information leading to knowledge and
truth about the natural world, in hindsight it seems utterly
terly tragic that their logical and objective methodology
instead *invented* a mechanical description of an earth that
exists nowhere in nature outside the twentieth-century
mind.[1] But of course this description succeeded only too
well as a rationale for ultimate control. Even when the
great rain-forest crisis erupted in 1988, the initial reaction, accepted by almost everyone at the time, was to develop a gargantuan monitoring system and thus dominate
the environment more thoroughly than it was already

dominated by those who were chopping down all the trees. We look back on the twentieth century and find it difficult to believe the excesses visited upon the earth by human beings. Although each of us is now capable of feeling the great tuning of nature within his or her own heartbeat and so acting responsibly, it may still take another 150 years of healing before the pulse of a life-in-balance is able to resonate to its full critical potential.[2]

To help us better understand the experiential transformation that has swept through the human species, it seems relevant to offer a recap of an important event in the history of human/orca relations that occurred exactly a century ago, in 1986. This incident reflects many of the polarized and patently absurdist scientific sentiments of the time, while also offering a glimmer of the shamanic biology that would so forcefully erupt upon the scene twenty years later. Of course, I am referring to the celebrated case of the Pain of Whales.

On San Juan Island, Washington, back in the summer of 1986, a researcher was granted a permit by the U.S. Marine Mammal Protection Agency to shoot "cookie cutter" darts into forty-five orcas over a period of five years. The one-quarter-inch-wide, three-quarter-inch-deep sample lifted from the skin and blubber of the whale was to be analyzed to evaluate the level of pollutant chemicals as well as to determine the genetic relationships among the forty-five whales. The researcher hoped to provide "direct evidence that the gene pool of orcas is much smaller than could be determined by simply counting fins." At that time, mostly due to the human overfishing of salmon and the wholesale pollution-killing of sea lions (known as an incidental kill), the orcas numbered only 10 percent of what they do today. The forty-five constituted about half the contemporary orca population of Puget Sound. Surprisingly, the issuance of that permit generated the greatest amount of protest around the Sound since the oceanarium captures were at their peak a decade or so earlier. The objections ran the gamut from the then-radical concept that those whales deserved to exist without any more threat of human interference to the issue of whether or not the research had any lasting merit beyond serving a Ph.D. candidate in striving for a higher degree. At the heart of the immediate controversy lay the fact that those whales were seen and loved by hundreds of thousands of people. The very image of a scientist poised on the deck of a boat with bow and arrow aimed at the hide of one of "our orcas" was a matter of intense local concern, notwithstanding the purported value of the research involved.[3]

Both the Protection Agency and the researcher tried to allay public criticism by drawing attention to the permit provision stipulating the presence of an expert on board whose job it would be to report any negative reaction on the part of the darted specimen. If there were any such repercussion, then it was agreed that the project would be terminated immediately.

Unfortunately for the project advocates, the idea of an objective observer, hands gripped around a pair of binoculars, inscrutably possessed of some special access to the pain of whales opened up another can of worms. What within the orcas' behavioral store, the critics wanted to know, was going to constitute a negative reaction? Opinions varied. The whale might ram the boat. Or perhaps it would veer away from the archer at high speed.

Some students of orca behavior worried that the departing orca would simply keep on going, removing its entire pod from the darting area for a long time to come. There was a well-documented precedent for that scenario. One Puget Sound orca haunt had become the site of choice for mounting oceanarium captures. By the time of the proposed darting, twelve years later, the whales still chose to avoid that area.

In fact, there were many examples of cetaceans reacting succinctly to harassment from humans. Near Maui, researchers had documented the now-extinct humpbacks shunning a former nursery site soon after commercial waterskiing operations started up.[4] And in Alaska this same humpback stock had been documented in its outright exodus from Glacier Bay. The issue was presumed to be aggressive and noisy whale-watching boats. Power boats were banned, and the whales returned. In both incidents the whales communicated a message that the humans were able to read.

But what if, the darting detractors wanted to know, the message were not so clear? What if, for example, a darted whale, a formerly friendly whale, stopped venturing within one hundred yards of boats and instead drew the line at three hundred yards?[5] What if this subtle change in behavior were to go unnoticed for a year? Would anyone be able to state unequivocally that the new pattern sprang directly from the point of a dart sinking three-quarters of an inch into flesh and blubber? And given the off-chance that such a conclusion were reached, would it be enough reason to terminate a project already well under way?[6]

In search of a relevant precedent for such decisions, let us consider the contemporary (1980s) case of the gray whale that surfaced just underneath a whale-watching skiff, spilling all of its human occupants into the sea. One man suffered a heart attack and died. Some observers of gray whale behavior concluded that the huge animal was just acting frisky. After all, there were many instances of grays venturing right up alongside small boats to permit whale watchers to stroke their gnarly skin. Other commentators disagreed, pointing to the fact that the species was once called "devilfish," a name given to the grays by nineteenth-century whalers who often witnessed the whales capsizing their longboats.

Which version to believe? Here was an outwardly similar display observed in episodes 150 years apart by humans who held very different intentions toward the grays. Who was capable to judge the essential difference between friskiness and defense? Who would feel confident enough to pool the relevant information and then render an *objective* verdict?

There was another piece of background information that deserves special mention here. It involved the orca pods that reside just a few hundred miles north of San Juan Island in Johnstone Strait, British Columbia. In August 1983, a local fisherman was observed taking pot shots at two orcas. Both animals were wounded, neither one died.[7] In the days that followed, local researchers seemed to agree that not only those particular animals, but in fact the entire extended family of whales went into retreat whenever humans attempted to draw near. This withdrawal conveyed in whale body language a message the humans were able to read. But as the days turned into weeks, the message grew hazy. The ability to discern it became dependent on the methodology utilized by the observer. Those scientists employing "invasive techniques," e.g., zooming up on the whales in motorboats, following the pods for hours at a time, now noted that behavioral patterns had returned to normal. But those researchers who employed "benign techniques," e.g., observing from a stationary base, permitting the whales to initiate contact, continued to note changes throughout the entire next summer. One longtime researcher believed that the pod never did recover from that shooting.[8]

Those citizens who rallied against the darting of the Puget Sound orcas have provided us with key statements in the early phase of the invasive/benign debate. This split acquired its critical significance when people realized that the field methodology of choice affected the researcher's fundamental ability to observe the whales. If the whales did not choose to congregate near a land-based station, then some forms of benign research could not be performed at all. Thus, benign research might best be understood as a method that permitted the whales a role as active participants.[9] By contrast, the invasive researcher preferred to exercise an anthropocentric control, motoring up on an orca pod to carry out whatever study he or she wished to undertake. The whale was considered to be a specimen. But there was one severe catch to the invasive method: the orcas never vocalized as much, or as significantly, when there were noisy motorboats nearby.[10] So, whatever data an invasive researcher was able to buy through the power of a fast motor, he or she had to pay for with a diminution of the whales' own signals.[11] The field methodology of choice not only affected the ability to observe, but also biased the behavior patterns of the whales themselves. In other words, unless invasive studies were specifically geared to measure the effects of invasive studies, all the data were tainted. Or on still another level, here was one of the first cases of Heisenberg's uncertainty principle as applied to the field of marine biology.[12]

The darting program certainly followed the invasive model. A crew was to motor up alongside an orca, draw a crossbow, shoot a tethered arrow, watch for any immediate response, and finally return to shore again. The official government monitor for the program would thus be privy to any short-term and outwardly negative communication on the part of the whale. But inevitably, the subtle, long-term variations would elude him or her.[13]

It seemed that the program could have benefitted from the input of a simultaneous study employing the more participatory techniques of benign research. Unfortunately, the Puget Sound orca community traveled far and wide within a very expansive body of water brimming with human sightseers who followed them closely in motorboats. By comparison, the Johnstone Strait orca community resided within a relatively small semiwilderness area, which is why so much benign research was practiced there. Most of the Johnstone Strait researchers were quick to point out that the environment of Puget Sound was too clamorous to permit any kind of long-term benign study.

It is noteworthy that of seven research groups strung out along the fiord of Johnstone Strait, six of them cosigned a letter sent to the Marine Mammal Protection Agency on the very eve of the darting decision, asking that the permit not be granted. Yet despite the fact that the letter reflected a veritable roll call of active orca researchers, the permit was granted anyway.[14]

The split in methodology had generated an ethical as well as a perceptual delineation about what did and what did not constitute valid whale observation. All of the protagonists, darter and protester alike, were faced with the classic tale of Rashomon applied to marine mammal science: the witnesses to the same incident each reporting a different string of events, recalling a different defendant, choosing an entirely different verdict. No human being was capable of rendering a rational judgment about an orca's subtle and long-term reactions to a "cookie cutter" dart— especially not an expert in marine mammal science. The data the researcher desired would be the data he or she perceived.

Given this built-in confusion, this subjectivity as it were, the very idea of a scientist arriving at a judgment based upon objective evidence became highly suspect.[15] The issues seemed to undermine the very foundations of zoology. At the time, field biology was best described as the objective observation of animal behavior. Conversely, where there was no objective observation, there could be no field biology.

As in the birth of any morphogenetic field, there was suddenly a plethora of similar paradoxes forcing both scientists and nonscientists to conclude that "objective observation" was a hoax that did not and could not exist. Field biology had been profaned. Likewise, the stage was quickly set for the emergence of a new paradigm where humans and the rest of nature were osmotically connected and interpenetrating. But shamanic biology, with its focus upon planetary healing through tuning, was such a disruption to the established worldview that it would be nearly twenty-five years before it replaced so-called objective observation.

The principal investigator for the darting project attempted to defend himself by stating that, in his opinion, the darting would most likely have no effect on the orcas whatsoever. For example, said he, when fishermen in Alaska shot at orcas repeatedly with high-power rifles, the whales still refused to turn away from the longlines toward which they were headed.[16]

Several benign biologists disagreed. The movements of the wounded whales could only be construed as *inexplicable* behavior on the part of a very beleaguered pod of orcas. The dissenters concluded that the darter would do far better to presume one more example of a behavioral reaction that eluded the comprehension of the observers. After all, the fishermen who were doing the shooting also reported that they had expected some reversal in direction. No one mentioned the fact that orcas spend about three-quarters of their life underwater. (Wave telequatics, which occurs entirely underwater, would not be discovered until 2029.)

Many benign biologists started to look askance at the intentions of the Marine Mammal Protection Agency. The MMPA had attempted both to safeguard the Puget Sound orca population as well as to mollify a suspicious public by proclaiming the merits of an "expert" whose job it would be to judge "a reaction." But who, the detractors wanted to know, was going to pose as an expert? Certainly none of the cosigners of that ineffectual protest letter. And what reaction would be judged? A reaction from the whales, or from the judges?

By that time, however, it was already becoming evident that there would be no reaction, and in fact no darting program in Puget Sound. The Sierra Club Legal Defense Fund sued the Marine Mammal Protection Agency.[17] Another judge, a federal judge this time, found for the plaintiff and revoked the darting permit altogether, stating that the potential harm to the orca population far outweighed the potential benefits of the program. She concluded that the Marine Mammal Protection Agency had erred in granting such a permit without first seeking an environmental impact study. The young researcher, for his part, went off to South America, where word has it he soon commenced his darting program with the cooperation of the Argentine government.

The results of that study have been lost to history.

NOTES

EDITOR'S NOTE: The account of the Puget Sound research proposal is based on an actual happening. Parts of this story were used by the Sierra Club Legal Defense Fund in their suit to halt the darting program.

1. It is now extremely difficult for us to grasp the twentieth-century worldview that depicted nonhuman species as unpossessed of any powers of perception beyond the bare rudiments of consciousness. Immersed as humans were within the deadness of that view, how easy it was to go about the late-twentieth-century business of eradicating so many species.

2. For a comprehensive account of the osmotic revolution, read *What the Orcas Said* by Virginia Coyle (New York: Beluga Books, 2052).

3. In 1986, zoologists working under the paradigm of objective observation were still construed as the stewards, managers, and definers of nature for the rest of civilization. Because of their mindset, neither morphic nor osmotic phenomena ever received serious scientific investigation. One result was that horticulturalists actually believed it was they who were creating new vegetable forms by controlling the parameters of plant reproduction. By contrast, our current comprehension of garden vegetables as conscious symbionts—tuning into the resonant emotions of their human parasites as a fundamental evolutionary strategy—would have seemed hopelessly anthropomorphic at that time. As the osmotic proverb tells us: Tomatoes are us.

4. One can only surmise how the irresistibly beautiful and very wide-band songs of the humpbacks might have speeded up the osmotic tuning of the planet. Unfortunately, pirate whalers took the last of the species sometime around the turn of the century.

5. This is exactly the strategy utilized by the Cuvier's beaked whales for more than a century. Long considered one of the rarest of all cetacean species, suddenly, in 2026, more than 400,000 Cuvier's whales appeared along the Japanese east coast to commence their own still inscrutable version of tuning osmosis.

6. If the answers to such questions now seem more than obvious, remember that most of the men and women who studied whales in those days viewed the whale as a "specimen," which is an archaism variously translated as "object," "commodity," or "source of income."

7. Guns that shot bullets were, of course, still legal at that time. In certain societies, their use as weapons to kill wild animals expressed the shooter's claim to manliness. Because the orcas were so huge, so obviously harmless, and yet possessed of such a ferocious reputation, utilizing them as living targets developed into a kind of macabre game among boaters. By 1986, as many as 80 percent of the whales in Johnstone Strait had bullet scars.

8. The distinction between "invasive" and "benign" would provide the underpinning for the Shamans' Movement which emerged as the general paradigm within biology by the year 2015.

9. Developing synchronously with the "invasive/benign" debate, the closely related "participant/specimen" debate revolved around the issue of whether or not the pursuit of knowledge was reason enough to impose "studies" upon animals. The Specimen school believed that it was ethically permissible for a scientist either to capture or control an animal on the one hand, or disrupt its wild lifestyle on the other, in the cause of gathering information that might be useful to human culture. The Participant school believed that animals must be permitted all the rights of land, protection, and privacy enjoyed by human beings. It was only after the "six causes plague" of 1997 that human numbers dwindled enough to make realistic the Participants' call for reapportionment of wilderness and human habitation. As I write, dramatic new evidence is surfacing that describes that plague as a chemically triggered cleansing meted out by Gaia as a balancing mechanism.

10. By 1990, whale vocalizations were mostly construed as an elementary form of communication. In the spirit of the time, most scientists believed that the careful collection of data, assisted by the ubiquitous human-based computer, would someday spew up the hoped-for rosetta stone—the translation of whale language into English. It wasn't until the year 2000 that whale vocalizations were understood instead as an amalgamation of music, pure experiential mathematics (akin to a Bach fugue devoid of the limitations of gravity), and osmotic game-playing. One such game, synchronous breathing, adopted

by humans, was among the first realistic alternatives to pandemic drug abuse and became all the rage at teenage parties during the Twenties.

11. What would be formally "proven" in a series of papers first presented in 1991 was already well established among benign researchers in 1986.

12. A hundred years ago most scientists considered Heisenberg's theory to be applicable exclusively to quantum mechanics and possessing little or no relevance to field biology. Although his famous principle has since lost most of its original import as a mathematical interpretation of quantum mechanics (a dead end if ever there was one), it has gained as the metaphysical cornerstone of shamanic biology. Also, it is entirely too easy to forget that, in their own time, neither Heisenberg nor Einstein were considered to be aesthetic theorists. But then, a hundred years ago aesthetics was utilized primarily as entertainment. Also, a hundred years ago, science, economics, and especially politics were imbued with the cultural and ideological import now exclusively reserved for the aesthetics of osmotic tuning.

13. In 1986, the concept of osmotic tuning was only hinted at by some of human culture's more eccentric mystics. The government observer in the darting case, who was almost certainly neither eccentric nor mystical (by 1986 standards), could not have had any idea that the distress introduced by the darting would create a dissonance in the orca's osmotic focal point, which would upset that individual whale's own life purpose as well as the entire planet's nanopsi balance.

14. Ironically, the sole missing signature on that petition belonged to a young researcher whose own permit had been rescinded just the year previously for unnecessary harassment of orcas in the cause of collecting data.

15. It would be thirty more years before that extraordinary document "The apology from science to culture" would be issued by the Fifth International Congress of Shamanic Science. To quote: "Objective Observation was introduced by eighteenth- and nineteenth-century industrial ideologues as a means to separate human beings from nature. Its utilization thus insured a philosophical foundation for the continuing exploitation of natural resources. Its primary tenet is that human beings are like gods, transcendent to, and above nature. But we are not as gods, nor are we above the insuperable unity of the biosphere that wholly supports our mortal existence. . . . Let it be known that recent discoveries in morphic resonance and osmotic tuning have demonstrated that scientific objectivity is an absurd ruse. All participants in the drama known as life on earth are tuned as a musical instrument. The actions of all beings affect all beings all of the time."

16. Easily explained as an attempt by the orcas to retain their community tuning rhythm despite the threat of bullet wounds and even individual annihilation. Twentieth-century humanity had no way to perceive the intellectual and emotional responsibility assumed by the whales (and the songbirds, lemurs, elephants, etc.) in tuning the metabolism of the earth. For example,

one can only speculate how the "six causes plague" might have metamorphized differently had not Japanese whalers exterminated the last of the blue whales at about the same time.

17. One of the last of the establishment environmental groups, the Sierra Club was also considered one of the best. However, after the worldwide "six causes plague" depleted human population by nearly half, all organizations, including environmental groups, became drastically decentralized. This has led to the bioregional territories of the late twenty-first century.

Hunting a Christmas Tree

✳

BARBARA DEAN

N MY EARLY YEARS OF LIVING on this square mile of northern California wilderness, I often traveled to Michigan for the holidays to share Christmas with family. But for nearly a decade now, faced with more travel than I like during the rest of the year as part of my work as editor for an environmental publisher, I have chosen instead to stay home and celebrate alone or with a few friends.

On this oak-dotted hillside, my life is defined by wildness and solitude. Most days, my face-to-face interactions with other humans are limited to two-minute exchanges about the weather with the mail carrier. Although the workweek brings long-distance collaboration with authors and colleagues, my immediate daily relationships are not with people, but rather with animals and the landscape.

In this place and within this quasi-hermit life, miles from city lights and store windows, Christmas is a celebration that is restored to its pagan roots. The winter solstice has become part of my holiday preparations, lending a timeless dimension to the season and extending its observance beyond the human community.

After fall's bustling activity, the dark time of the year

arrives quietly, with shadows creeping up the hills across the river a little earlier each day. The ground squirrels disappear underground early in November, about the same time that the oak trees begin to loosen their grip on dying leaves. The white-tailed deer munch acorns behind my house and then stroll into the open field, where slanting sunlight glances off coats grown thick against the cold. In the main meadow, the resident family of coyotes, also splendid with new fur, prowl for lagging ground squirrels. A flock of wood ducks has arrived at the pond in a great rush of flapping wings, to remain through the winter. By December, the raging gusts of late fall winds have stripped the trees bare.

For me, less daylight and colder temperatures mean fewer hours for more chores: I need to take a break from my desk in midafternoon to split tomorrow's firewood and carry it in to the stoveside. There is barely time to take a walk with Nandi, my Rhodesian Ridgeback, into the meadow and through the forest, before darkness closes in.

One Sunday morning, Nandi and I venture into the meadow's crisp stillness to cut fragrant Douglas fir boughs from young trees on the hillside just to the north of my house, luminous red-berried holly from the bushes near the Big House, dusky mistletoe that is attached to the white oak halfway down the meadow. Walking home, laden with the smells and colors and shapes of the season, thinking about decorating the house, my feelings for Christmas mix with quiet anticipation of the light's return.

More days pass and my inner sense of promise grows. Finally the solstice is here: darkness and light are equal, and then the light stretches out, a natural blessing that embraces this place and all creatures who dwell within it. And then as the solstice turns toward Christmas, the light without is met by light within, and the season becomes whole.

This year, I am late for everything. It's December 23d and although the solstice has come and gone, not a single fir bough drapes the window ledges. The press of last-minute work has delayed my usual preparations—but this week-end I will catch up. Throughout a busy week, I have aimed myself toward this day, which I have set aside for getting my Christmas tree.

The morning is overcast, the temperature unusually cold for northern California. In the meadow, the night's frost still clings to the dead stalks of last spring's grass. Calling for Nandi, who is always ready for an adventure, I reach for my jacket, gloves, and then the bow saw that hangs from a nail on the outside back wall of my house. The day is quiet, the natural sounds muted by the heavy air. Nandi looks at me expectantly, wondering if she will get to choose the way. But, no, today I am the one who knows where we are going, and so she follows my cue, as I move toward the cold side of the gentle slope to the north of the house.

Despite my love for Christmas, cutting a tree is always a daunting project. This square mile of remote mountain land was logged almost thirty years ago, and although it is important to me that my Christmas tree come from this place that has become the ground of my life, I also want the second-growth forest to flourish. So I must find a tree in a group that needs thinning or one that has started in such poor soil that I doubt it will thrive. The problem, of course, with choosing a tree from a close-growing group is that nearly always it is also scrawny or lopsided. Wild trees don't have the groomed fullness and symmetry of those in Christmas tree farms.

And yet I want a tree that comes close to my perfect vision from childhood. Each year, as I walk over the land in the months before Christmas, I make mental notes of the young Douglas firs. This fall my wanderings have led me again and again to the tree we are walking toward today, a tree that I have watched for years. The tree is about the right height—six feet—and about the right diameter, as far as I can tell. The deer have browsed the branches, a natural pruning that helps them to grow full. Most important, the trunk of this tree grows only two feet from the trunk of another. Either one of these trees would probably grow better without the other. I can't tell for sure whether or not the apparent fullness of "my" tree is partly the branches of its neighbor. "Mine" may after all be lopsided once it stands by itself. But I don't think so. I think this young fir will be just right.

As I have passed the tree in the last months, I have been nodding to it, getting to know it, measuring it in my mind's eye for its spot in my house. The years of watching it grow have established a familiarity between us, at least on my part. I have visited this tree during summer's searing heat, on fall days when mist hung in the air, and in the frosted quiet of winter. I have felt the tree's prickly needles, circled its small gray trunk with my hands. This tree and I have been neighbors: the same winds that have rustled its needles have blown through my hair; I know the deer who have browsed its branches; the same wary bobcat, brilliant hummingbirds, and family of raccoons have encountered us both.

After so much time and shared experience, I have a particular feeling for this particular tree—and here is where the difficulty is. For I am about to kill it.

At times like this, I wonder whether living in this near-wilderness has rendered me unfit for twentieth-century life. When I was a child, Christmas tree-cutting adventures with my family were a high point of the season; we children would race around the hill, choosing the "best" tree, always wanting Dad to cut the biggest. I don't remember that the scruples I struggle with now were any part of those days.

But years of living in this wild place have changed me in ways that I could not reverse even if I wanted to. Among the changes, those pressing on me today are an awareness of the individual essence of this tree and the terrible knowledge that all life depends on death.

I am not planning to eat this tree, of course. Rather than feeding my body, the tree will feed my soul. But the distinction blurs. The central paradox, the truth that is at the heart of all life on earth, remains.

The interplay of life and death is everywhere here: in a postseason fly caught and eaten in a spider web above my desk; in the deer bones, freshly gnawed in the canyon across the stream; in the oak leaves, fallen and now decaying in a mat behind the house. I have been a vegetarian for more than twenty years, which I once thought exempted me from the violence that accompanies the securing of food. But a few weeks of working in the garden my first summer here—weeding, transplanting, thinning, harvesting—did away with that comforting illusion. Picking a blackberry may not kill the bush, but what about pulling up a carrot? Besides, I soon grew uncomfortable with the notion that even a berry might not have a life.

Each death is clearly part of sustaining another life, and, just as clearly, my own survival depends on being part of this chain every day in one way or another. Most of the time, I understand this inescapable reality well enough to justify my own role. But sometimes the darkness at the heart of that logic breaks through, and I face what seems an intolerable truth.

Perhaps it is because of Christmas, because of the feeling of ceremony that hovers in the air, because of the season's unusually fragile veil between spirit and nature—whatever the reason, today my killing of this tree seems to epitomize my life's dependence on the death of another life. Today this seems to me a profound and chilling mystery, not easily accommodated in the soul. And nothing in my own upbringing has taught me how to make peace with it.

As I stand in front of this tree that I have chosen, it occurs to me that, despite living alone, I am lonely here only at times such as this, when my emotions seem to isolate me from my own culture, from the traditions I have received and experienced since childhood. Those traditions have served me well in the part of my life that engages the twentieth century. But I seem to live a parallel life here, one that constellates primal emotions, for which I often find myself deeply unprepared.

Soon after moving to the country, the intensity of my feelings for this land caught me by surprise. Looking for insight, I sought out books about the Native Americans who first lived in these hills, and then about other cultural groups that lived close to the earth, reaching back to the earliest hunter-gatherers. In the descriptions of people who depended directly on the natural world for food and shelter and whose stories and rituals revealed an intimacy with the plants and animals sharing their lives, I found human traditions that offered a framework for my own feelings.

Since I don't eat meat and most traditional hunters are male, knowledge of the substance and texture of life for hunting cultures might not seem, on the surface at least, to be very relevant to my life here. But something has compelled me to continue to read about the hunter, to learn about the experience of the hunt, and to explore as much as possible the hunter's mind through the writings of philosophers and anthropologists and some contemporary hunters.

I realize now that it must be this fundamental truth that life depends on killing—this central fact of life that is sidestepped by my own cultural tradition—that has pulled me to the hunter. Without fully understanding why, I have been seeking insight into the mind and conscience of someone who faced this dilemma every day.

As I stand here in this place that has become part of the outer skin of my soul, I understand that the emotions that assault me now—sorrow, guilt, anticipation—are an original chemistry, just as timeless and universal as the bond between human and nature. Over the years, I have read the accounts of hunting rituals, preparations, and taboos, with the assumption that the careful actions were aimed at petitioning success in the hunt. But now I wonder if another purpose wasn't just as important. The rituals must also have been a way to help the soul justify its part in the cycles of life and death.

I think back over the months of looking for this tree—of stalking it. I realize that I have searched for the right tree with some part of my mind during every walk through the woods, no matter what the season. The hunt inspired me to explore new trails into different parts of the forest. My awareness was sharpened, my senses of observation fine-tuned: I deduced which areas must have good soil, where the trees grew thick, and which were too rocky or thin to feed healthy branches. I noticed how and where the land was reseeding itself, where the deer grazed the trees. The arc of my honed attention pulled me into and connected me with the landscape.

In the early days of the hunt, when many different trees caught my fancy, I remember feeling startled at how my perceptions would change from day to day: a tree that seemed perfect one day would look all wrong the next. My shifting moods made me uneasy. From the tree's point of view, I held the power of life and death, and it was a small leap of imagination to project my fickleness onto the powers that regulate my own life. If I could decide to kill this tree instead of that one, almost by whim, what would keep my life from being snuffed out by an equal fluke of fate— by a bolt of lightning, a forest fire, a lurking rattlesnake?

At the time, I thought I had stumbled onto the origins of superstition. If the universe is random, ruled by fancy, there is no safety in skill or logic; one needs luck. Infused

with a sense of the randomness of fate, the magical thinking that is at the heart of what we call superstition makes
sense.

But Richard K. Nelson, who for many years has lived
with and studied the Koyukon people of the Alaskan forest, explains in *Make Prayers to the Raven* that "luck" to
those native hunters means something quite different from
my interpretation. For the Koyukon, "luck" is kept by observing elaborate codes of behavior based on respect for the
watchful world of nature. The understanding of the world
that underlies their idea of "luck" is not one of random interactions, but rather a sentient, interrelating, living web
of plants, animals, and landforms that themselves have a
specific spiritual presence. For the Koyukon and other native cultures, the natural world is a powerful reality to
which human lives are linked by spiritual and moral
bonds.

This is a view of the world that lies deep in our collective
psyche and has become familiar to me over the years I have
spent on this hillside. Now, it coalesces with new meaning
as I recall my continuing search for the perfect tree, week
after week, how it finally led me to this tree, once and then
repeatedly, walk after walk. I remember that my feelings
shifted; in place of feeling the randomness of fate, I had a
feeling of rightness about this tree. I began to understand
something that had never made sense to me before—how
a hunter could feel that an animal offers him- or herself to
be killed. With my intuition that this tree was "right"
came a feeling that the tree and I were both part of some
larger pattern of life within which our small lives
intersected.

And so I stand here, in front of this tree I have chosen. My reflections have left me feeling mostly at peace with my part in this event. But the moment of the cutting is still harrowing.

While Nandi investigates something under a fallen madrone, its smooth red skin sparkling with frost, I hold this tree's small trunk firmly with my left hand. I place the saw at the base of the tree, close to the ground, so no stump will be left. As I pull the blade slowly through the tree's flesh, I am careful not to let its teeth wound the tree alongside, the one that I hope will benefit from less competition on this slope.

In the winter stillness, the rasp of the saw echoes down the length of the canyon. I wonder if other trees are listening, knowing. Despite my sense of rightness about this tree-cutting, the experience is not the clean and neat ritual I might hope for. The saw gets stuck, I feel clumsy, I grumble as I struggle to pull the blade. But in a few minutes, the violence is done. I lift the tree from its roots and hold it here, in my hand. The silence closes in again.

Nandi comes over to sniff what I have done. The small tree is still fresh with life; I can smell it, too. Breathing the juice of the fir into my lungs, I feel regret, gratitude—and something else. A hint of doubt. What if I have made a mistake? What if, after all, I have misinterpreted the signs; what if I have killed in error?

If a Koyukon hunter does something that offends the spirit of other life forms, even out of ignorance, he will pay for his mistake with a loss of luck and perhaps with some acts of conscious atonement. Some mistakes—say, a lapse of attention, a miscalculation—can mean hunger or even death. Today, the possibility of error does not put me in physical danger, but feels threatening nevertheless: the knowledge that I might have erred unintentionally shakes my feeling of "rightness" and colors it with angst.

I understand in this flare of doubt that however much I may think I know about this land and its trees, about how trees grow and what they need to live, I will never know enough about the profound complexities of life on earth to be sure that I perform this act—that I kill—with moral certainty. The conviction of my human inadequacy expands within me.

And then, somehow, from somewhere, another emotion sweeps over me, and I am enveloped by a sweet and transforming humility, a feeling so unexpected that the experience can only be called a moment of grace. This feeling, which transcends the hunt and yet is utterly rooted in its essence, brings a sense of resolution to the impossible dilemmas with which I have been wrestling. I finally understand that humility is the key. Only through humility can the soul make peace with the terrible necessities of survival.

Getting to my feet, I carry the tree to the path, so I can take a good look. Yes, its branches are thick enough all the way around, as I had hoped. Before we turn toward home, I nod to the place from which I have taken the tree, give the tree a chance to bid farewell too. Then I hoist the trunk and needled limbs to my shoulders. While my head bobs among the sweet-smelling branches, Nandi dances ahead, and my boots crunch frost on the trail. Christmas feelings spread through the winter air.

The tree seems heavier by the time home comes into view, and my shoulders are weary as I lean it against the back wall of the house. Inside, I have already moved the furniture to its Christmas configuration, so that the tree will have the place of honor in front of the sunny south-facing windows. With some struggle, I carry the tree into the house and plant it firmly in the big earthen pot, filled with wet dirt. To help the tree stay straight, I fasten a wire from its trunk to the window knob.

The Koyukon believe that the being who is killed retains its power for some time, so the body is handled with great respect. I have no doubt that this small tree still holds its power: I can feel its energy, sense how naturally the tree becomes the focus of the room.

With Christmas music playing, I decorate the tree. First, the twelve-volt Christmas tree lights, new this year, the first Christmas of my solar-powered system. Next, the gold star on the tree's highest point. Then, one by one, I hang the animal ornaments—birds near the top, heavier pieces like the polar bear near the bottom, just as my mother always does. After the animals are all in place, I add the olive wood stars, the straw angels, the crocheted snowflakes, and the needlepoint figures. I stand back, look at the tree from another angle, then move a few pieces that don't seem quite right.

Deacon, my resident cat, watches these activities with barely restrained glee. He remembers the dangling snow-flakes from last year and the year before—and is only biding his time before leaping to catch one. Nandi looks from Deacon to the tree and back to me, remembering, too, ready in her turn to pounce on the cat as soon as he moves. I am thinking that this is how time is knitted together, how one year connects with the next, in memories that spawn stories that will shape the future. Already this household has begun to create its Christmas traditions.

Finally, nearly every branch holds something. I pour myself a glass of eggnog, sit on the couch nearby, and plug in the lights. Both Nandi and Deacon have settled temporarily, curled on the couch by my side. Peace and beauty fill the room. My love for the little tree moves within me.

The tree holds for me the wonder of the season, linking multiple layers of meaning and memory: the perfect Christmases of childhood; my adult experience of Christmas as a time when daily stresses recede and life becomes whole; collective memories of ancient rituals welcoming the return of the light. Gazing at the little tree, I am filled with gratitude for the gift of new life, new light, both within and without.

During the next ten days, as I go about the activities of Christmas—baking cookies, sweeping the floor, preparing a meal for friends—within the aura of the star- and animal-bedecked tree, I find myself contemplating the pattern of the hunt. In particular, I muse about the humility I felt—a feeling that I understand is part of a "right relation" to the largest powers of life, to God. Where, I wonder, did it come from?

I realize that the moment emerged from the convergence of many things: my wish for a Christmas tree, my attraction to this particular tree, my sense that the tree was a sentient being—and the inexplicable feeling that my life and the natural life of this place are linked, a sense of connection that has been quickening within me for twenty years.

Casting back, again, to what I know of hunting cultures, I understand that all the traditions of the hunt—prehunting rituals that attune a larger awareness, the code that admonishes killing only out of need, the respect given to the prey, the careful use of every part of the killed animals—derive from this central sense of connection. The hunter knows that all life is bound together by powers too subtle and complex to be fully understood. Humility, I think, must begin in this knowledge of sacred connection and be nourished by daily intimacy with the powerful, interrelated, living world.

And yet, for me, the act itself—this paradoxical, impossible act of taking a life—released the feeling. I contemplate again the moment, let myself sink again into the experience, with all its emotion and contradiction, trying to understand why. And I finally see that in this moment of the kill, the hunter stands at the intersection of the most profound of opposites—life and death. He knows not only that those opposites are linked—indeed that one becomes the other—but also that his life depends on being part of the transformation, part of the intimate, mysterious, ongoing communion of all life. I know that there are other ways to experience life's Oneness, but I wonder if this truth is ever so immediate, so palpable, so full of feeling as in the hunter's act.

I wonder what happens to a culture such as ours that avoids the direct experience of the kill. Psychologists would say that denial of such a fundamental guilt—guilt that another life has to end in order for one's own to continue—sets the stage for self-righteousness. On a more conscious level, without the deep knowledge of human capacity for error that is part of the traditional hunter's experience, it becomes much too easy to think that we can *know* enough to perform right action.

The archetypal hunter's wisdom seems especially important now, when we are beginning to repair our relationship with the natural world. The sciences of ecology and conservation biology are leading that work, with new and enlightening explanations of the complex connections of all life. But in order to understand how those connections *feel*, I think we must turn to the ancient hunter. The scientist, by training, describes the processes of life from a distance; the hunter's perspective, on the other hand, is from *within* life's web. Without the hunter's sense of being personally connected with and dependent on the natural world, without the demanding, transforming humility that is part of the hunter's soul, it seems to me that our efforts to repair the damage we have done, to restore the world and ourselves within it, will surely be marked by hubris and failure.

I think of these things each evening for the next ten days, as I plug in the tree's tiny, solar-powered lights, curl up on the couch, and gaze at the tree. In those moments of reflection and also during the day, when I sit down to a meal, I find that the shift of perspective I experienced in front of the tree in the woods has stayed with me. The essentials of my twentieth-century life—preparation and consumption of food, splitting and burning of firewood—seem starkly congruent with those of the ancient hunter. The archetypal hunter emerges in my consciousness, a powerful mentor for my own life's journey.

By the time New Year's Day has come and gone, the

tree's needles are dry, and its energy seems to be diminished. It is time to move into a new season. On a morning bright with sun, I carry the tree to the leaf-covered earth under the towering bay tree behind my house. In the next months, I will watch the tree's needles turn brown and fall to the ground, see beetles and small ants penetrate the fragile gray bark and carve tunnels in the tree's flesh. Spiders will weave webs among the twigs, where they will catch and eat spring flies. By June, snakes will begin to crawl over and under the tree's naked limbs. Quail will search for bugs in the earth between the branches, and Deacon will stalk the mice who scurry under the tree on their way to homes in the meadow grass. The sun and wind and rain will fall on the little tree as it slowly becomes earth, passing through the bodies of beetles and earthworms, as the tree feeds the layers of new life it now holds, as the new lives live and die and feed each other.

Manatees and the Metaphors of Desire

※

CHARLES BERGMAN

S HE TOUCHED ME WITH A SUD-
den, unexpected intimacy. A large
manatee, she had been sculling across
the bright limestone bottom of Crys-
tal River, in Florida, near the springs that feed the pellucid
waters of the manatee sanctuary. When she saw me above
her, she plumped slowly to the surface like a dirigible, rotating indolently to face me, seeming to linger through
each movement. I braced for the encounter.

Her approach was slow—an infinitely sweet, infinitely
guileless address. She looked vaguely like a walrus, with
her flat, whiskered nose and duffel-bag body. Her trun-
cated snout and large, prehensile lips revealed some of her
distant and ancient relation to the elephant. Her skin, gray
and leathery, reminded me in its roughness of a cracked ce-
ramic plate. Sunk deep into her face, her pinprick eyes
seemed much too small for her immense bulk. She looked
out at me from within a blubberous body, through the
bleary film over her eyes.

Except in a spectacularly homely way, you could not call
her beautiful. But her trust and openness were irresistible,
endearing. As she paddled the water with her splayed flippers, I could see the bones moving beneath the skin like

the fingers inside a child's mittens. On her skin, short and delicate hairs wavered in the water. Manatees are tactile creatures. They love to touch, and these sparse hairs increase the manatee's sensitivity.

She treaded toward me, within inches of my face. Still, I was not prepared for what she did. With a gentle and startling thud, she banged into my face mask with her bristled snout. It was as surprising as a first kiss, and just as memorable.

This manatee had come toward me like an idea taking shape. In her steady approach, she became an increasingly significant presence. She evoked in me a powerful desire for more, though I could not tell what it was at the time that I wanted more of. In the intimacy of the encounter, I felt what I have often felt in my experiences with wild animals—that there is something lacking in our ability to account for moments like these.

The feeling of estrangement and the desire to know nature grow with the awareness of the loss of nature in our time. I had come to the Crystal River to study manatees as part of the research for my book on endangered animals. Swimming with this manatee gave me a sense for how I might begin to create new kinds of relationships with animals. I do not think we can ever know other creatures completely, but I do believe we can achieve relationships richer in intimacy and intensity than those we are now capable of.

Usually, with wild animals, I am a spectator, watching them from a distance. With this manatee in the Crystal River, however, I was in her element, swimming with her in a slow-motion process of discovery. I must have been a comical sight: my cheeks squished inside a face mask and my lips almost orange on a cold winter morning. She seemed to like peering at me. Bound in a mutual gaze, we floated together in the water, mask to massive snout.

Even though manatees are famous for their gentleness, I confess I felt uncomfortable. Through my face mask, I could see only a small circumference, in a kind of tunnel vision. The manatee started to drift to the left, inspecting me. Her hulking and harmless being seemed at peace in the warm waters, like a gentle sea-Buddha, and her motions were elegant in their simple, casual drift. With her round tail flipper, big as a manhole cover, she propelled herself toward my left, behind me. With a hint of panic I found myself sculling almost frenetically to keep her within the narrow field of view afforded by my face mask. I bent myself in contortions at the waist to keep facing her, kicking stupidly, absurdly, with my flippers. But I could not match her moves in the water. I started to lose sight of her as she slid behind my back. I did not want her behind me. Something about her unguarded easiness made me feel slightly ashamed. I suddenly felt tyrannized by this need to see.

It was a strange moment. The recollection of being in the water, straining to keep an utterly innocuous manatee within the frame and periphery of my face mask, has stayed with me. I continue to mull the disquiet I felt in the encounter. I have come to believe that the nervousness I felt while swimming with this manatee was related to my need to *see* her, because that is how we have learned to relate to animals—largely through the eyes. Our knowledge of creatures is dominated by metaphors of perception—especially seeing and hearing. For us, to see is to grasp, and affirm, reality. The true way to know animals, we imagine, is through the eyes. Think of birdwatching. Or wildlife photography. Both activities try to satisfy the need to know the creatures through the act of seeing and the illusions of the visual image. And these metaphors have implications for the way we relate to creatures. If the language of science gives us pictures of the world out there, it is perceptual metaphors that give us images of our particular relationships with the world. So trained are we, however, in knowing through these metaphors that we cannot see them as metaphor. We can barely imagine any way of relating to another except through the senses.

Yet the metaphors we have inherited for understanding animals have left a strange gap, a lack of immediacy, between us and them. I believe that it is through the creation of new metaphors that we can begin to move into, and pioneer, the hollow spaces between us and the animals we live among.

I love to watch wildlife. Yet I often have had the vague and slightly disturbing sense that watching wildlife is akin to voyeurism. With the manatee, I suddenly felt as if I had been caught looking—as if I had been staring through a one-way window, and with a slight shift of focus, had suddenly seen my own eyes staring back at me. It was as though the manatee had revealed a part of our relationship ordinarily invisible to me.

As both Freudians and voyeurs know, looking can be an act of power. It is much the same pleasure that an audience has at a play, spectators who see more than can any of the characters on stage. Being seen, however, reverses the relation, and brings with it a greater sense of vulnerability.

This we might call the politics of perception, or the psychology of the gaze.

We live in a post-Galilean age, an age inaugurated by advances in vision and observation. Its great symbol might easily be the telescope. We feel most comfortable with the kinds of intellectual authority that are expressed in metaphors of vision—when our ideas are "clear," for example, when we "see things well," when we are "lucid" in our language. We like to be "focused" in our thinking and to have good "insights." The great age of scientific advances, the Age of Reason, is called the Enlightenment.

With the emphasis on perceptual metaphors in the West has come the sense that we are separate from the world. The seer is distinct from the seen, and there is a distance between the subject and the object. Hans Jonas, the philosopher who wrote *The Phenomenon of Life*, shows the implications of the modern dependence on vision, and he might have been describing my reaction to the manatee: "Thus vision secures that standing back from the aggressiveness of the world which frees for observation and opens a horizon for elective attention. But it does so at the price of a becalmed and abstract reality denuded of its raw power."

Perceptual metaphors define a relationship, even if we are unaware that they are doing so. Oddly, it is as if we actually grant existence to other creatures through our eyes. How else can we explain our strange discomfort at not knowing whether an animal exists or is extinct—like the black-footed ferret or the ivory-billed woodpecker? We are reluctant as a culture to protect them until we have seen them, and if we cannot see them, we cannot even prove whether they are extinct—the perfect paradox for an empirical age. How else can we account for the reluctance to set aside chunks of habitat, like national parks in Alaska, for animals most of us may never see? It explains why we remain vulnerable to the old argument that only a few people will get to see these creatures, and what good is that? Until we see them, we somehow fondly believe, they do not exist for us.

The manatee, as described in literature and history, is an example of the way that perceptual metaphors and cultural images define our relationships with nature. Manatees belong to the order of Sirenia. It is an unlikely association, given their homeliness, but they are sirens. By the Middle Ages, sirens had become confused with fishlike mermaids. In their early Greek incarnation, though, sirens were bird-like women who lulled men with their music and led them to destruction.

The classic story of humans and sirens comes from the *Odyssey* of Homer. The story provides, I think, an almost archetypal image of Western man responding to nature. The ancient Greeks emphasized clear vision and hearing in knowing nature—the name of the great cultural hero, Prometheus, means "foresight." Perceptual metaphors figure prominently in Homer's story, as Odysseus positions himself in his encounters with nature.

In Book Twelve, Homer describes the seductive appeal of the sirens. With Greek foresight, Odysseus warns his men sailing home with him of the danger ahead and tells of the strategy given to him by Kirke (Circe):

> Kirke foresaw for us and shared with me,
> so let me tell her forecast: then we die
> with our eyes open, if we are going to die,

> *or know what death we baffle if we can. Seirenes*
> *weaving a haunting song over the sea*
> *we are to shun, she said, and their green shore*
> *all sweet with clover; yet she urged that I*
> *alone should listen to their song. Therefore*
> *you are to tie me up, tight as a splint,*
> *erect along the mast, lashed to the mast,*
> *and if I shout and beg to be untied,*
> *take more turns of the rope to muffle me.*

Odysseus stuffs beeswax into his sailors' ears, and as they row, he listens to the song of the sirens:

> *Sweet coupled airs we sing.*
> *No lonely seafarer*
> *Hold clear of entering*
> *Our green mirror.*

Odysseus is ravished by the sirens' song, and cries out to his men to untie him. They do not. Odysseus hears the sirens but is prevented from succumbing to their "lovely voices," which would "sing his mind away on their sweet meadows lolling." He avoids their "green mirror." Instead, he sees truth beneath their delusiveness, death beneath their loveliness: "bones of dead men rotting in a pile beside them and flayed skins shrivel around the spot."

In the sirens, two images are combined into one symbolic representation: animals and females, birds and women. They are the projected image of desire—the desire inspired by nature, and the desire inspired by women. The story serves to evoke this desire for an entire culture, only to demonstrate how to manage and control it. Homer portrays Odysseus listening to the sirens and clearly seeing their beauties and their threats. But he has himself bound to the mast, hearing yet not responding to the loveliness of the song. The image is itself eloquent and seductive. Nature is to be perceived from a distance. It can then be defeated through rationality and restraint. There is authoritarianism in the image as well—Odysseus can hear and see the loveliness in nature, but the men he commands must not. They bow over their oars, their ears are stuffed with beeswax. They neither see nor hear.

Many centuries later, another traveler voyaged through strange lands and reported seeing sirens. On his first voyage to the New World, Christopher Columbus made what is now regarded as the first sighting by a Westerner of a West Indian manatee. On January 9, 1493, he was coasting along the shores of Haiti. He wrote in his journal that three "mermaids" were observed from the ship. Without a trace of irony, and only a hint of doubt, he reports that these creatures rose high out of the sea. "They were not nearly as beautiful as painted," Columbus wrote, "although to some extent they have a human appearance in the face."

How could Columbus, the preeminent explorer, look at blunt-nosed and bewhiskered manatees and imagine that he saw mermaids? In this journal passage, we are given an intimate glimpse of Columbus's mind and his way of seeing as he is confronted with something genuinely new in the world—it is a rare and wonderful moment. He interprets what he sees through the cultural images he carries with him. Not only is perception a basic metaphor in the West for knowing the world, but metaphors, cultural images, guide the way we perceive. Columbus transformed his physical perception of manatees through a cultural image, the mermaid, itself a transformation of the Greek image of desire.

Desire—the same desire that was felt but resisted by Odysseus, that is symbolized in the mythic siren, that was evoked for me by the manatee in the Crystal River. This is not the desire to know nature as it exists in our eyes only. However much the eyes have given us, they also confine us to know creatures by their surfaces and grant them a strange anonymity. Our relations with animals have been largely one-sided—us seeing them. We need to begin to incorporate into our thinking about animals a sense of reciprocity.

Conversation and dialogue—we already have available to us new metaphors for reconstructing our relationships with animals. These metaphors have taught us to rethink human interactions over the last half century, to move from authoritarian relations to more interactive and democratic ones. If perceptual metaphors stress accurate representation and knowledge, conversational metaphors stress relationship and emotional meaning. This greater intimacy requires recognizing our own role in defining relationships—being honest about the ways in which our own prejudices and needs, fears and desires, shape our responses to the world. It requires a sensitivity not only to the information we acquire about animals and their visible externals, but also to what is essential in them—their inner lives, what we would call the "character" of a creature, if it were human. We cannot hold ourselves back from exploring what is real because it is not reducible to absolutes. If we want to redeem the nature we have lost in our time, we must begin to articulate much more clearly what nature means to humans, why we need nature, realizing always that our understanding is necessarily provisional, part of the complex and unending process of naming the world and finding our places in it. A sense of dialogue in our dealings with animals can help us to supplement our present knowledge with wisdom, to discover those animals that are the living analogies of the heart.

The same manatee that made me aware of my discomfort because of my need to see her also showed me how my experience of animals might be enlarged. It was an unusually cool day on the Crystal River. Steam played over the surface of the cloud-darkened river. The slack drift of the waters had a hypnotic, almost narcotic tranquillity to it. While the manatee swam in her slow career around me, I tried to open myself to this creature, tried to imagine how she must experience the world.

Almost everything we know about manatees appeals to that part of us that longs for a peaceful, unhurried approach to life. Once, she settled toward the bottom, as if luxuriating in these warm waters, and then rose again with an effortless buoyancy. Breaking the surface with just her nose, she sent up a swoosh of breath in a small feathery spray. I got the feeling that she moved not through water but through the medium of a dream, swimming in a kind of aquatic somnambulance. I could not help but wonder what notions, flitting like fish through the streams of her thought, were able to curl her lips in such a self-satisfied smile.

I stayed in the water for over an hour. I felt changed by the manatee as I swam with her. She embarrassed me out of my sense of superiority. Although she was homely, her appearance mattered less and less the longer I was with her in the water. I quit struggling to watch her, and we just drifted. She swung around behind me and banged into my back with the tender thump of fifteen hundred pounds. She nuzzled my sides and chest with her nose, as if she were smelling me. She seemed to want to know me through smell and feel.

I like to think of myself as the author of my own experience—as if my life were a story that I am writing. But with the manatee, there could be no illusion that I was the author of the encounter. This was her drama, and my role was unfolding as I took part. She dived below me, came up, and bumped into my belly. She rolled over, sinking. Then, like a huge and slowly spinning bubble, she bobbed toward me again and nudged my side. Wafting her flat round tail, she spiked toward the bottom, where she tumbled onto her back with an elephantine magnificence. In her superbly languid torpor, she rose toward me once more, coming at me from an angle with all her engaging, unpretentious bulk. Her face was eloquent with curiosity, playfulness, and the serene vulnerability of things that simply are what they are.

I felt honored by her trust, just as I am honored when another human being reveals a part of himself or herself to me. Dialogue explicitly tries to diminish the barriers that separate one from another, humans from nature. I tried to apprehend this manatee with the only quality that enables us to understand the life of another, whether human or animal, as they might experience it themselves—empathy. She made me feel expanded, as if, swimming to her rhythms, I had pushed back some personal boundaries.

The manatee had, as it were, extended an invitation to intimacy. I was in her waters. This was not Odysseus's resistance and restraint, but trust; not distance, but engagement; not authority, but dialogue. With a touch that was barely perceptible, she brushed her snout against my face mask, and we spun together in a dreamy, balletic swirl, lost in an impromptu, naked moment.

Contributors

※

DAVID ABRAM is an ecologist, educator, and free-lance magician who has exchanged magic with tribal sorcerers in Indonesia, Nepal, and North America. He lectures frequently on ecology and the philosophy of science, and his essays have appeared in *The Ecologist*, *Environmental Ethics*, and other publications.

CHARLES BERGMAN is the author of *Wild Echoes: Encounters with the Most Endangered Animals in North America*, which examines the meaning of nature as it is increasingly defined by absence and loss. He teaches in the English department at Pacific Lutheran University and lives in Tacoma, Washington.

SUSAN POWER BRATTON is a plant ecologist active in park and wilderness protection. She has written on conservation biology, landscape history, and Christian environmental ethics and is the author of two books, *Christianity, Wilderness, and Wildlife* and *Six Billion and More: Human Population Regulation and Christian Ethics*.

BARBARA DEAN is executive editor at Island Press and the author of *Wellspring: A Story from the Deep Country*. "Hunting a Christmas Tree" is part of a work in progress.

DAVID EHRENFELD is the author of *The Arrogance of Humanism* and the editor of *Conservation Biology*, a journal for professional biologists. He teaches ecology at Rutgers University. His "Raritan Letter" appears regularly in *Orion*. He lectures widely on subjects ranging from Judaism and the environment to the overmanagement of modern society.

JOHN ELDER is the author of *Imagining the Earth: Poetry and the Vision of Nature*, coeditor of *The Norton Book of Nature Writing*, and series editor for the Concord Library of Beacon Press. He teaches English and environmental studies at Middlebury College.

J. RONALD ENGEL is professor of social ethics at Meadville/Lombard Theological School and chair of the Ethics Working Group of the World Conservation Union. He is the author of *Sacred Sands: The Struggle for Community in the Indiana Dunes* and coeditor with Joan G. Engel of *Ethics of Environment and Development*.

ROBERT FINCH is the author of three collections of essays about Cape Cod. The most recent is *The Cape Itself*, with photos by Ralph MacKenzie. He is the coeditor of *The Norton Book of Nature Writing*.

WILLIAM R. JORDAN III is outreach and publications manager for the University of Wisconsin-Madison Arboretum, a founding member of the Society for Ecological Restoration, and editor of *Restoration and Management Notes*. He is often called on to speak on ecological restoration and its meaning for the relationship of human beings to nature.

WALLACE KAUFMAN'S writings and travel preferences often take him to Latin America and the Soviet Arctic, where his chief subject continues to be the human struggle both to develop and respect the natural environment. He is the author of books on the American shoreline, housing, and the Amazon valley.

BARRY LOPEZ lives in Oregon with his wife, Sandra, a book artist. He is an essayist and short story writer and a contributing editor at *Harper's* and *North American Review*. He is the author of *Arctic Dreams*, for which he received the National Book Award, *Of Wolves and Men*, and several collections of fiction. His most recent books are *The Rediscovery of North America* and *Crow and Weasel*, an illustrated fable.

GARY NABHAN is an ethnobotanist and the author of three books on the plants and peoples of the desert Southwest, including *Enduring Seeds* and *Gathering the Desert*, for which he won the John Burroughs Medal for natural history writing. He is cofounder and research director of Native Seeds/SEARCH and a recent MacArthur Fellow.

JIM NOLLMAN is the founder and principal investigator of Interspecies Communication, an organization conducting research in musical communication with animals of various species, among them orcas, deer, howler monkeys, and most recently, beluga whales. He has written about his work in *Dolphin Dreamtime* and *Spiritual Ecology*.

BRENDA PETERSON is the author of two recent collections of essays, *Nature and Other Mothers: Reflection on the Feminine in Everyday Life* and *Living by Water: Essays on Life, Land, and Spirit*, as well as three novels. Her new novel is titled *Duck and Cover*. She lives on Puget Sound in Seattle.

DARRELL ADDISON POSEY has been engaged in ethnobiological research among the Kayapó Indians of Brazil since 1977. He is president of the International Society for Ethnobiology and senior advisor to the Minister for the Environment of Brazil. One of his current interests is protecting the intellectual property rights of indigenous peoples.

SCOTT RUSSELL SANDERS'S most recent book, *Secrets of the Universe: Scenes from the Journey Home*, has been published by Beacon Press. His previous collection of essays, *The Paradise of Bombs*, won the Associated Writing Programs Award for Creative Nonfiction. He teaches in the English department at the University of Indiana.

CONTRIBUTORS

PETER SAUER is a fellow of the Myrin Institute and a member of the *Orion* editorial board. He is writing a series of field guides to American landscapes.

JOHN R. STILGOE is the author of *Metropolitan Corridor: Railroads and the American Scene* and *Borderland: Origins of the American Suburb*, among other books. He is Robert and Lois Orchard Professor in the History of Landscape at Harvard University. He is presently writing a history of the North American seashore landscape.

TERRY TEMPEST WILLIAMS is a naturalist in residence at the Utah Museum of Natural History and the author of six books about the Southwest. Her first book, *Pieces of White Shell*, won the Southwest Book Award. Her most recent book is *Refuge: An Unnatural History of Family and Place*.

ANN ZWINGER'S natural history writing has received many awards, including the John Burroughs Medal. Her most recent books are *Aspen: Blazon of the West* and *The Mysterious Lands: The Four Deserts of the United States*. She has also illustrated several books of natural history. She is currently at work on a book about the Colorado River in the Grand Canyon.